NEAR DEATH

CREATED BY JAY FAERBER & SIMONE GUGLIELMINI

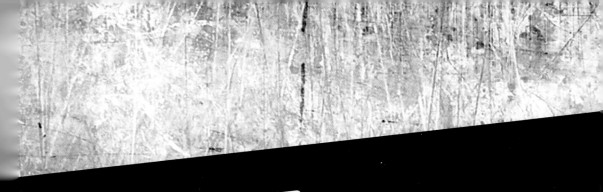

STORY **JAY FAERBER**

ART **SIMONE GUGLIELMINI**

COLOR **RON RILEY**

LETTERS **CHARLES PRITCHETT**

COVERS **TOMM COKER & DANIEL FREEDMAN**

BOOK DESIGN **DREW GILL**

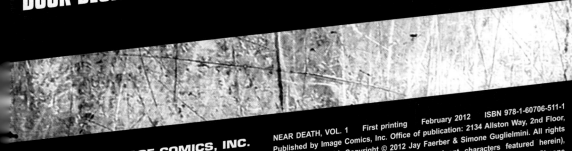

IMAGE COMICS, INC.
Robert Kirkman - chief operating officer
Erik Larsen - chief financial officer
Todd McFarlane - president
Marc Silvestri - chief executive officer
Jim Valentino - vice-president

Eric Stephenson - publisher
Todd Martinez - sales & licensing coordinator
Jennifer de Guzman - pr & marketing director
Branwyn Bigglestone - accounts manager
Emily Miller - administrative assistant
Jamie Parreno - marketing assistant
Sarah deLaine - events coordinator
Kevin Yuen - digital rights coordinator
Tyler Shainline - production manager
Drew Gill - art director
Jonathan Chan - senior production artist
Monica Garcia - production artist
Vincent Kukua - production artist
Jana Cook - production artist
www.imagecomics.com

NEAR DEATH, VOL. 1 First printing February 2012 ISBN 978-1-60706-511-1
Published by Image Comics, Inc. Office of publication: 2134 Allston Way, 2nd Floor,
Berkeley, CA 94704. Printed in the United States. For information regarding the CPSIA
on this printed material call: 203-595-3636 and provide reference # EAST – 425930
International Rights Representative: Christine Meyer — christine@gfloystudio.com

VOLUME ONE

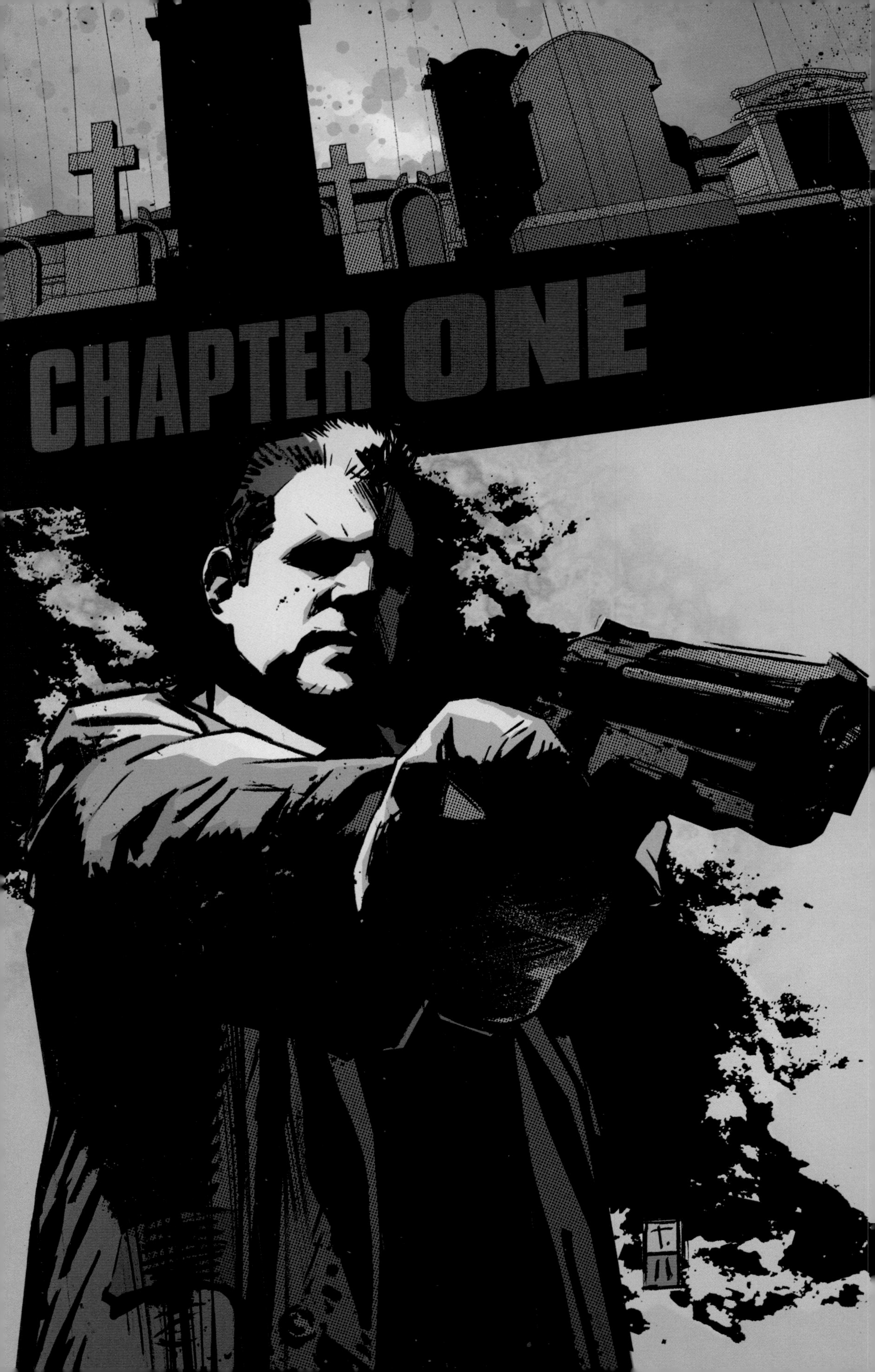
CHAPTER ONE

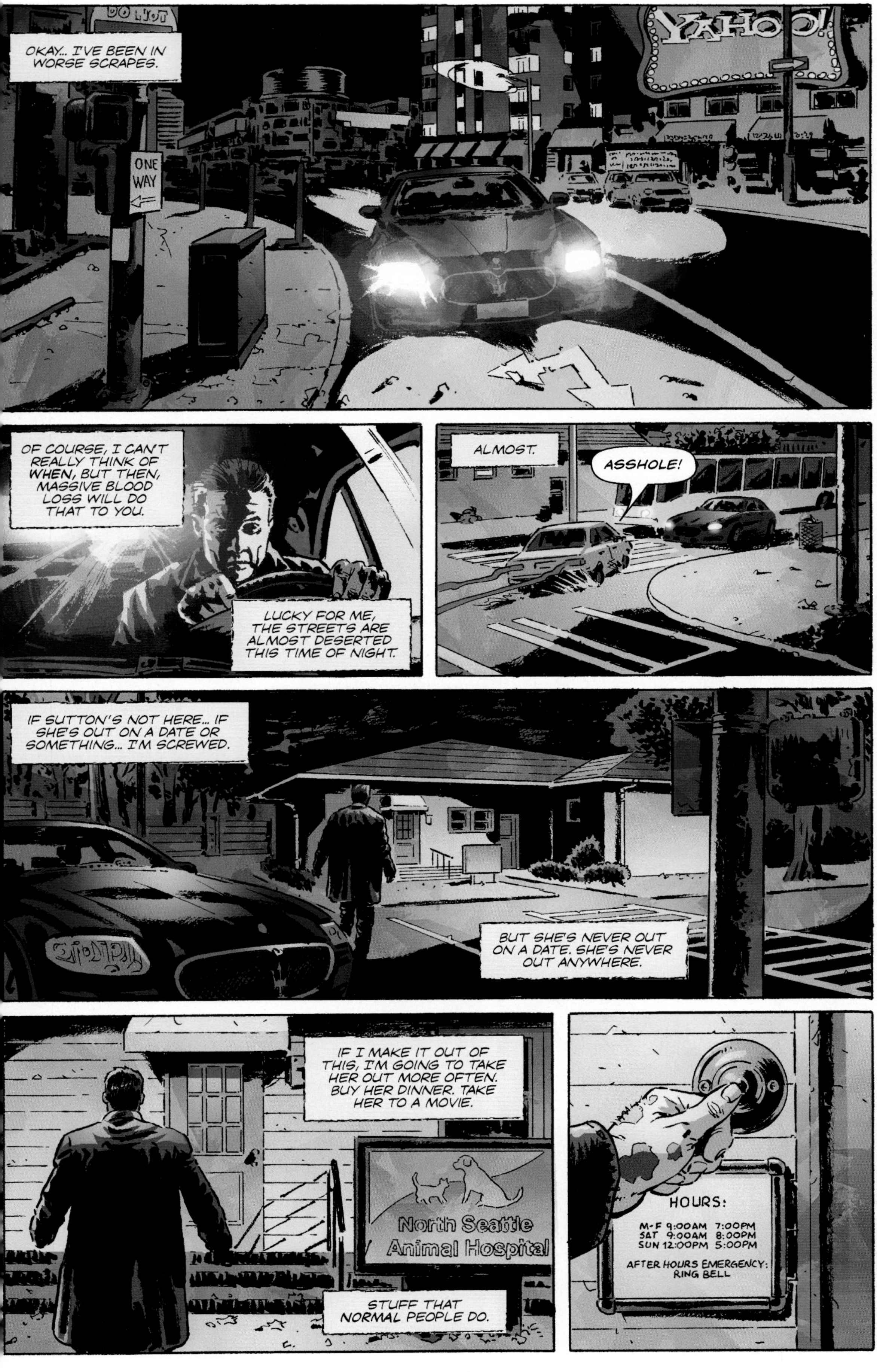

OKAY... I'VE BEEN IN WORSE SCRAPES.
YAHOO!
ONE WAY
OF COURSE, I CAN'T REALLY THINK OF WHEN, BUT THEN, MASSIVE BLOOD LOSS WILL DO THAT TO YOU.
LUCKY FOR ME, THE STREETS ARE ALMOST DESERTED THIS TIME OF NIGHT.
ALMOST.
ASSHOLE!
IF SUTTON'S NOT HERE... IF SHE'S OUT ON A DATE OR SOMETHING... I'M SCREWED.
BUT SHE'S NEVER OUT ON A DATE. SHE'S NEVER OUT ANYWHERE.
IF I MAKE IT OUT OF THIS, I'M GOING TO TAKE HER OUT MORE OFTEN. BUY HER DINNER. TAKE HER TO A MOVIE.
North Seattle Animal Hospital
STUFF THAT NORMAL PEOPLE DO.
HOURS:
M-F 9:00AM 7:00PM
SAT 9:00AM 8:00PM
SUN 12:00PM 5:00PM
AFTER HOURS EMERGENCY: RING BELL

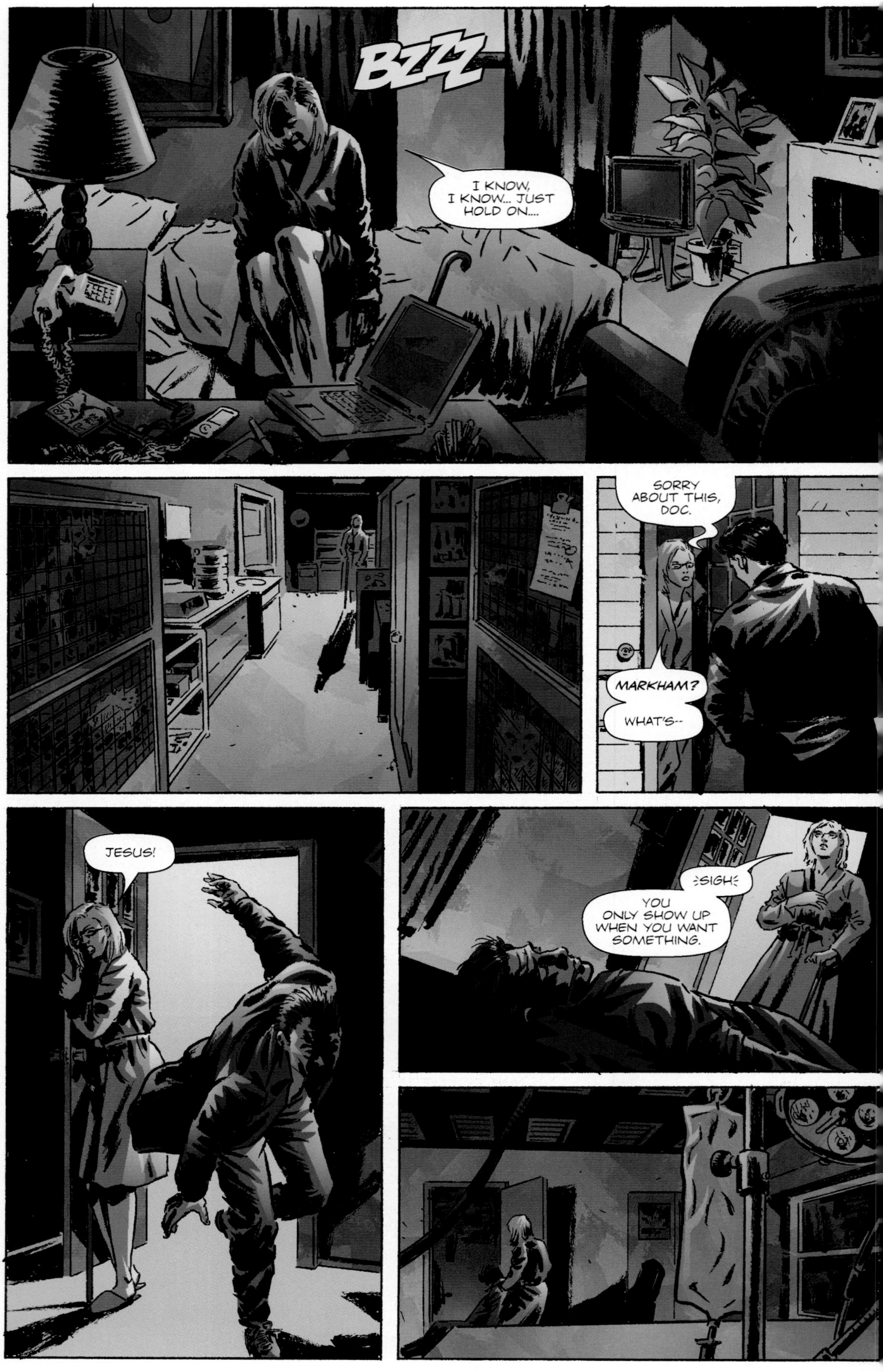

BZZZ
I KNOW, I KNOW... JUST HOLD ON....
SORRY ABOUT THIS, DOC.
MARKHAM?
WHAT'S--
JESUS!
SIGH
YOU ONLY SHOW UP WHEN YOU WANT SOMETHING.

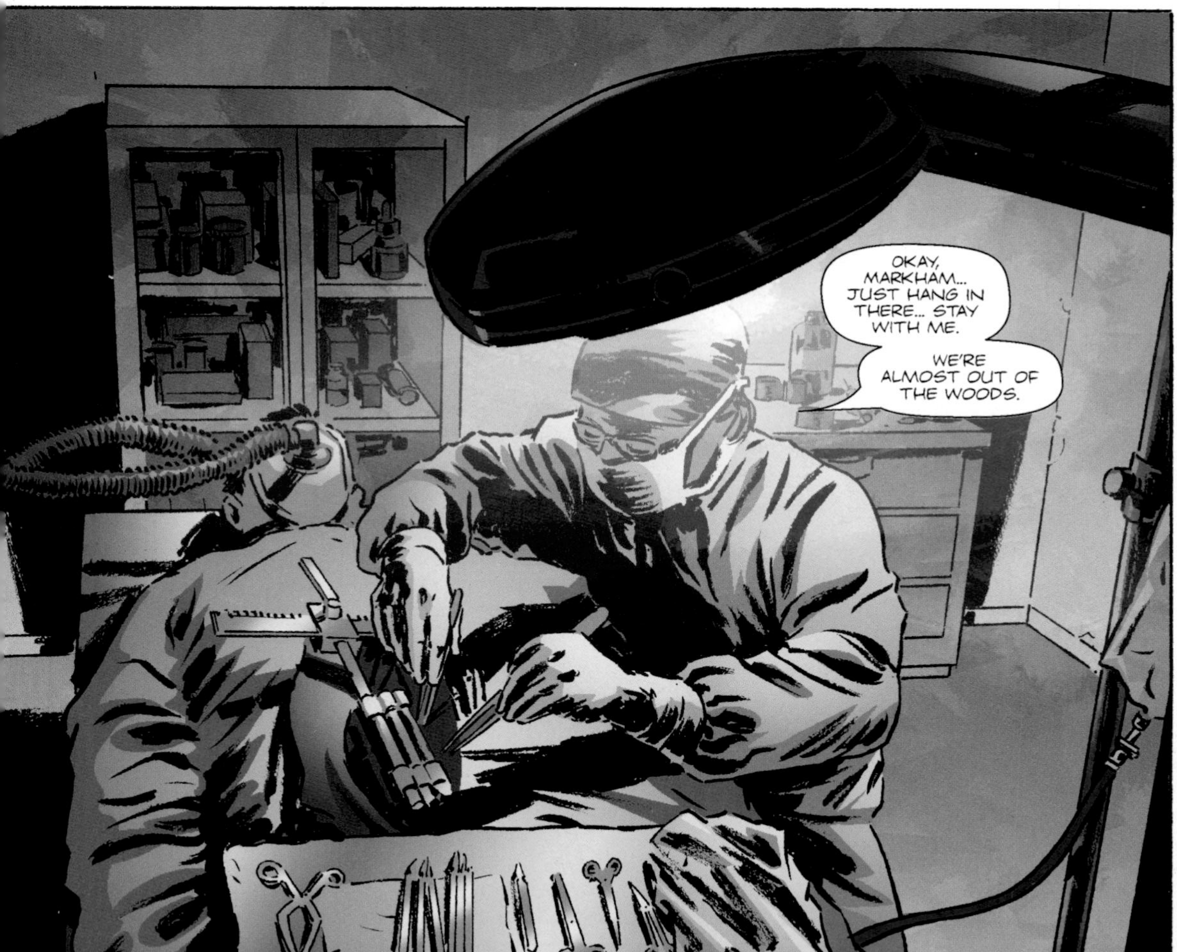
OKAY, MARKHAM... JUST HANG IN THERE... STAY WITH ME.
WE'RE ALMOST OUT OF THE WOODS.

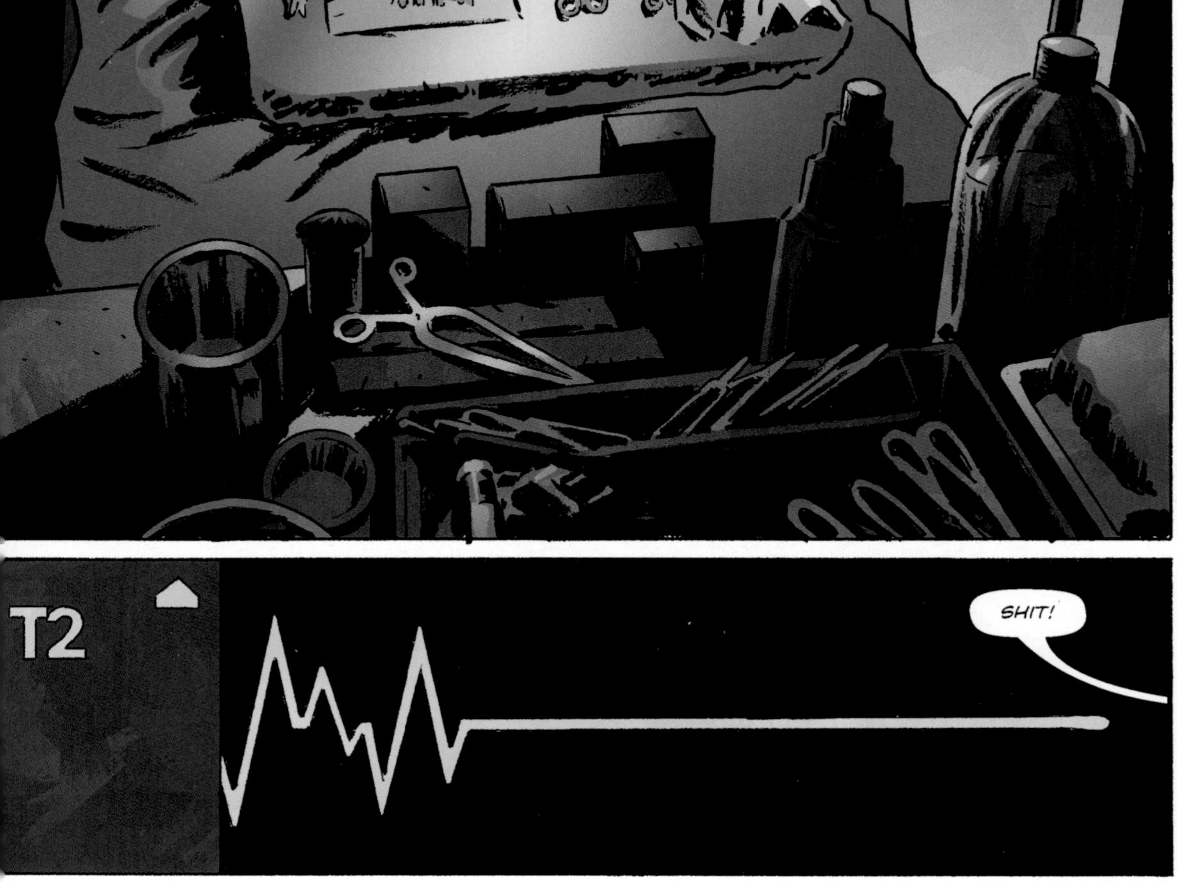
T2
SHIT!

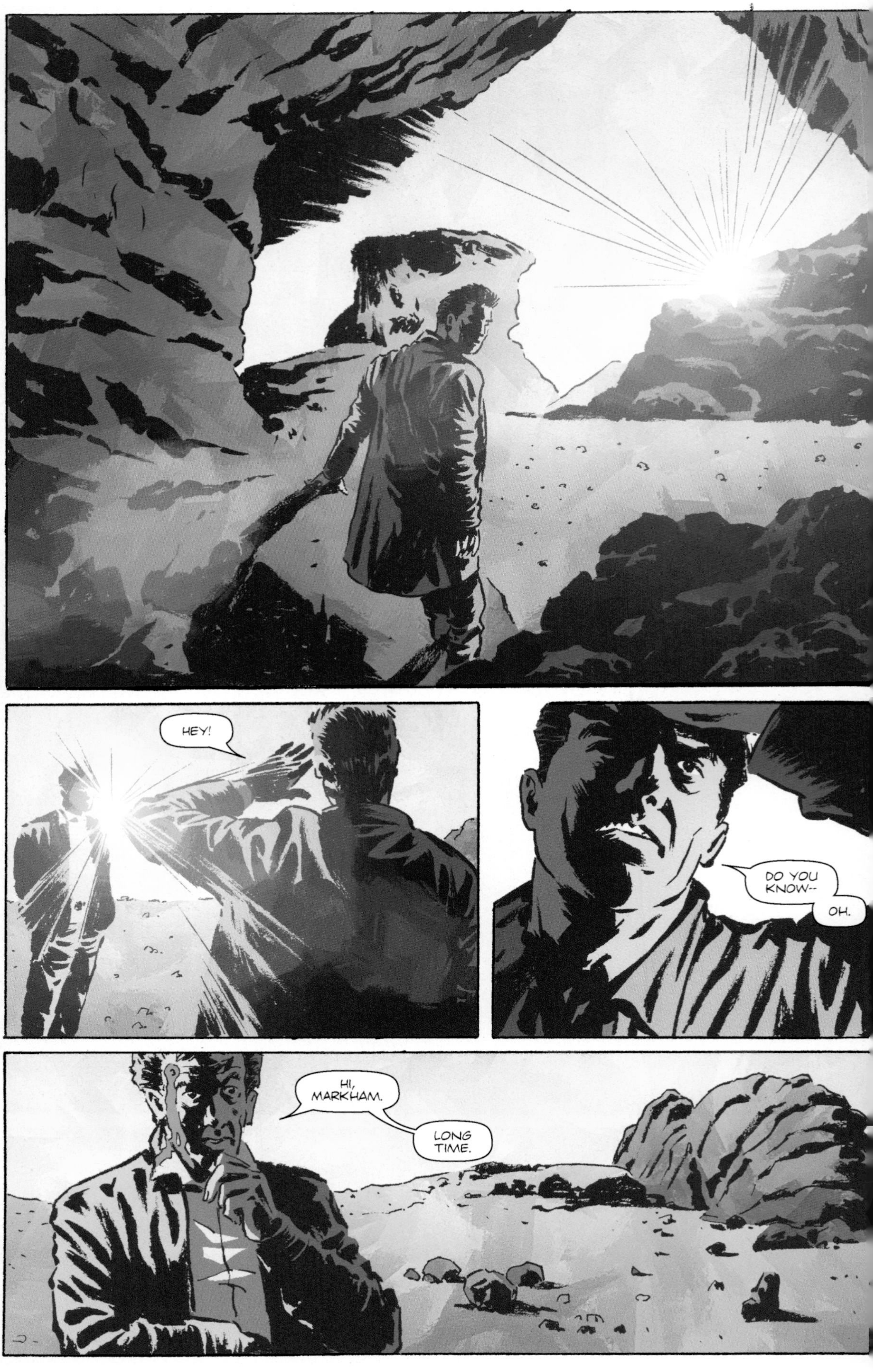
HEY!
DO YOU KNOW--
OH.
HI, MARKHAM.
LONG TIME.

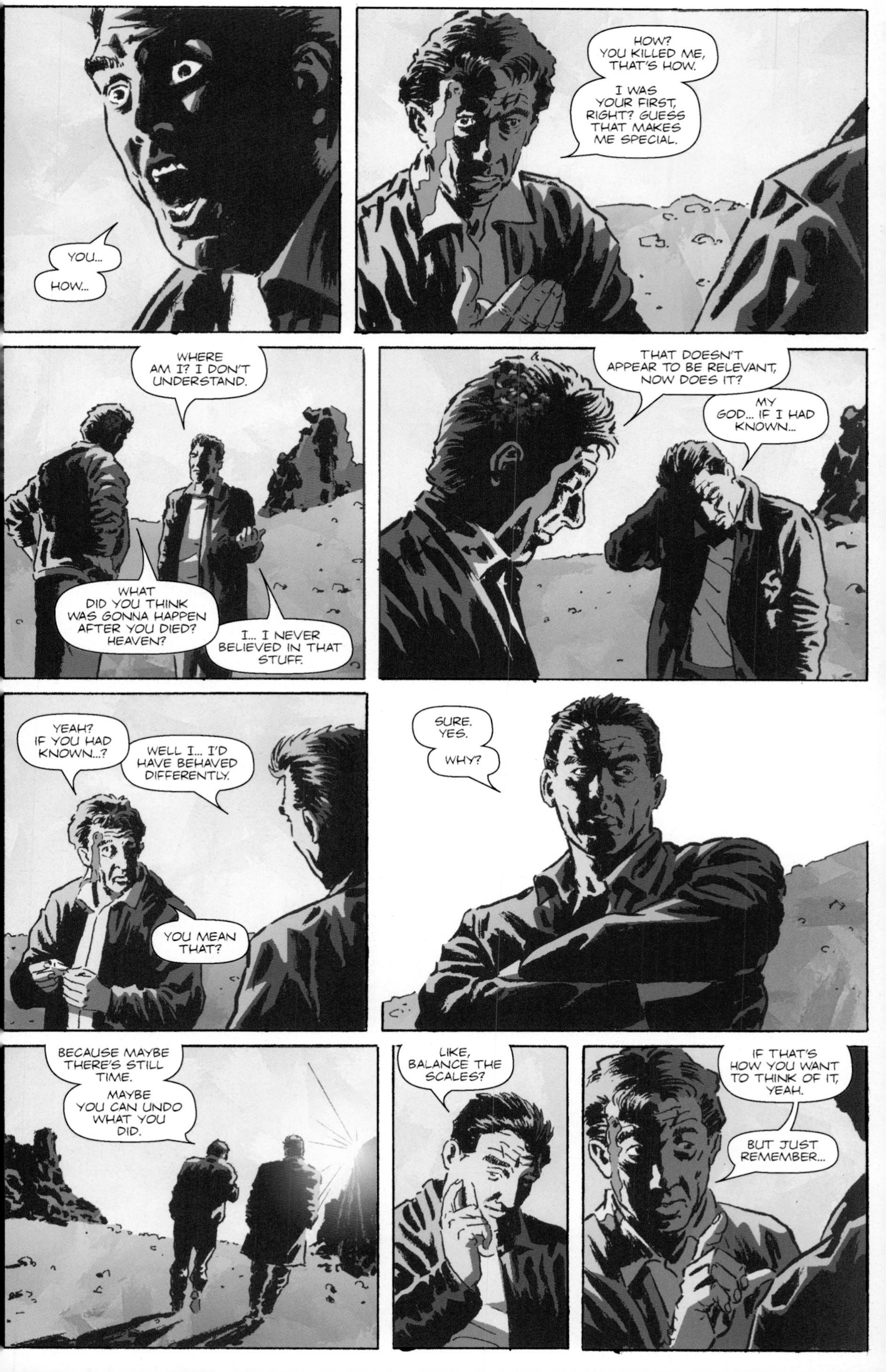
YOU...
HOW...
HOW? YOU KILLED ME, THAT'S HOW.
I WAS YOUR FIRST, RIGHT? GUESS THAT MAKES ME SPECIAL.
WHERE AM I? I DON'T UNDERSTAND.
WHAT DID YOU THINK WAS GONNA HAPPEN AFTER YOU DIED? HEAVEN?
I... I NEVER BELIEVED IN THAT STUFF.
THAT DOESN'T APPEAR TO BE RELEVANT, NOW DOES IT?
MY GOD... IF I HAD KNOWN...
YEAH? IF YOU HAD KNOWN...?
WELL I... I'D HAVE BEHAVED DIFFERENTLY.
YOU MEAN THAT?
SURE. YES.
WHY?
BECAUSE MAYBE THERE'S STILL TIME.
MAYBE YOU CAN UNDO WHAT YOU DID.
LIKE, BALANCE THE SCALES?
IF THAT'S HOW YOU WANT TO THINK OF IT, YEAH.
BUT JUST REMEMBER...

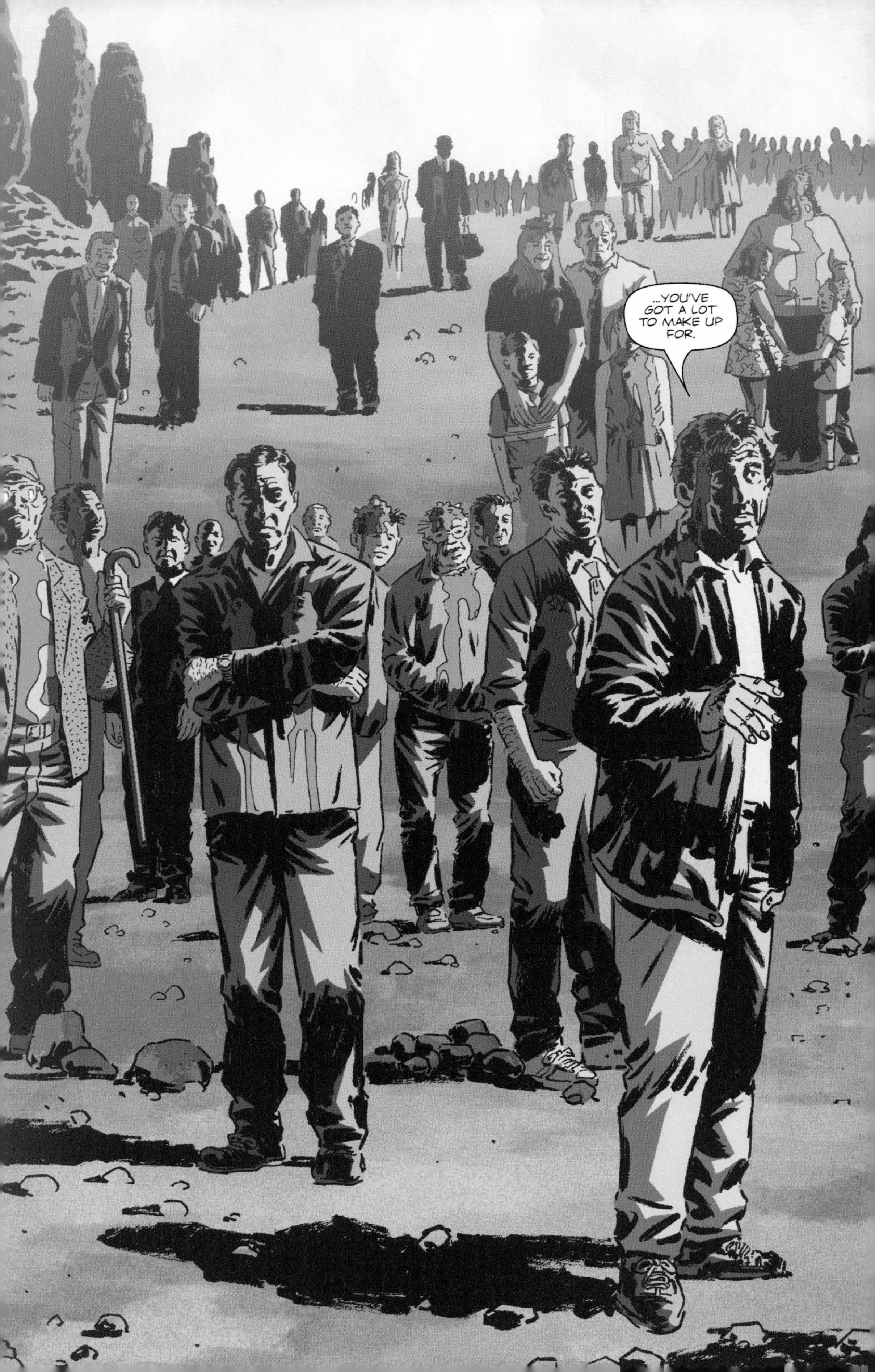
...YOU'VE GOT A LOT TO MAKE UP FOR.

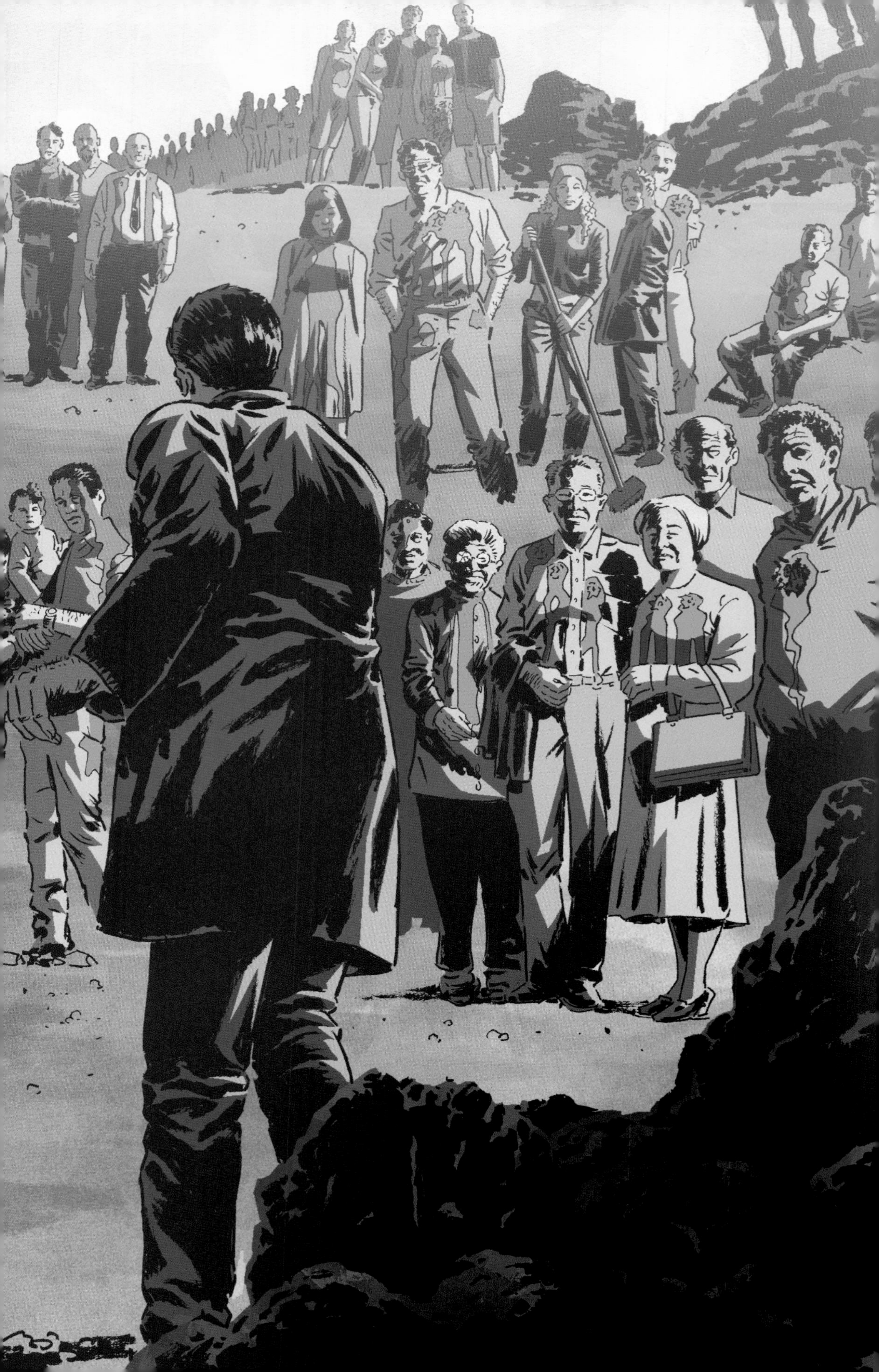

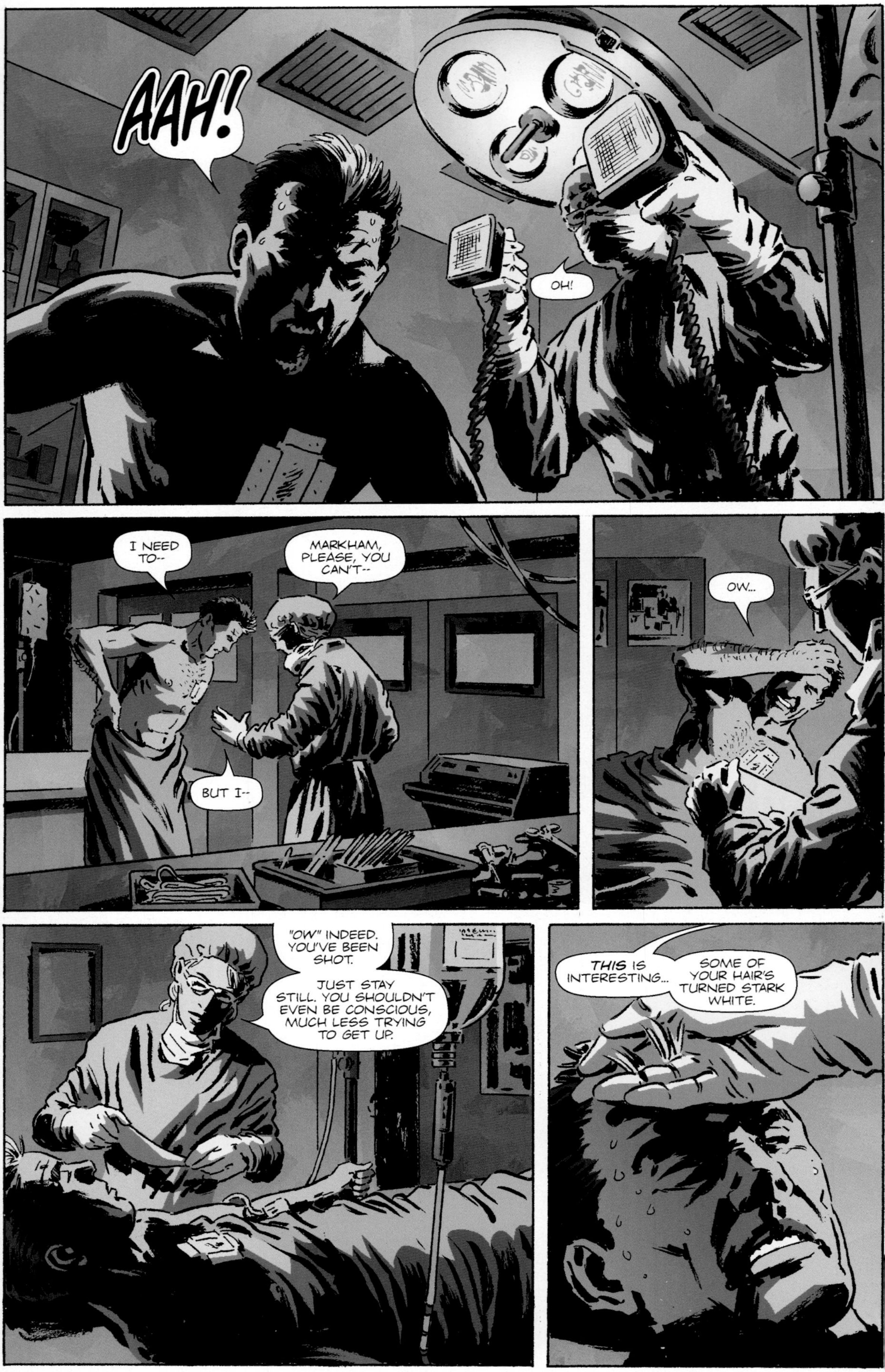
AAH!
OH!
I NEED TO--
MARKHAM, PLEASE, YOU CAN'T--
BUT I--
OW...
"OW" INDEED. YOU'VE BEEN SHOT.
JUST STAY STILL. YOU SHOULDN'T EVEN BE CONSCIOUS, MUCH LESS TRYING TO GET UP.
THIS IS INTERESTING...
SOME OF YOUR HAIR'S TURNED STARK WHITE.

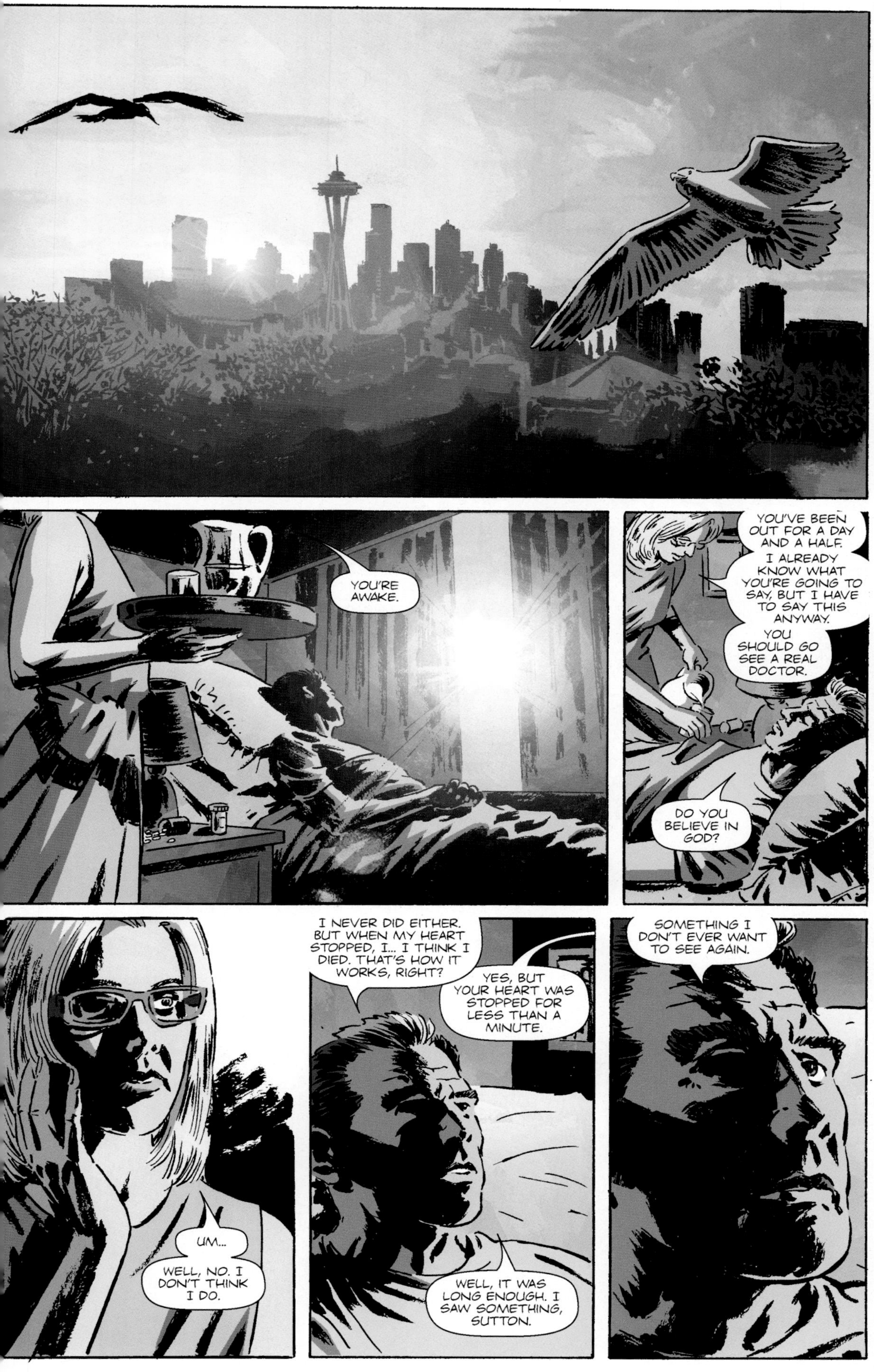
YOU'RE AWAKE.
YOU'VE BEEN OUT FOR A DAY AND A HALF.
I ALREADY KNOW WHAT YOU'RE GOING TO SAY, BUT I HAVE TO SAY THIS ANYWAY.
YOU SHOULD GO SEE A REAL DOCTOR.
DO YOU BELIEVE IN GOD?
UM...
WELL, NO. I DON'T THINK I DO.
I NEVER DID EITHER. BUT WHEN MY HEART STOPPED, I... I THINK I DIED. THAT'S HOW IT WORKS, RIGHT?
YES, BUT YOUR HEART WAS STOPPED FOR LESS THAN A MINUTE.
WELL, IT WAS LONG ENOUGH. I SAW SOMETHING, SUTTON.
SOMETHING I DON'T EVER WANT TO SEE AGAIN.

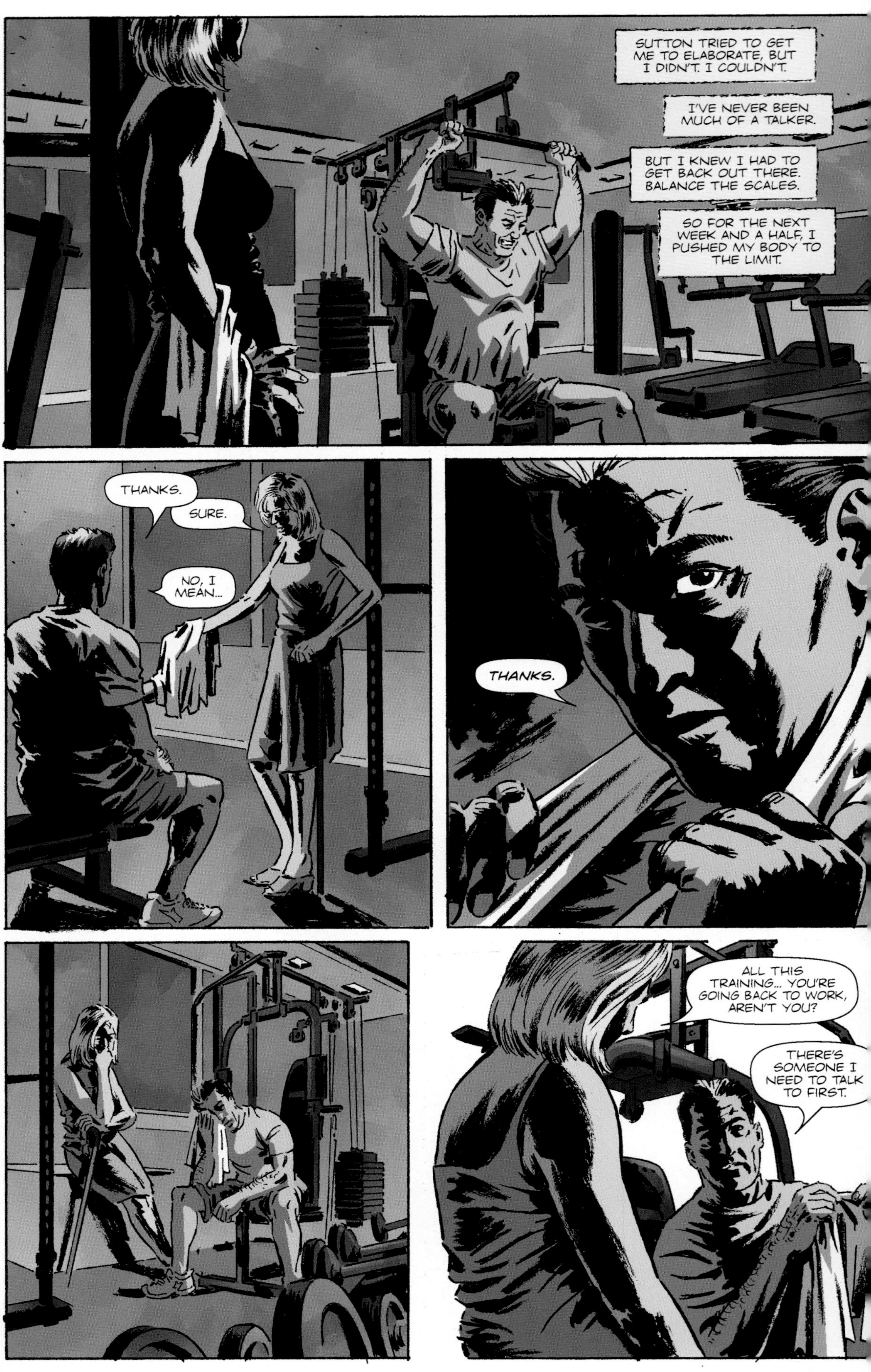
SUTTON TRIED TO GET ME TO ELABORATE, BUT I DIDN'T. I COULDN'T.
I'VE NEVER BEEN MUCH OF A TALKER.
BUT I KNEW I HAD TO GET BACK OUT THERE. BALANCE THE SCALES.
SO FOR THE NEXT WEEK AND A HALF, I PUSHED MY BODY TO THE LIMIT.
THANKS.
SURE.
NO, I MEAN...
THANKS.
ALL THIS TRAINING... YOU'RE GOING BACK TO WORK, AREN'T YOU?
THERE'S SOMEONE I NEED TO TALK TO FIRST.

MARKHAM. YOU'RE LOOKING GOOD FOR A GUY WHO ALMOST DIED.

THANKS, MAX.

I NEED TO KNOW ABOUT THE CONTRACT I WAS ON WHEN I GOT SHOT.

MR. NOVAK ALREADY GOT SOMEONE ELSE. YOU DON'T NEED TO WORRY ABOUT IT.

AS SOON AS YOU'RE FEELING UP TO IT, THERE'LL BE PLENTY OF WORK FOR YOU.

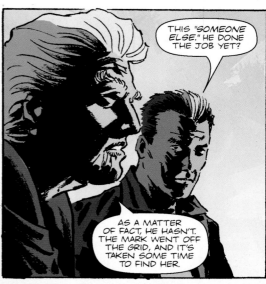

THIS "SOMEONE ELSE." HE DONE THE JOB YET?

AS A MATTER OF FACT, HE HASN'T. THE MARK WENT OFF THE GRID, AND IT'S TAKEN SOME TIME TO FIND HER.

BUT HE *HAS* FOUND HER?

GOT A LEAD ON HER YESTERDAY, YEAH. WHY DO YOU CARE? IT'S NOT YOUR CONCERN.

IT'S THE FIRST JOB I DIDN'T FINISH MYSELF. I'M HAVING A HARD TIME LETTING IT GO.

WHO'S MY REPLACEMENT?

YOU KNOW BREWSTER, RIGHT? OF COURSE YOU DO.

EVERYONE KNOWS BREWSTER. WELL, HE TOOK THE GIG.

AND HE'S MOVING NOW, I BET.

LIKE I SAID, HE GOT A LEAD ON HER YESTERDAY.

GOOD. I'M GLAD THE JOB'S IN GOOD HANDS. BREWSTER WILL COME THROUGH, NO DOUBT ABOUT IT.

SO WHAT ABOUT YOU? YOU READY TO TAKE SOME NEW JOBS?

NOT JUST YET. I'M STILL RECUPERATING, YOU KNOW? DOC SAYS I SHOULDN'T EXERT MYSELF.

BUT THANKS FOR TELLING ME ABOUT BREWSTER. I'LL SLEEP EASIER KNOWING HE'S ON THE JOB.

IF YOU SAY SO...

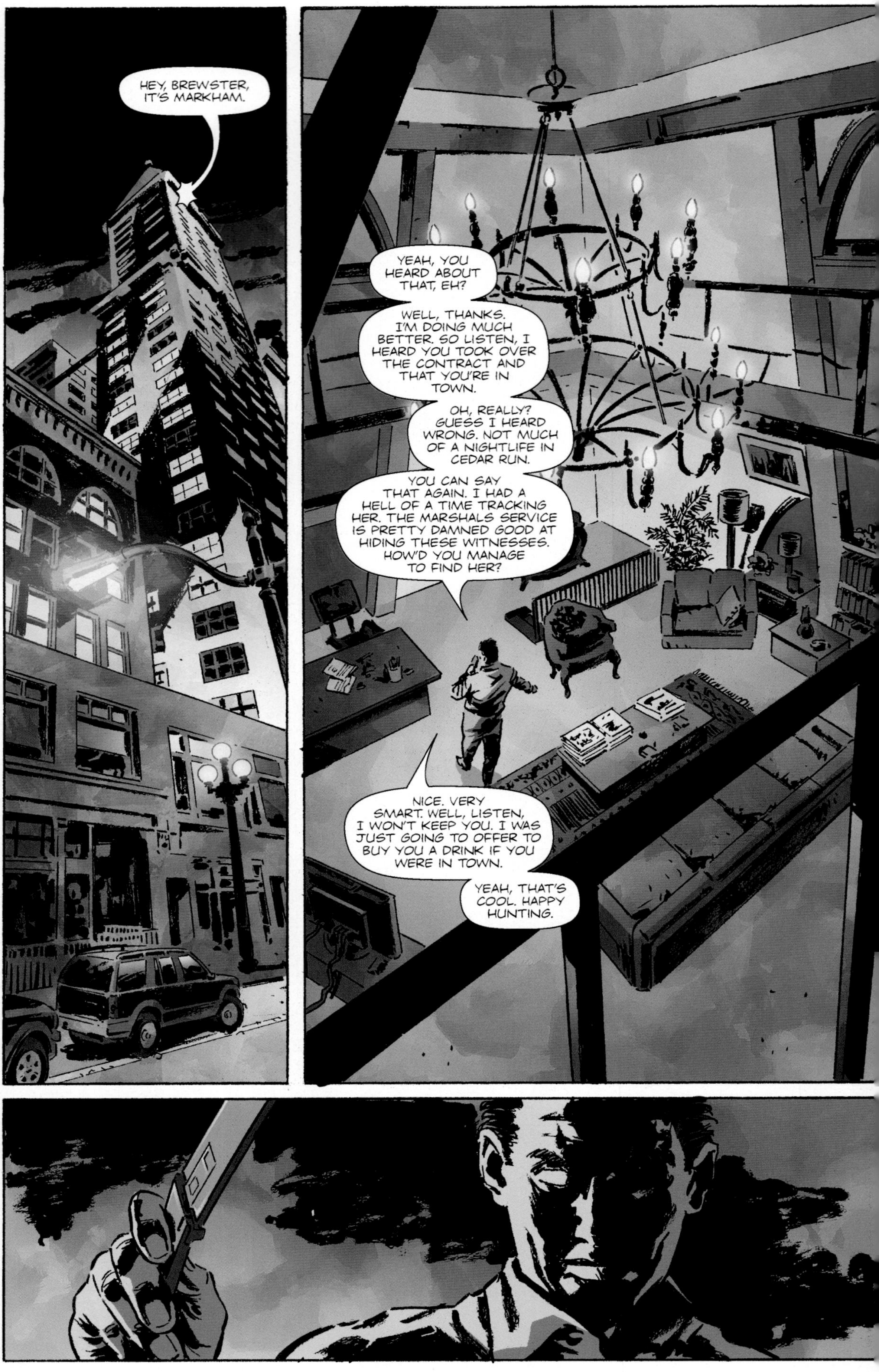
HEY, BREWSTER, IT'S MARKHAM.
YEAH, YOU HEARD ABOUT THAT, EH?
WELL, THANKS. I'M DOING MUCH BETTER. SO LISTEN, I HEARD YOU TOOK OVER THE CONTRACT AND THAT YOU'RE IN TOWN.
OH, REALLY? GUESS I HEARD WRONG. NOT MUCH OF A NIGHTLIFE IN CEDAR RUN.
YOU CAN SAY THAT AGAIN. I HAD A HELL OF A TIME TRACKING HER. THE MARSHALS SERVICE IS PRETTY DAMNED GOOD AT HIDING THESE WITNESSES. HOW'D YOU MANAGE TO FIND HER?
NICE. VERY SMART. WELL, LISTEN, I WON'T KEEP YOU. I WAS JUST GOING TO OFFER TO BUY YOU A DRINK IF YOU WERE IN TOWN.
YEAH, THAT'S COOL. HAPPY HUNTING.

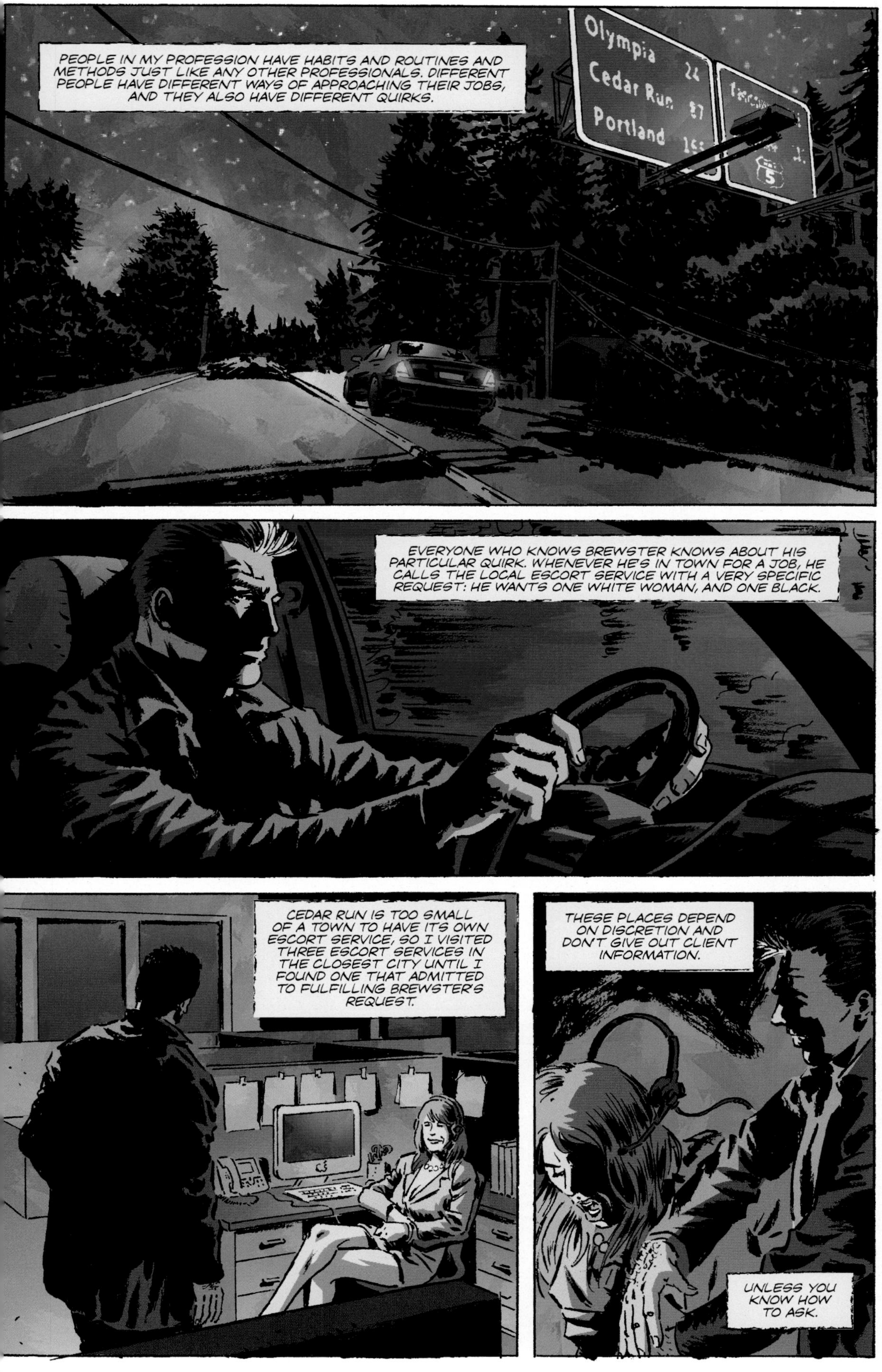
PEOPLE IN MY PROFESSION HAVE HABITS AND ROUTINES AND METHODS JUST LIKE ANY OTHER PROFESSIONALS. DIFFERENT PEOPLE HAVE DIFFERENT WAYS OF APPROACHING THEIR JOBS, AND THEY ALSO HAVE DIFFERENT QUIRKS.
Olympia 24
Cedar Run 87
Portland 165
5
EVERYONE WHO KNOWS BREWSTER KNOWS ABOUT HIS PARTICULAR QUIRK. WHENEVER HE'S IN TOWN FOR A JOB, HE CALLS THE LOCAL ESCORT SERVICE WITH A VERY SPECIFIC REQUEST: HE WANTS ONE WHITE WOMAN, AND ONE BLACK.
CEDAR RUN IS TOO SMALL OF A TOWN TO HAVE ITS OWN ESCORT SERVICE, SO I VISITED THREE ESCORT SERVICES IN THE CLOSEST CITY UNTIL I FOUND ONE THAT ADMITTED TO FULFILLING BREWSTER'S REQUEST.
THESE PLACES DEPEND ON DISCRETION AND DON'T GIVE OUT CLIENT INFORMATION.
UNLESS YOU KNOW HOW TO ASK.

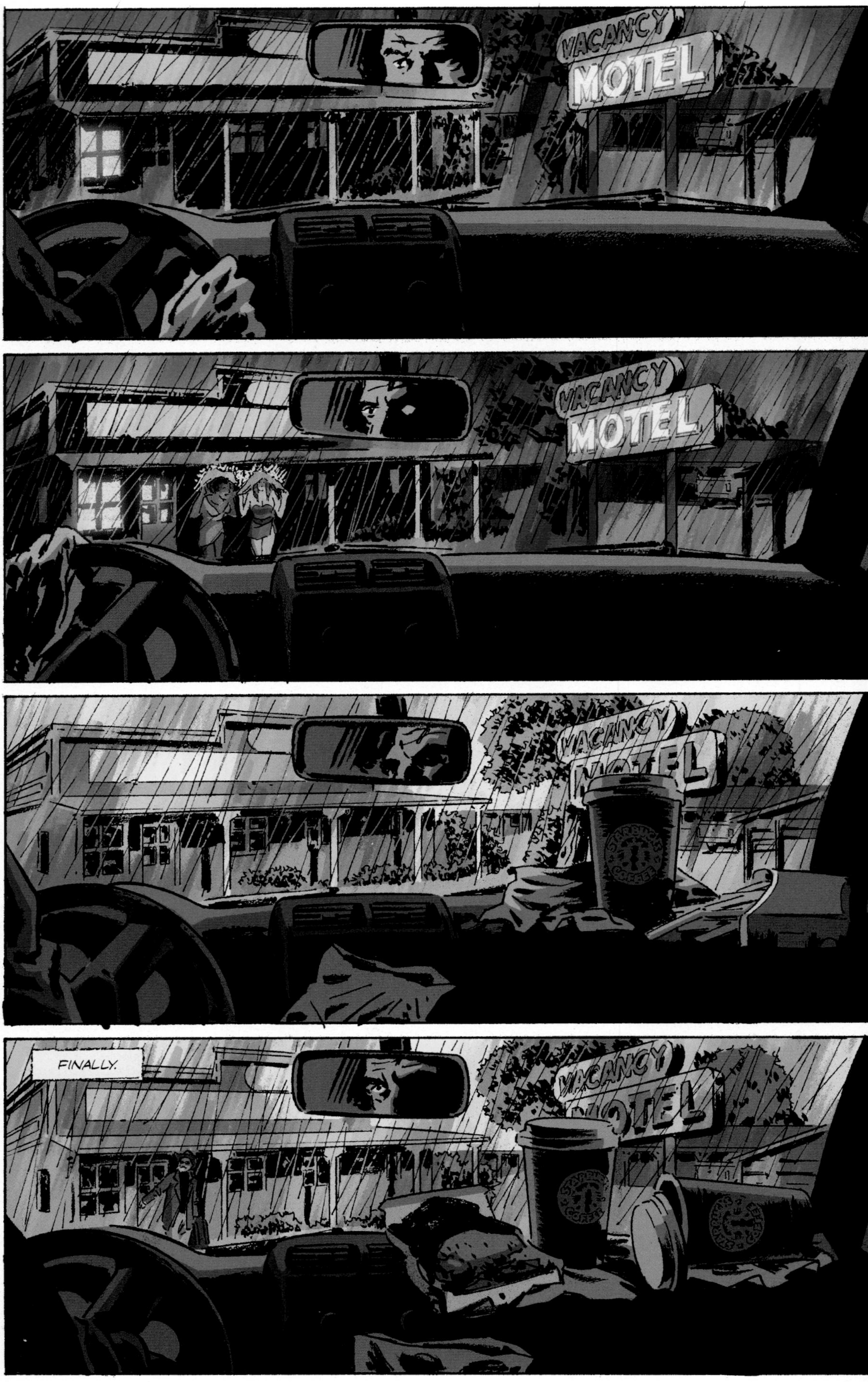
VACANCY
MOTEL
VACANCY
MOTEL
VACANCY
STARBUCKS COFFEE
FINALLY.
VACANCY

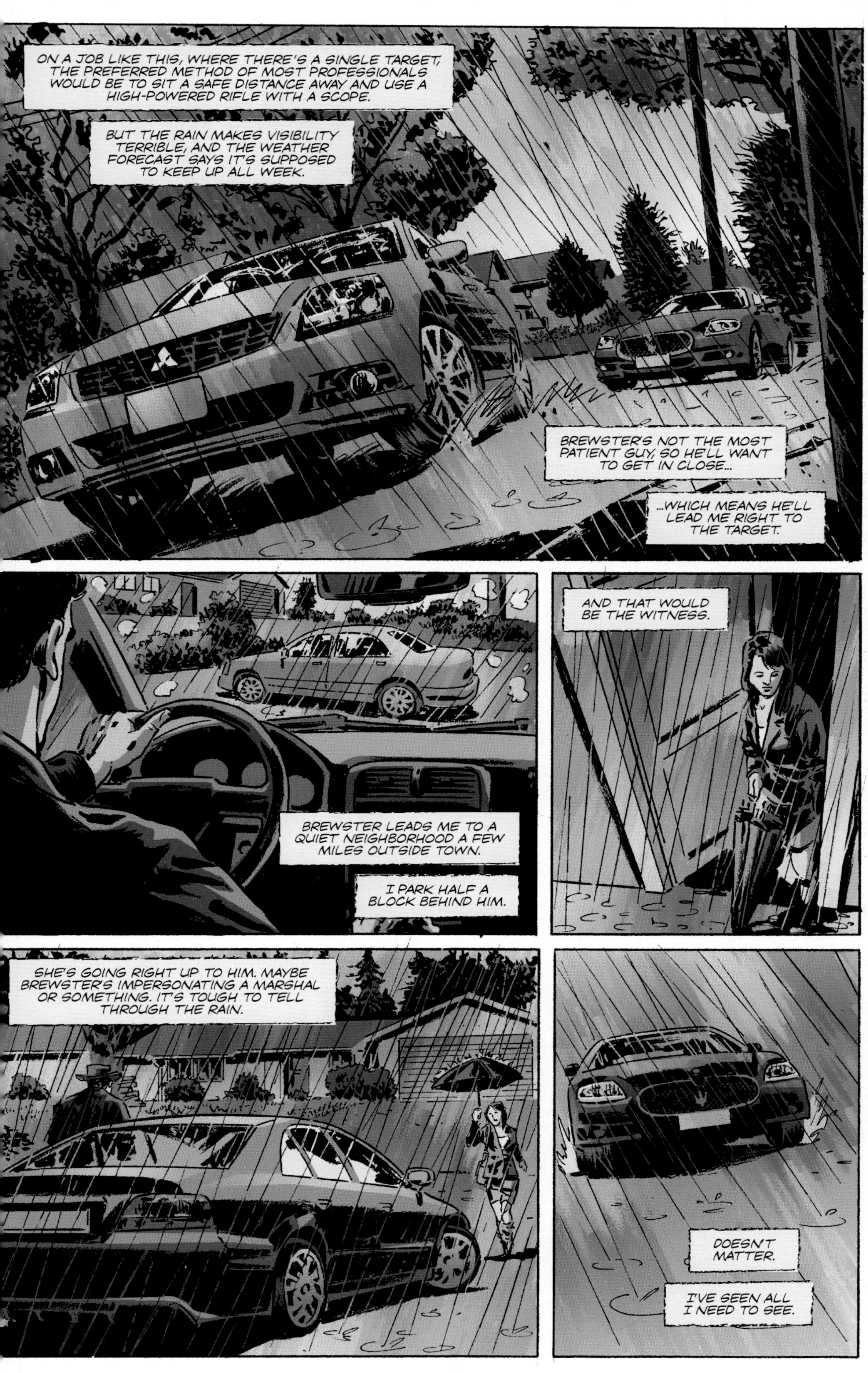
ON A JOB LIKE THIS, WHERE THERE'S A SINGLE TARGET, THE PREFERRED METHOD OF MOST PROFESSIONALS WOULD BE TO SIT A SAFE DISTANCE AWAY AND USE A HIGH-POWERED RIFLE WITH A SCOPE.
BUT THE RAIN MAKES VISIBILITY TERRIBLE, AND THE WEATHER FORECAST SAYS IT'S SUPPOSED TO KEEP UP ALL WEEK.
BREWSTER'S NOT THE MOST PATIENT GUY, SO HE'LL WANT TO GET IN CLOSE...
...WHICH MEANS HE'LL LEAD ME RIGHT TO THE TARGET.
BREWSTER LEADS ME TO A QUIET NEIGHBORHOOD A FEW MILES OUTSIDE TOWN.
I PARK HALF A BLOCK BEHIND HIM.
AND THAT WOULD BE THE WITNESS.
SHE'S GOING RIGHT UP TO HIM. MAYBE BREWSTER'S IMPERSONATING A MARSHAL OR SOMETHING. IT'S TOUGH TO TELL THROUGH THE RAIN.
DOESN'T MATTER.
I'VE SEEN ALL I NEED TO SEE.

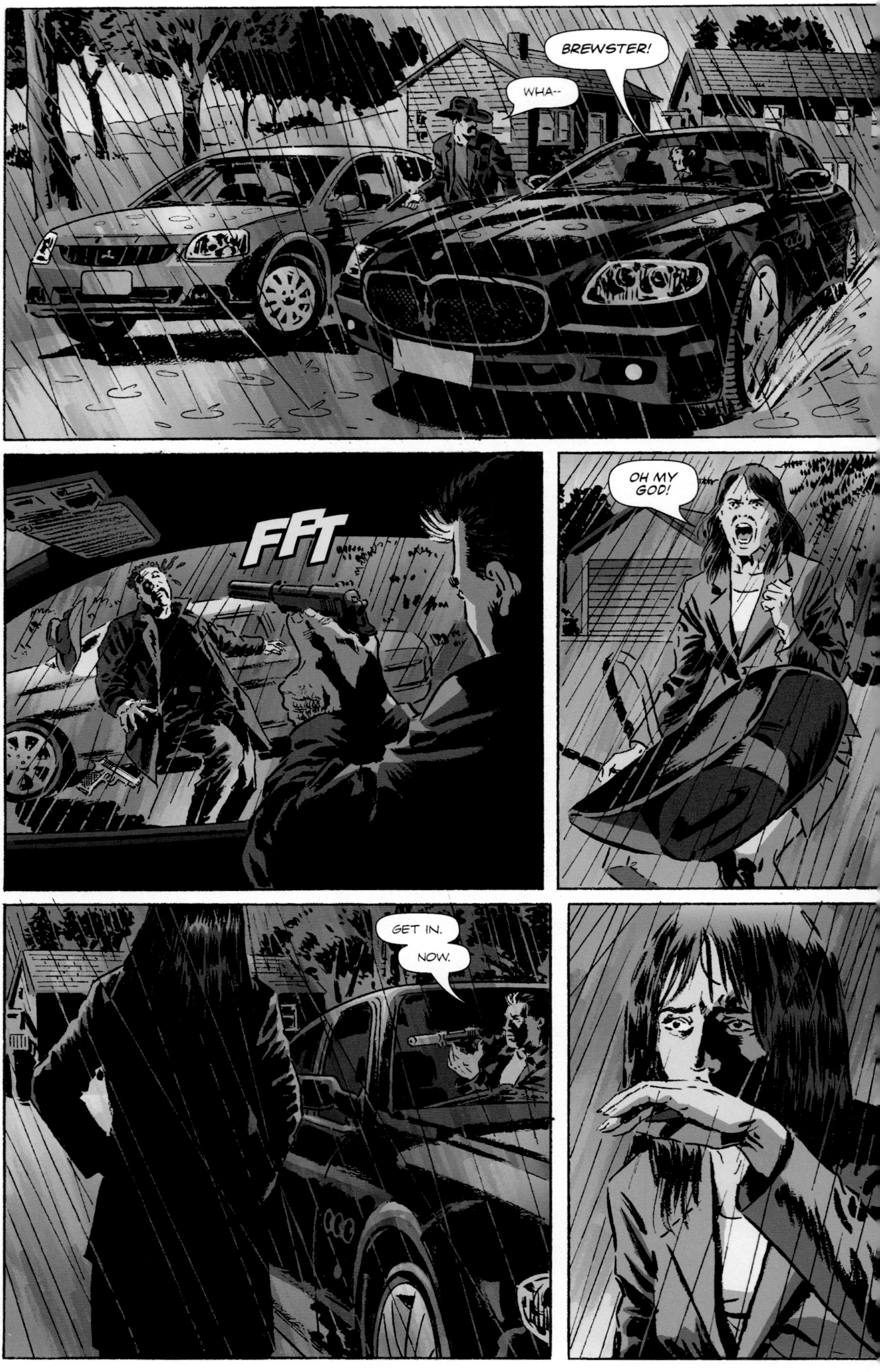
BREWSTER!
WHA--
FFT
OH MY GOD!
GET IN.
NOW.

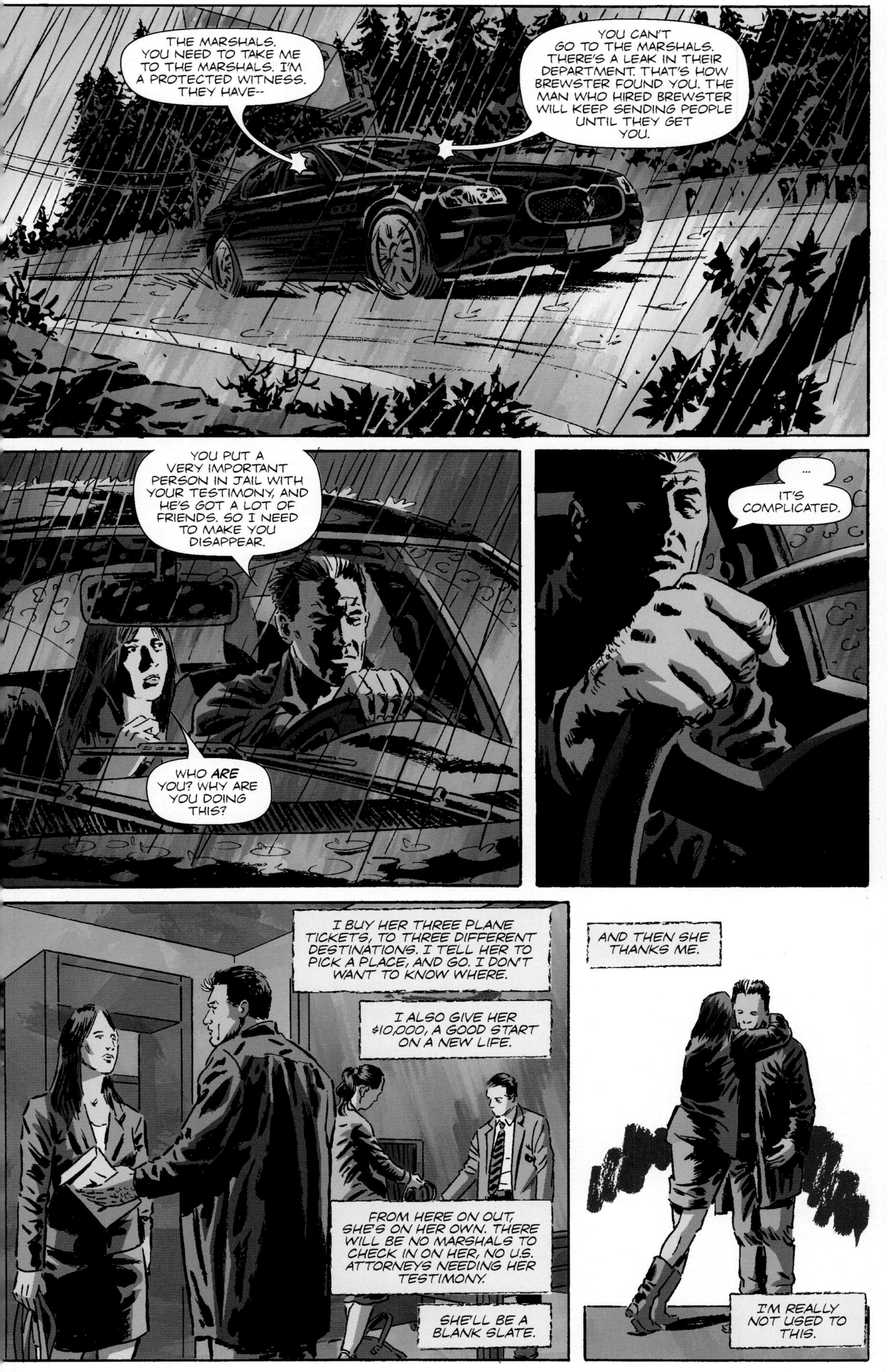
THE MARSHALS. YOU NEED TO TAKE ME TO THE MARSHALS. I'M A PROTECTED WITNESS. THEY HAVE--
YOU CAN'T GO TO THE MARSHALS. THERE'S A LEAK IN THEIR DEPARTMENT. THAT'S HOW BREWSTER FOUND YOU. THE MAN WHO HIRED BREWSTER WILL KEEP SENDING PEOPLE UNTIL THEY GET YOU.
YOU PUT A VERY IMPORTANT PERSON IN JAIL WITH YOUR TESTIMONY, AND HE'S GOT A LOT OF FRIENDS. SO I NEED TO MAKE YOU DISAPPEAR.
WHO ARE YOU? WHY ARE YOU DOING THIS?
...
IT'S COMPLICATED.
I BUY HER THREE PLANE TICKETS, TO THREE DIFFERENT DESTINATIONS. I TELL HER TO PICK A PLACE, AND GO. I DON'T WANT TO KNOW WHERE.
I ALSO GIVE HER $10,000, A GOOD START ON A NEW LIFE.
FROM HERE ON OUT, SHE'S ON HER OWN. THERE WILL BE NO MARSHALS TO CHECK IN ON HER, NO U.S. ATTORNEYS NEEDING HER TESTIMONY.
SHE'LL BE A BLANK SLATE.
AND THEN SHE THANKS ME.
I'M REALLY NOT USED TO THIS.

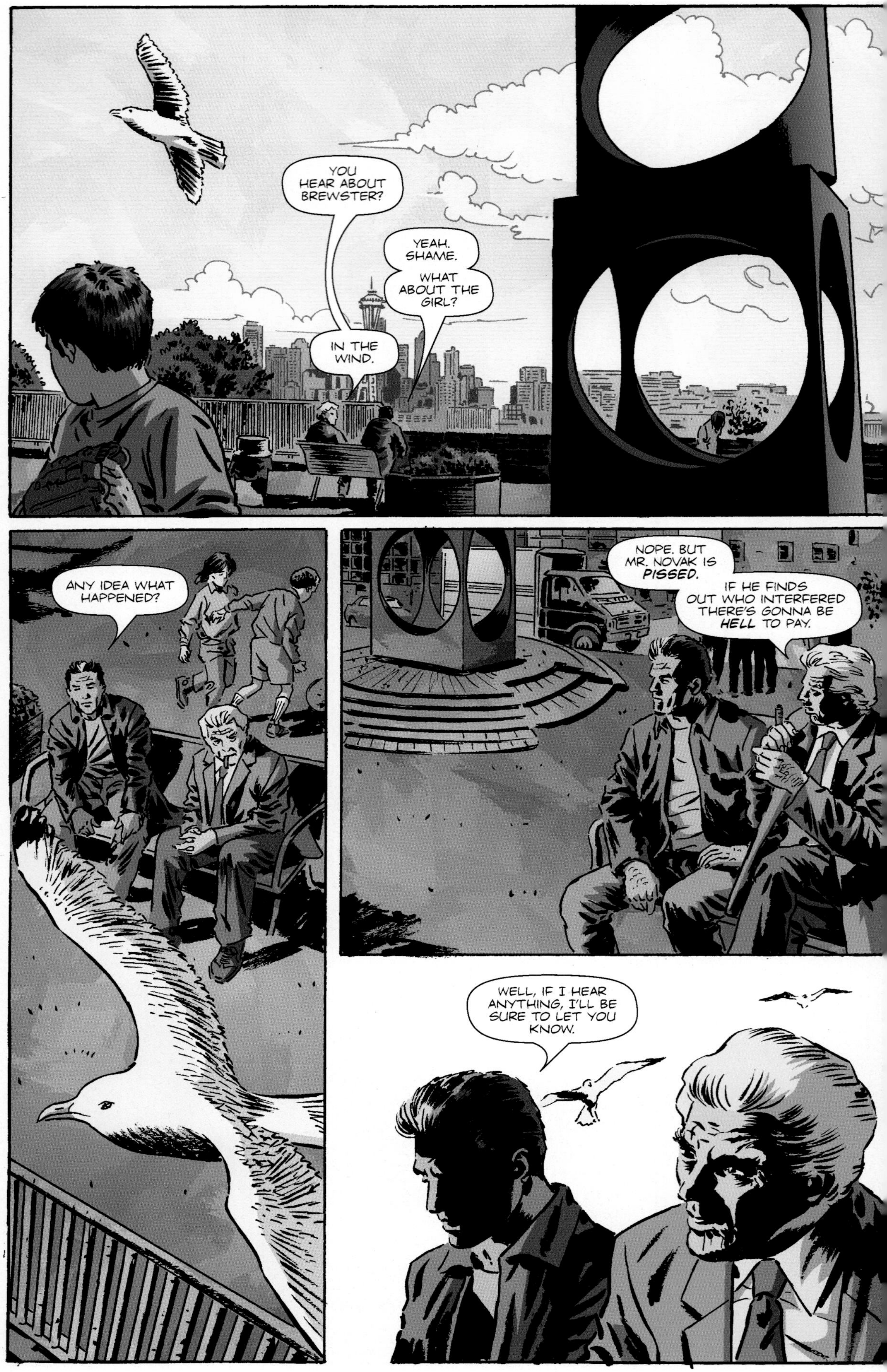
YOU HEAR ABOUT BREWSTER?
YEAH. SHAME.
WHAT ABOUT THE GIRL?
IN THE WIND.
ANY IDEA WHAT HAPPENED?
NOPE. BUT MR. NOVAK IS *PISSED.*
IF HE FINDS OUT WHO INTERFERED THERE'S GONNA BE *HELL* TO PAY.
WELL, IF I HEAR ANYTHING, I'LL BE SURE TO LET YOU KNOW.

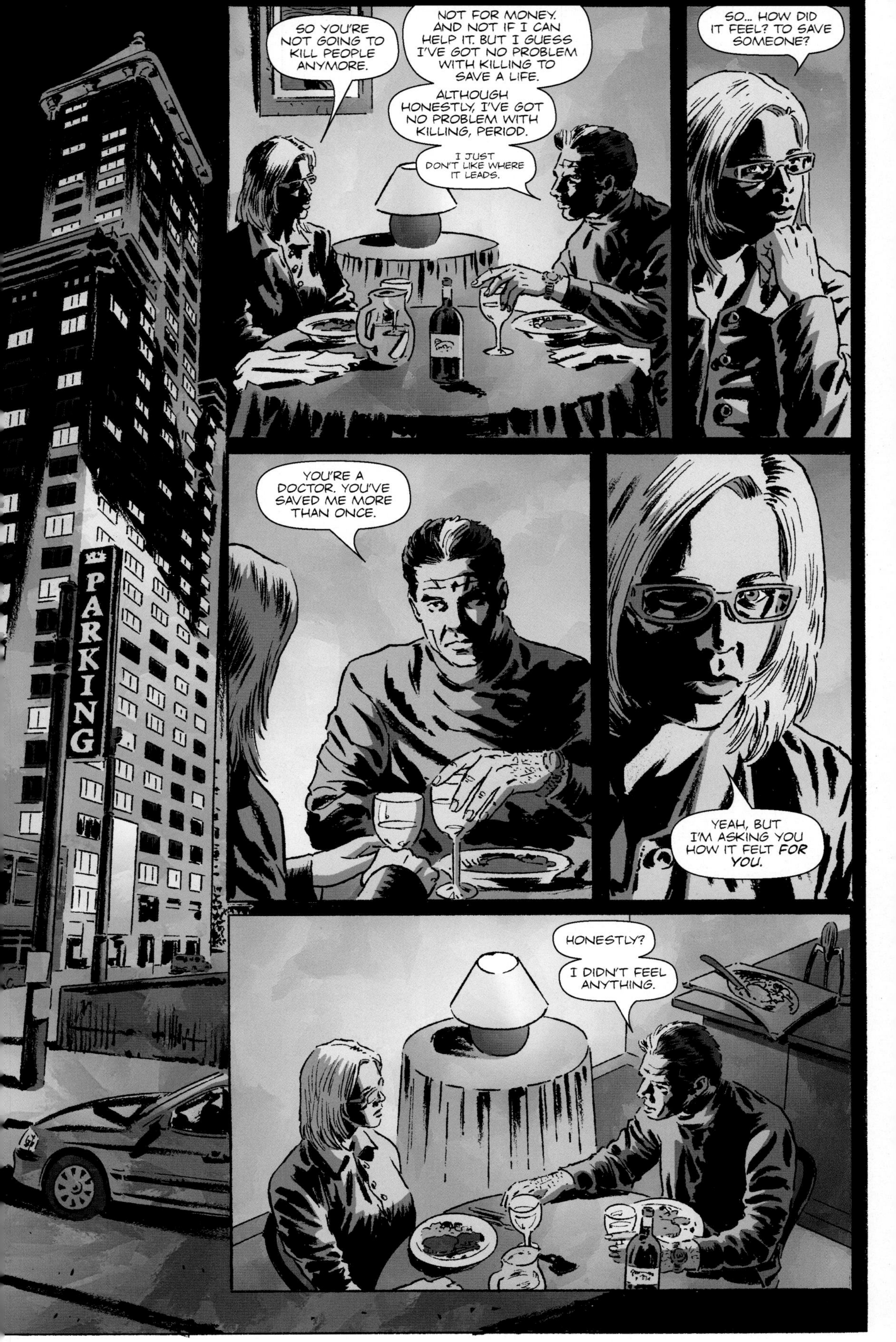
PARKING
SO YOU'RE NOT GOING TO KILL PEOPLE ANYMORE.
NOT FOR MONEY. AND NOT IF I CAN HELP IT. BUT I GUESS I'VE GOT NO PROBLEM WITH KILLING TO SAVE A LIFE.
ALTHOUGH HONESTLY, I'VE GOT NO PROBLEM WITH KILLING, PERIOD.
I JUST DON'T LIKE WHERE IT LEADS.
SO... HOW DID IT FEEL? TO SAVE SOMEONE?
YOU'RE A DOCTOR. YOU'VE SAVED ME MORE THAN ONCE.
YEAH, BUT I'M ASKING YOU HOW IT FELT *FOR YOU.*
HONESTLY?
I DIDN'T FEEL ANYTHING.

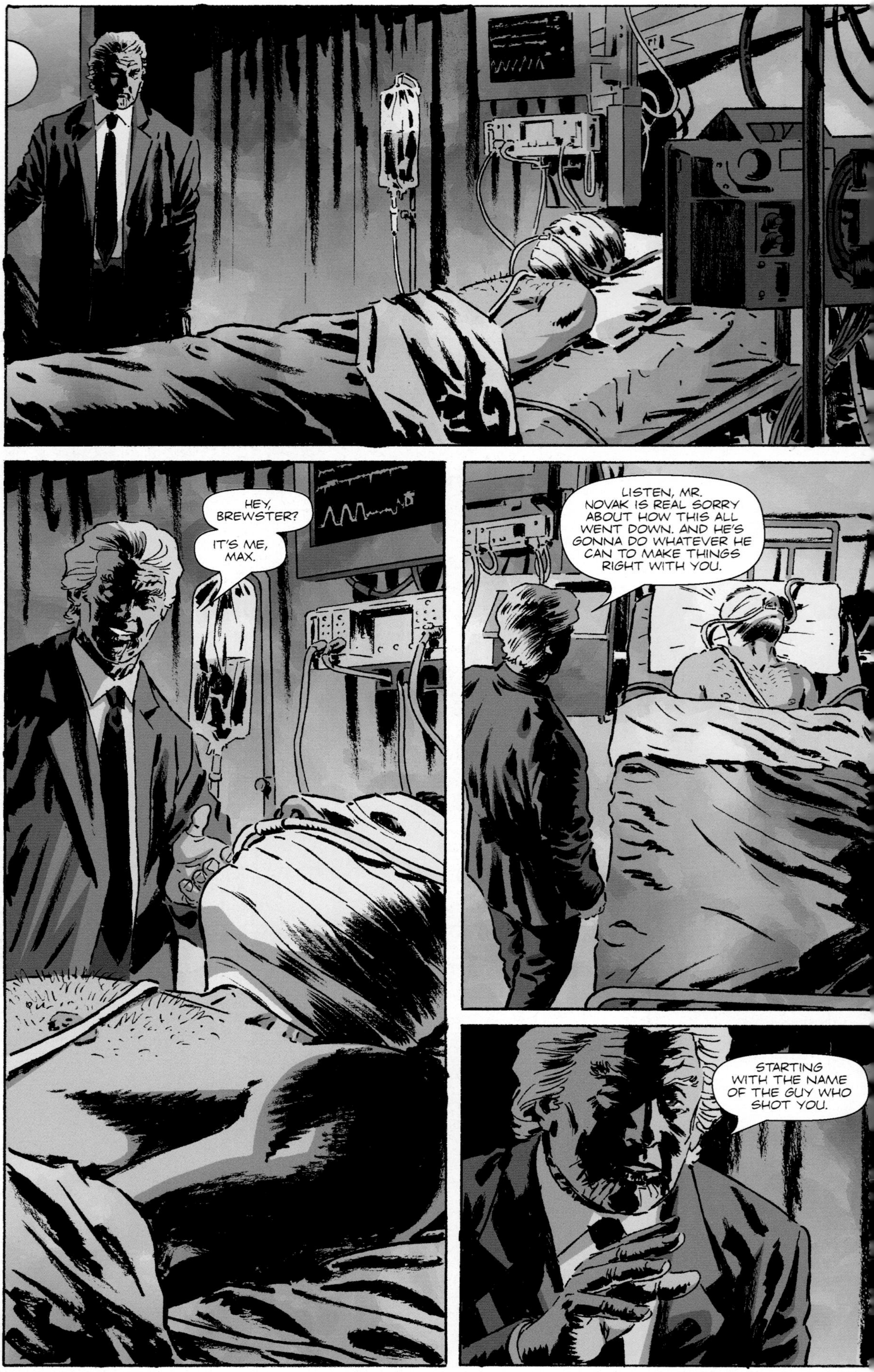
HEY, BREWSTER?
IT'S ME, MAX.
LISTEN, MR. NOVAK IS REAL SORRY ABOUT HOW THIS ALL WENT DOWN. AND HE'S GONNA DO WHATEVER HE CAN TO MAKE THINGS RIGHT WITH YOU.
STARTING WITH THE NAME OF THE GUY WHO SHOT YOU.

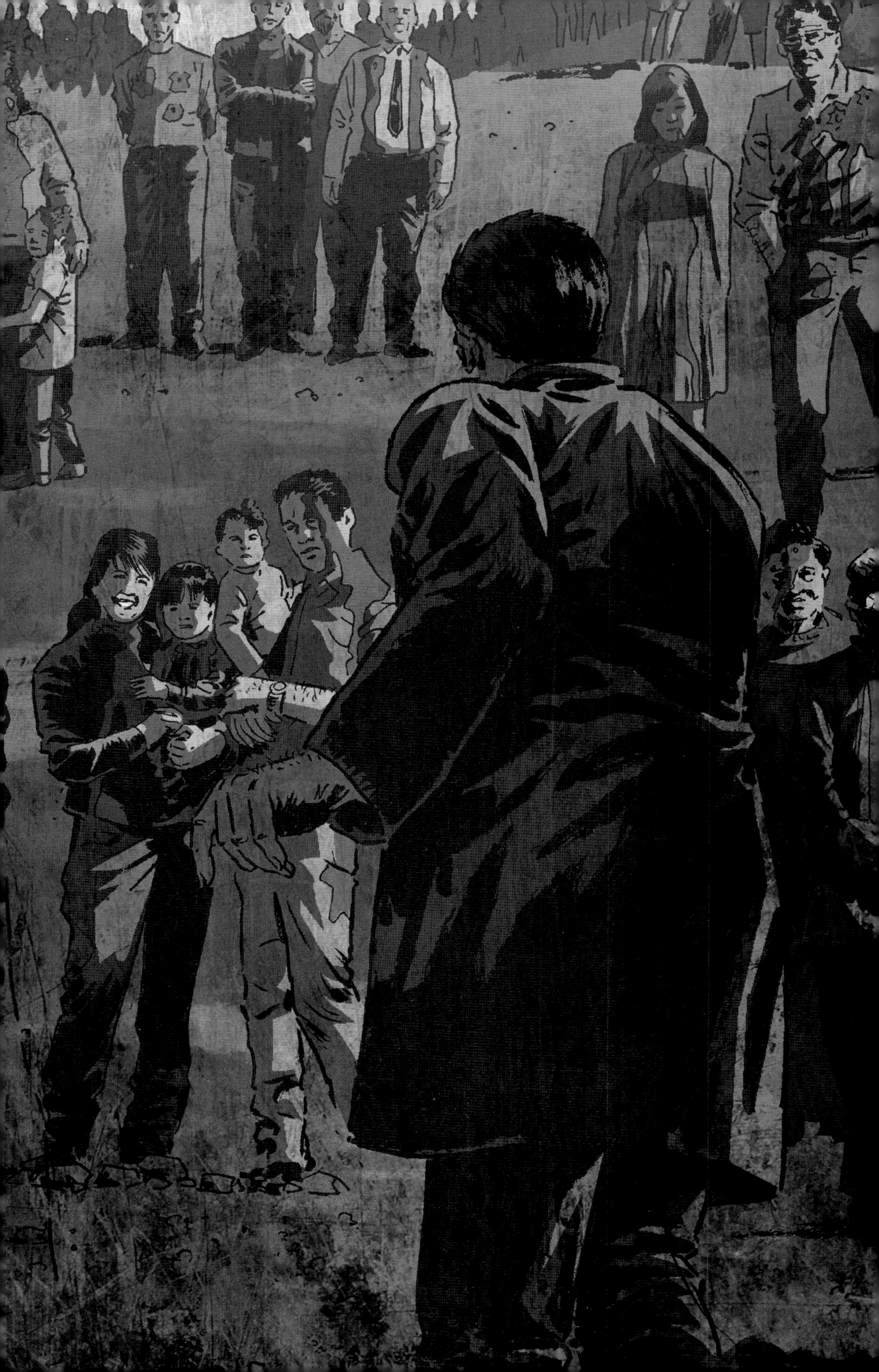

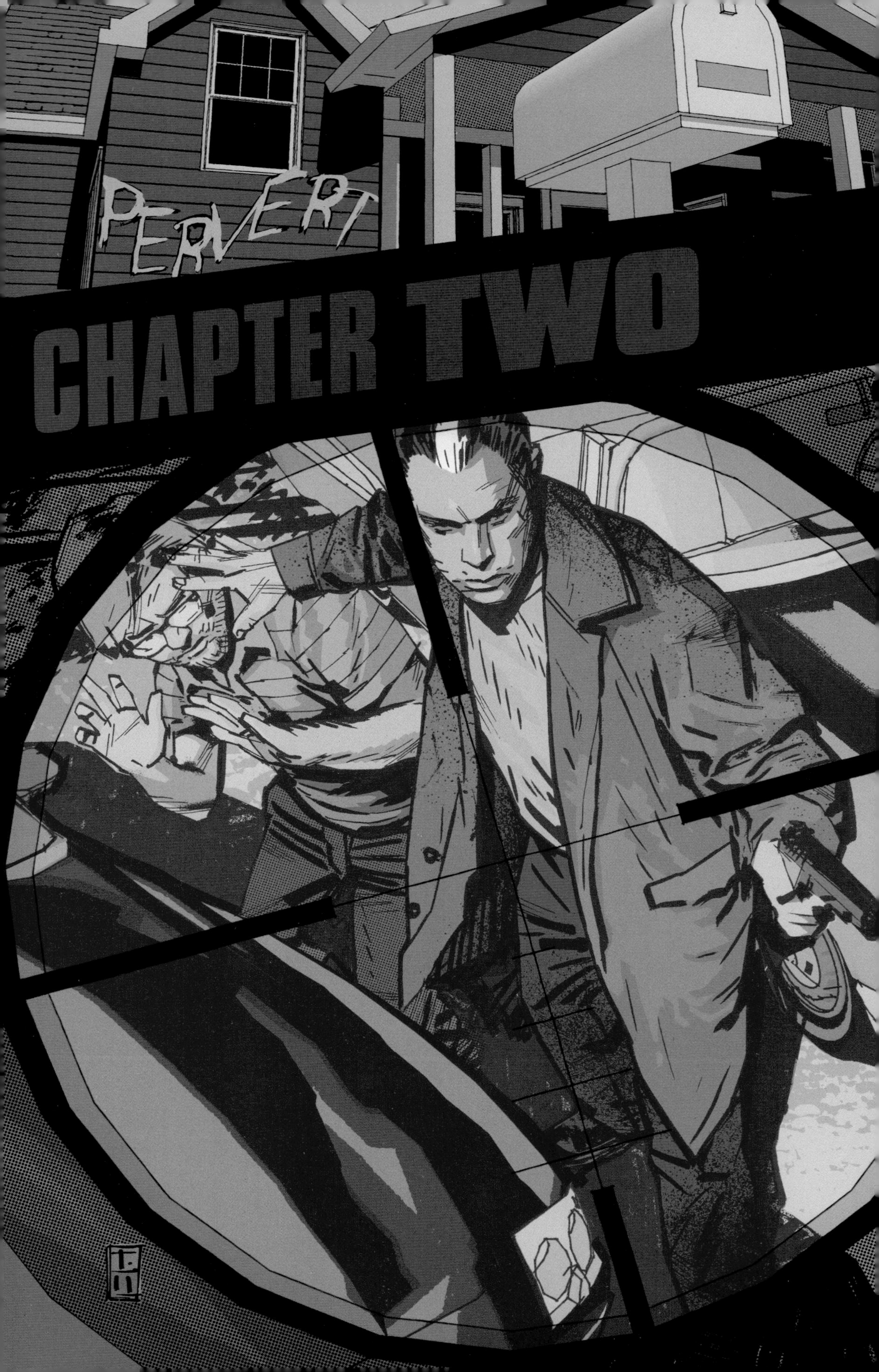
PERVERT
CHAPTER TWO

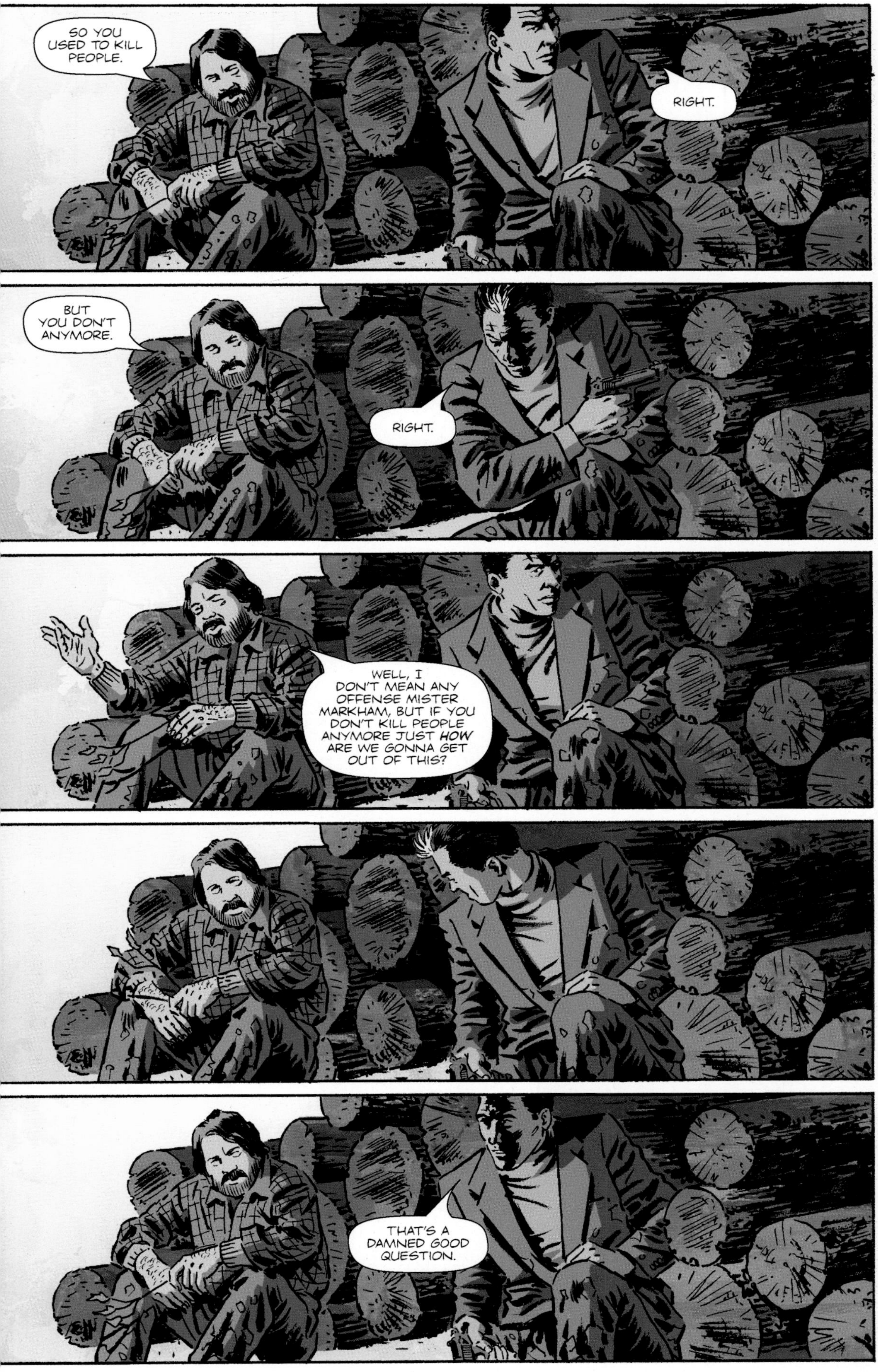
SO YOU USED TO KILL PEOPLE.
RIGHT.
BUT YOU DON'T ANYMORE.
RIGHT.
WELL, I DON'T MEAN ANY OFFENSE MISTER MARKHAM, BUT IF YOU DON'T KILL PEOPLE ANYMORE JUST *HOW* ARE WE GONNA GET OUT OF THIS?
THAT'S A DAMNED GOOD QUESTION.

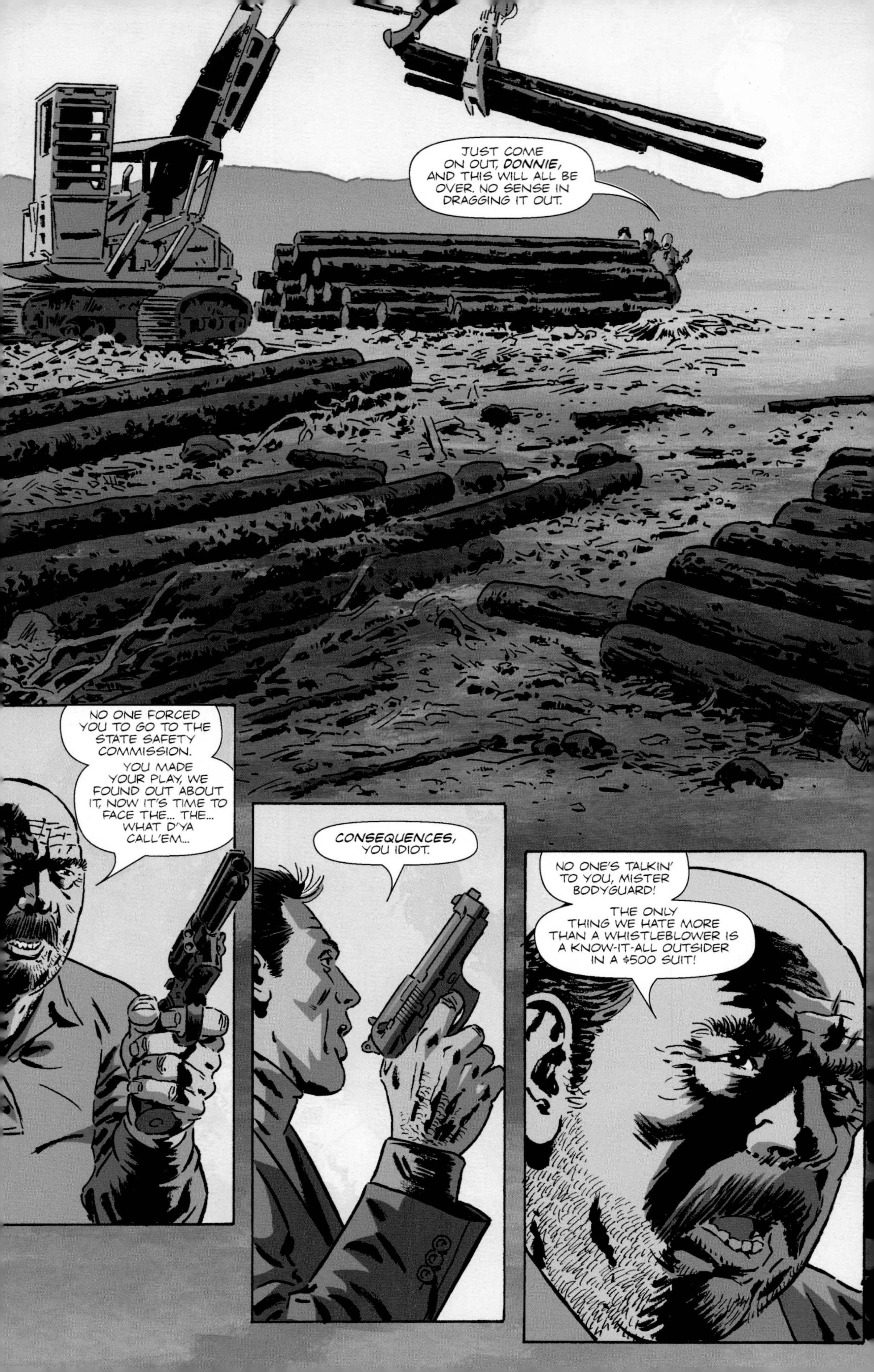
JUST COME ON OUT, DONNIE, AND THIS WILL ALL BE OVER. NO SENSE IN DRAGGING IT OUT.
NO ONE FORCED YOU TO GO TO THE STATE SAFETY COMMISSION.
YOU MADE YOUR PLAY, WE FOUND OUT ABOUT IT, NOW IT'S TIME TO FACE THE... THE... WHAT D'YA CALL'EM...
CONSEQUENCES, YOU IDIOT.
NO ONE'S TALKIN' TO YOU, MISTER BODYGUARD!
THE ONLY THING WE HATE MORE THAN A WHISTLEBLOWER IS A KNOW-IT-ALL OUTSIDER IN A $500 SUIT!

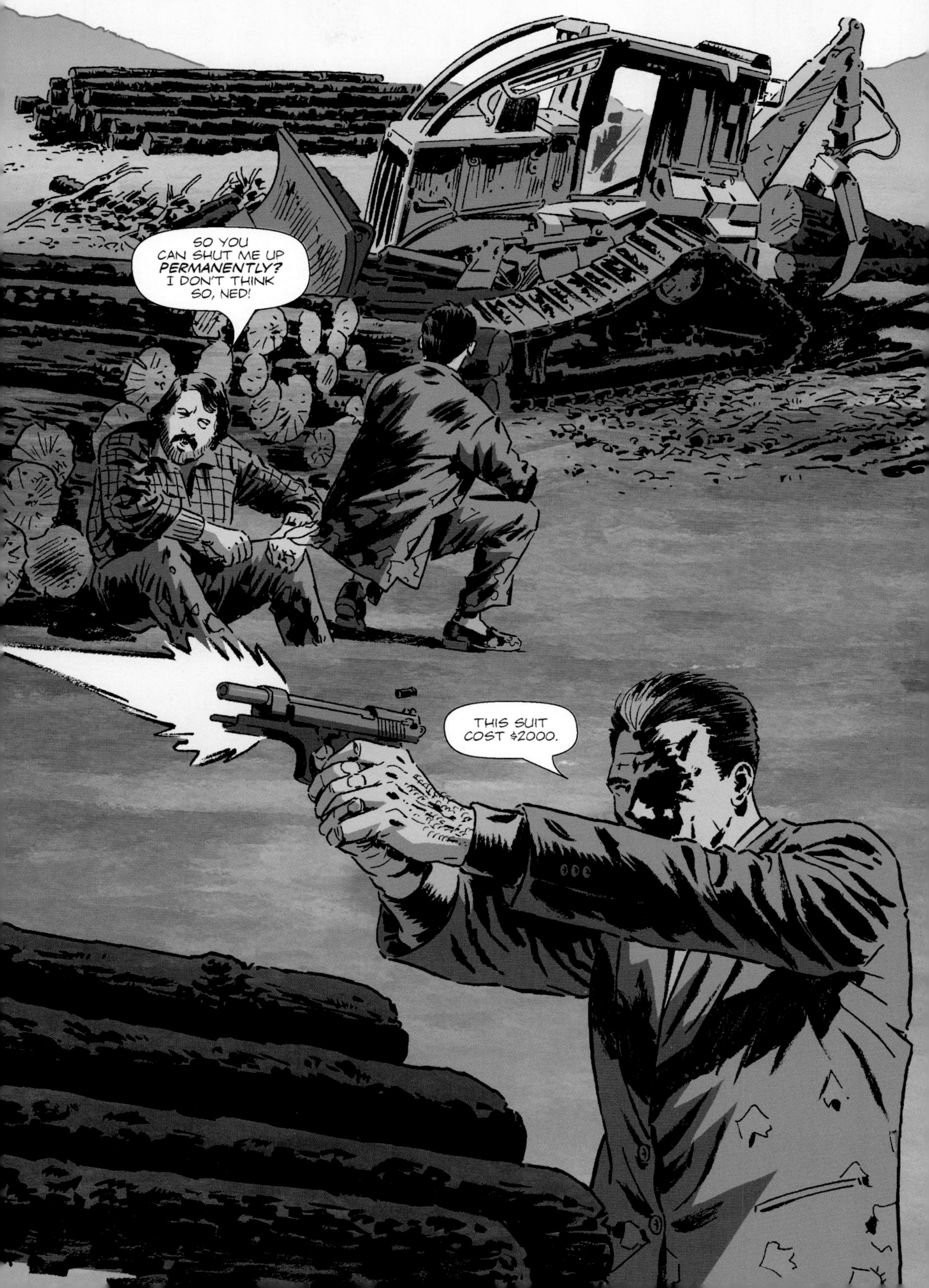
SO YOU CAN SHUT ME UP PERMANENTLY? I DON'T THINK SO, NED!
THIS SUIT COST $2000.

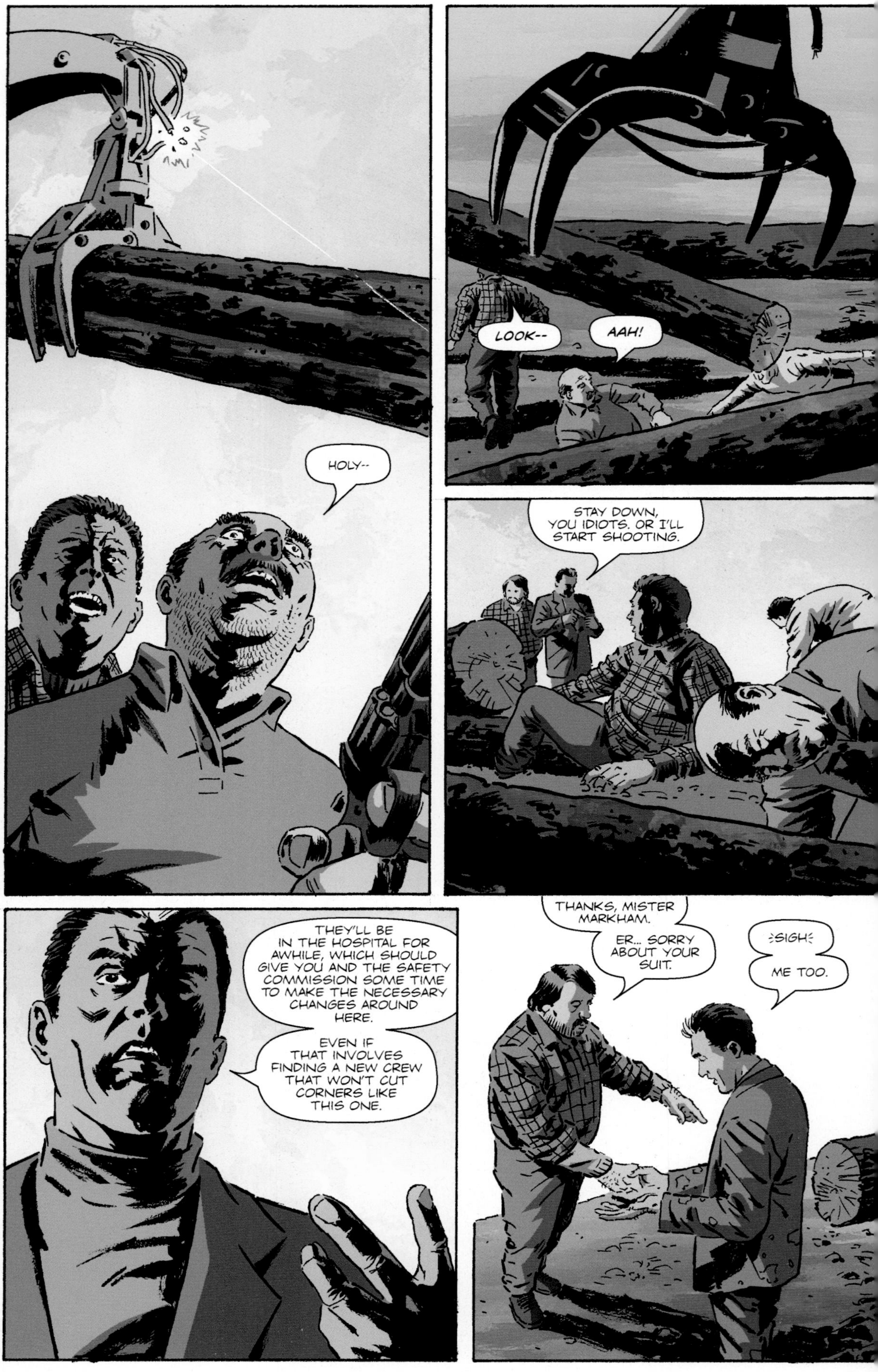
LOOK--
AAH!
HOLY--
STAY DOWN, YOU IDIOTS. OR I'LL START SHOOTING.
THEY'LL BE IN THE HOSPITAL FOR AWHILE, WHICH SHOULD GIVE YOU AND THE SAFETY COMMISSION SOME TIME TO MAKE THE NECESSARY CHANGES AROUND HERE.
EVEN IF THAT INVOLVES FINDING A NEW CREW THAT WON'T CUT CORNERS LIKE THIS ONE.
THANKS, MISTER MARKHAM.
ER... SORRY ABOUT YOUR SUIT.
SIGH
ME TOO.

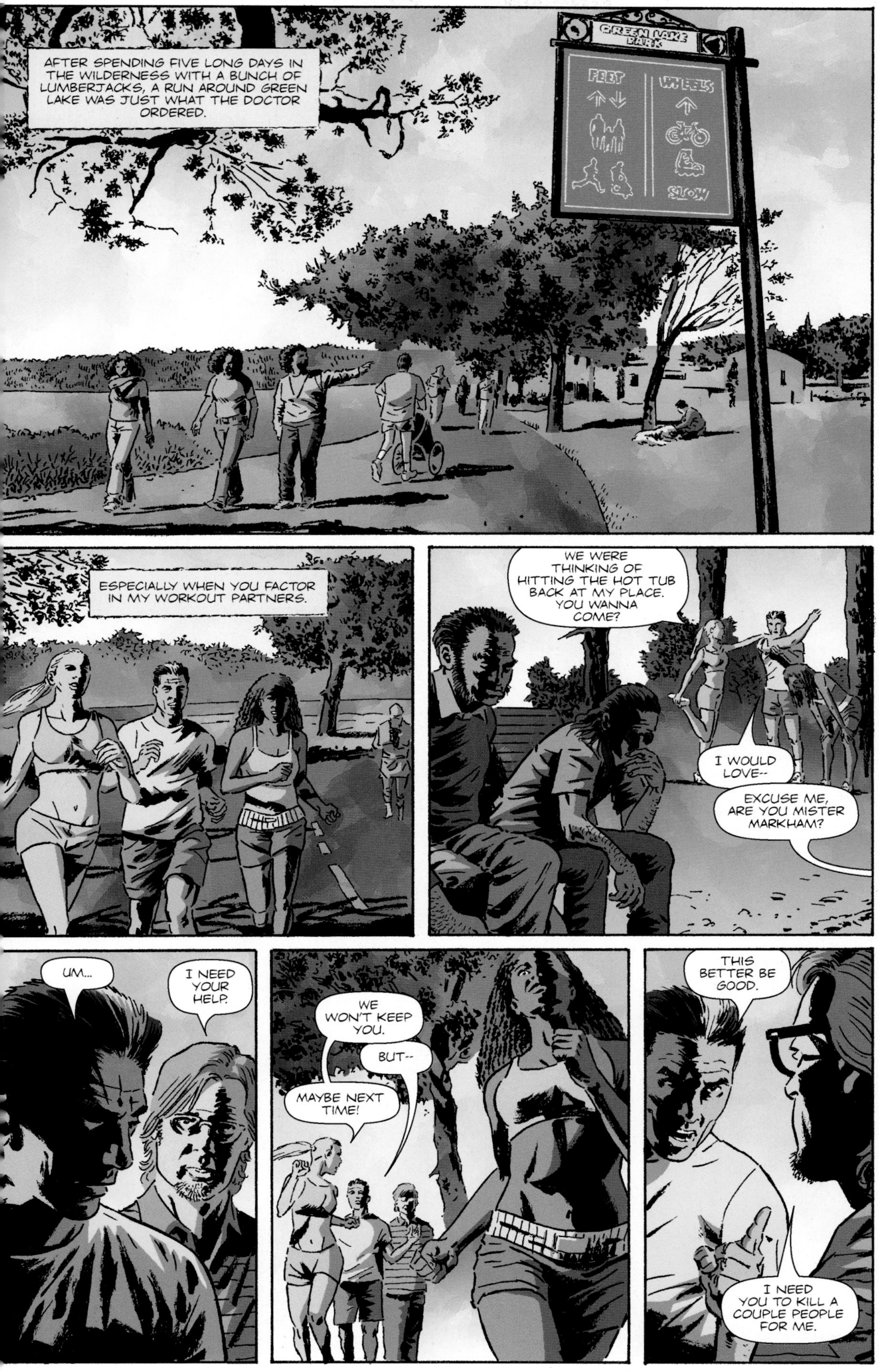
GREEN LAKE PARK
FEET
WHEELS
SLOW
AFTER SPENDING FIVE LONG DAYS IN THE WILDERNESS WITH A BUNCH OF LUMBERJACKS, A RUN AROUND GREEN LAKE WAS JUST WHAT THE DOCTOR ORDERED.
ESPECIALLY WHEN YOU FACTOR IN MY WORKOUT PARTNERS.
WE WERE THINKING OF HITTING THE HOT TUB BACK AT MY PLACE. YOU WANNA COME?
I WOULD LOVE--
EXCUSE ME, ARE YOU MISTER MARKHAM?
UM...
I NEED YOUR HELP.
WE WON'T KEEP YOU.
BUT--
MAYBE NEXT TIME!
THIS BETTER BE GOOD.
I NEED YOU TO KILL A COUPLE PEOPLE FOR ME.

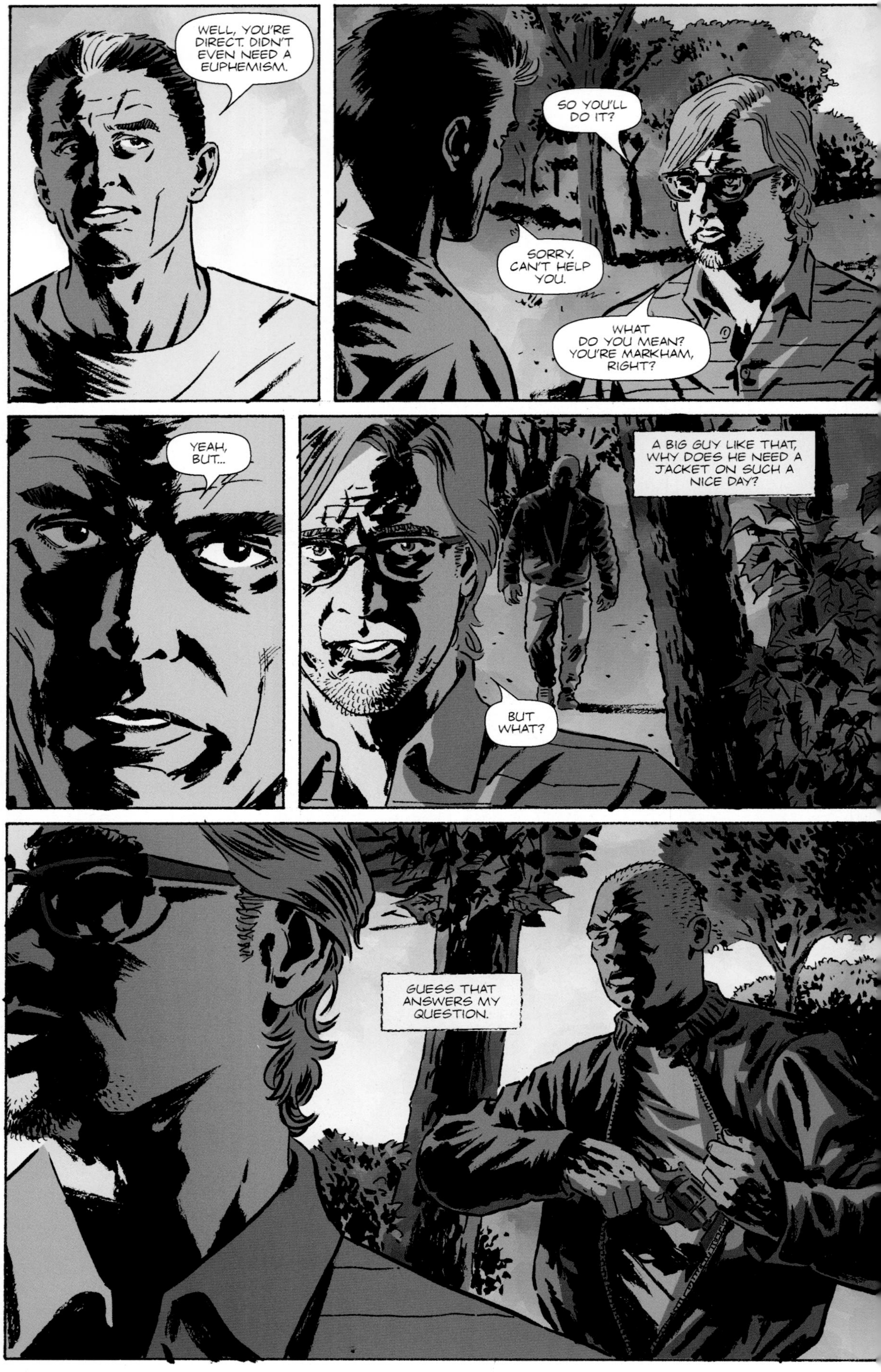

WELL, YOU'RE DIRECT. DIDN'T EVEN NEED A EUPHEMISM.
SO YOU'LL DO IT?
SORRY. CAN'T HELP YOU.
WHAT DO YOU MEAN? YOU'RE MARKHAM, RIGHT?
YEAH, BUT...
A BIG GUY LIKE THAT, WHY DOES HE NEED A JACKET ON SUCH A NICE DAY?
BUT WHAT?
GUESS THAT ANSWERS MY QUESTION.

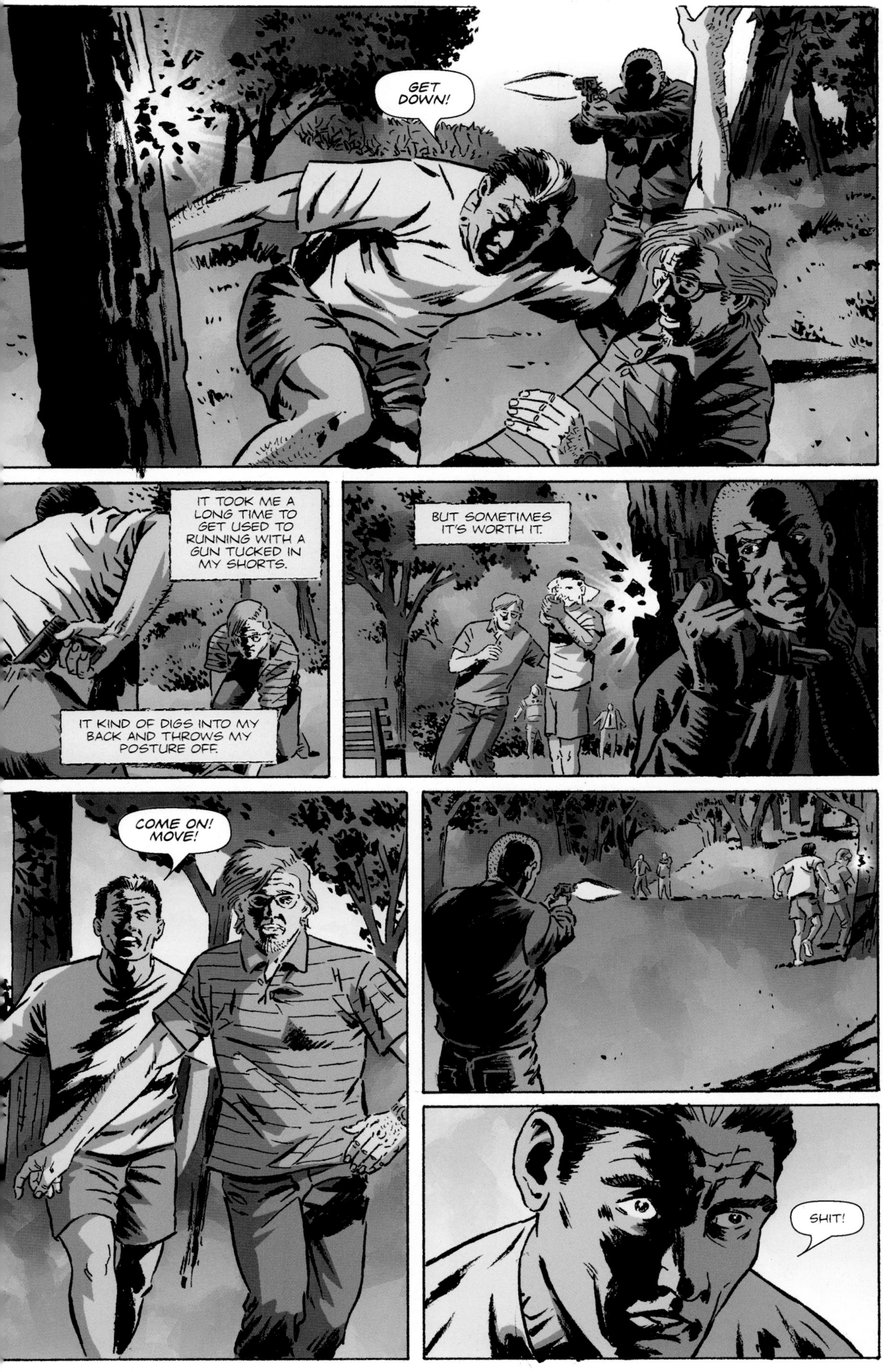
GET DOWN!
IT TOOK ME A LONG TIME TO GET USED TO RUNNING WITH A GUN TUCKED IN MY SHORTS.
IT KIND OF DIGS INTO MY BACK AND THROWS MY POSTURE OFF.
BUT SOMETIMES IT'S WORTH IT.
COME ON! MOVE!
SHIT!

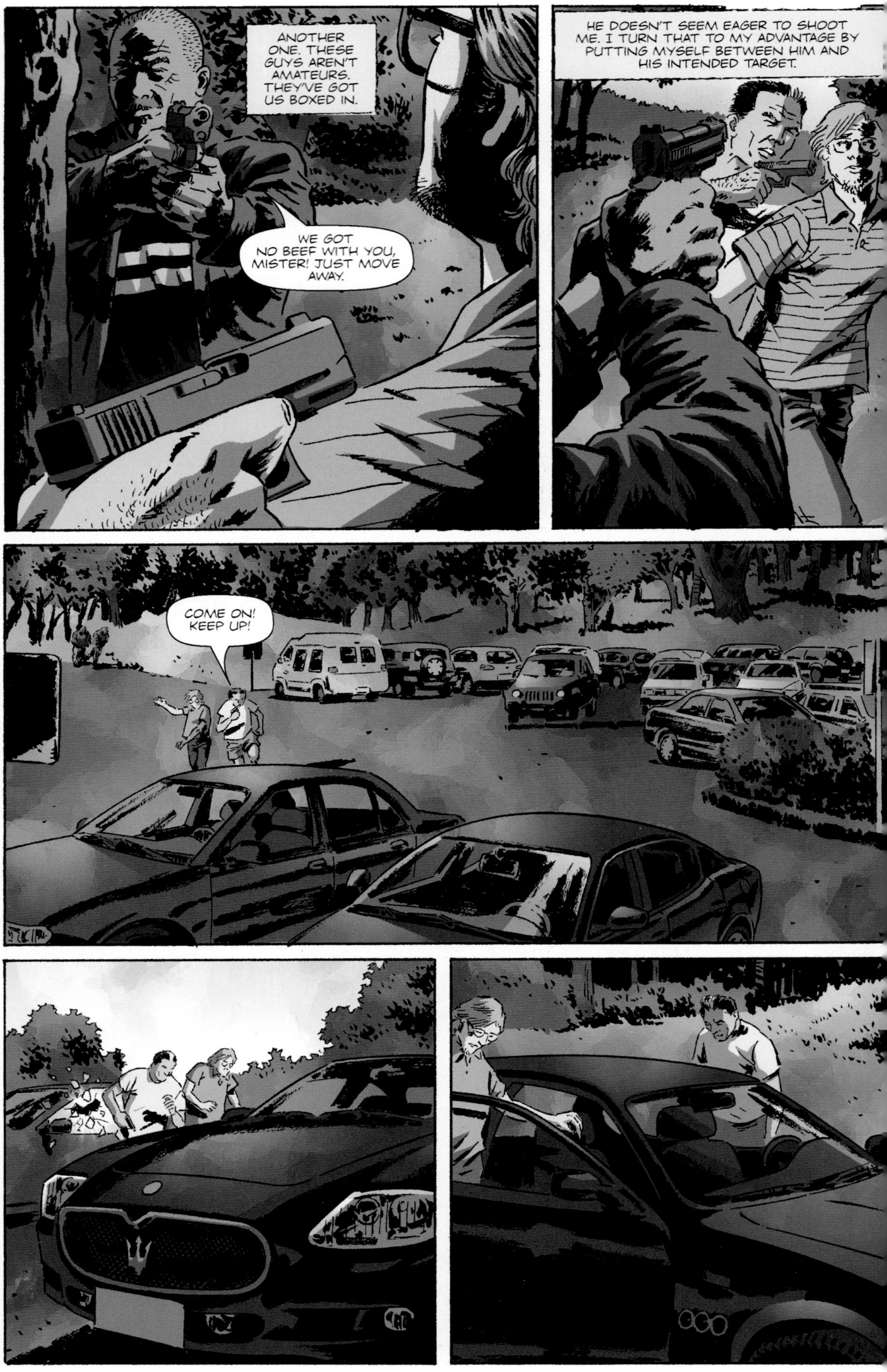
ANOTHER ONE. THESE GUYS AREN'T AMATEURS. THEY'VE GOT US BOXED IN.
WE GOT NO BEEF WITH YOU, MISTER! JUST MOVE AWAY.
HE DOESN'T SEEM EAGER TO SHOOT ME. I TURN THAT TO MY ADVANTAGE BY PUTTING MYSELF BETWEEN HIM AND HIS INTENDED TARGET.
COME ON! KEEP UP!

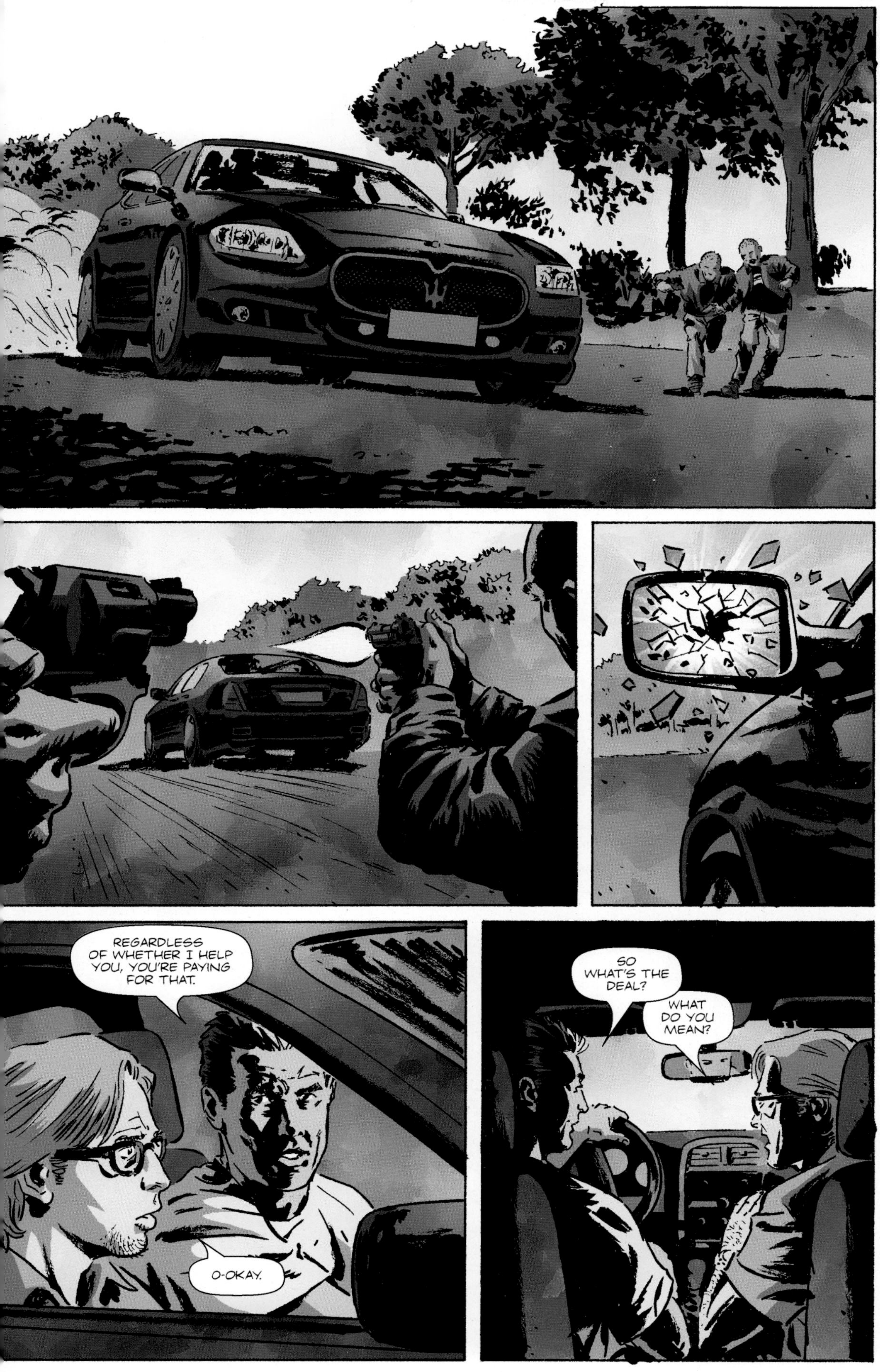
REGARDLESS OF WHETHER I HELP YOU, YOU'RE PAYING FOR THAT.
O-OKAY.
SO WHAT'S THE DEAL?
WHAT DO YOU MEAN?

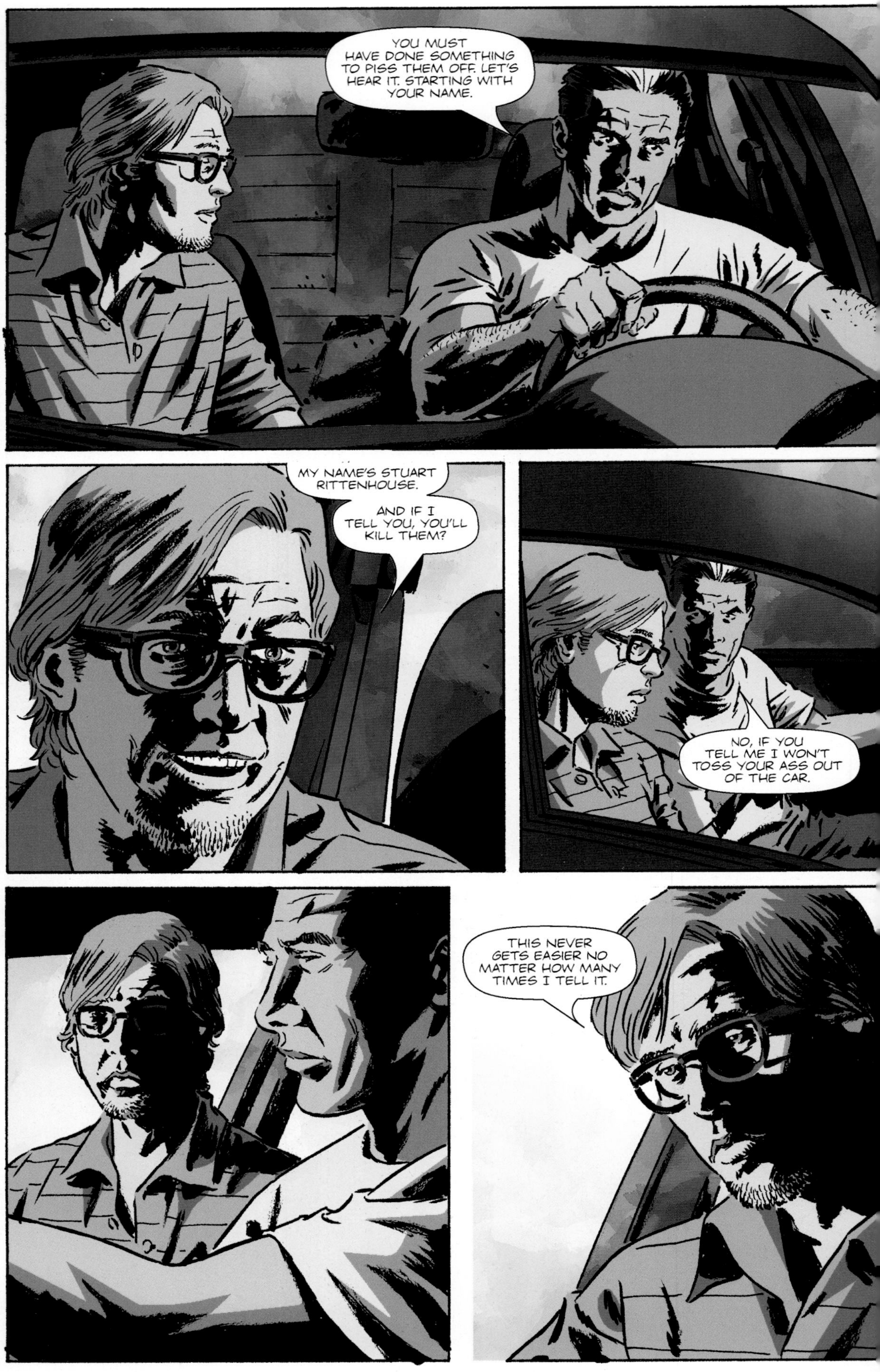
YOU MUST HAVE DONE SOMETHING TO PISS THEM OFF. LET'S HEAR IT. STARTING WITH YOUR NAME.
MY NAME'S STUART RITTENHOUSE.
AND IF I TELL YOU, YOU'LL KILL THEM?
NO, IF YOU TELL ME I WON'T TOSS YOUR ASS OUT OF THE CAR.
THIS NEVER GETS EASIER NO MATTER HOW MANY TIMES I TELL IT.

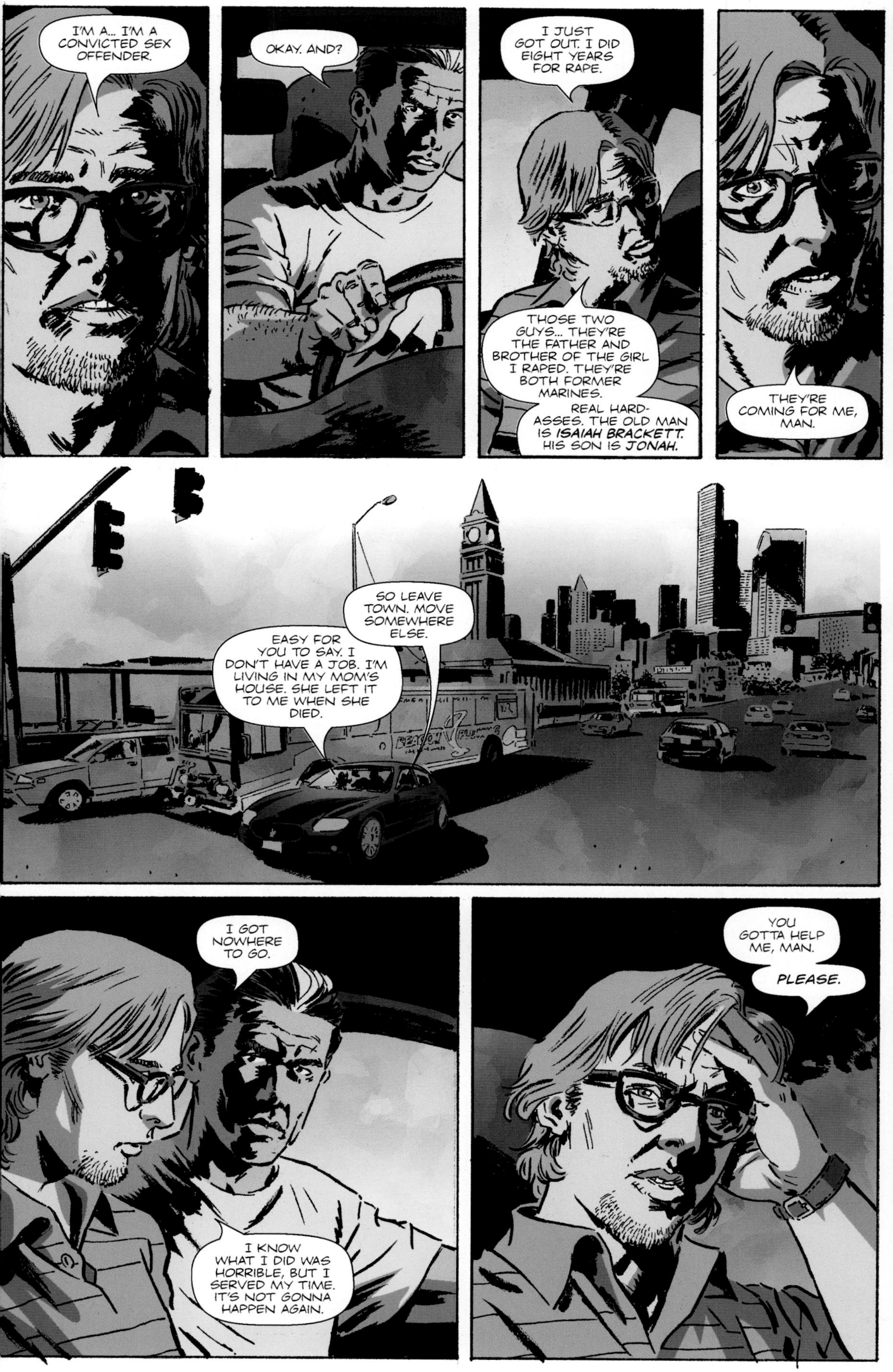
I'M A... I'M A CONVICTED SEX OFFENDER.
OKAY. AND?
I JUST GOT OUT. I DID EIGHT YEARS FOR RAPE.
THOSE TWO GUYS... THEY'RE THE FATHER AND BROTHER OF THE GIRL I RAPED. THEY'RE BOTH FORMER MARINES.
REAL HARD-ASSES. THE OLD MAN IS ISAIAH BRACKETT. HIS SON IS JONAH.
THEY'RE COMING FOR ME, MAN.
SO LEAVE TOWN. MOVE SOMEWHERE ELSE.
EASY FOR YOU TO SAY. I DON'T HAVE A JOB. I'M LIVING IN MY MOM'S HOUSE. SHE LEFT IT TO ME WHEN SHE DIED.
I GOT NOWHERE TO GO.
I KNOW WHAT I DID WAS HORRIBLE, BUT I SERVED MY TIME. IT'S NOT GONNA HAPPEN AGAIN.
YOU GOTTA HELP ME, MAN.
PLEASE.

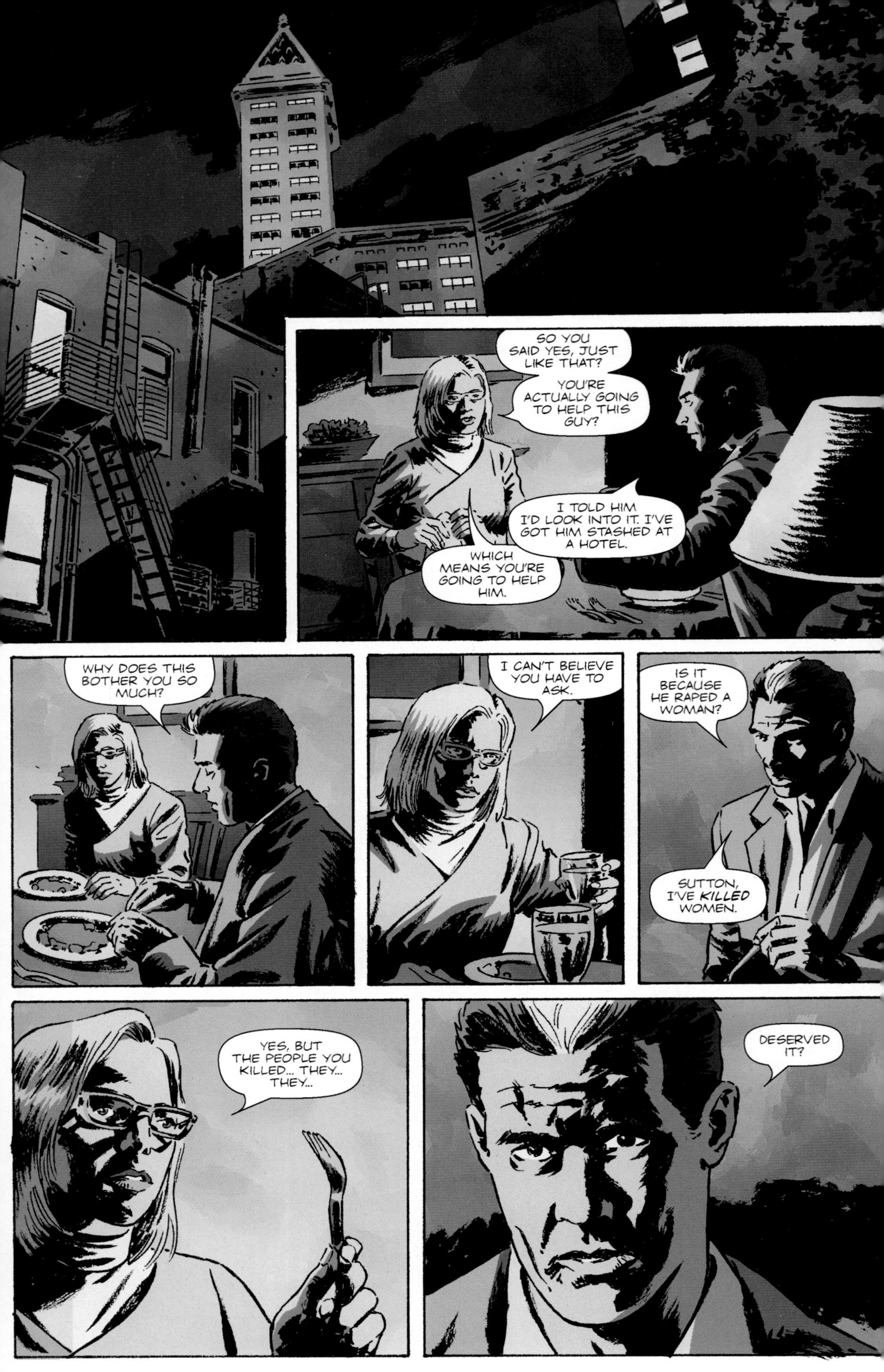

SO YOU SAID YES, JUST LIKE THAT?
YOU'RE ACTUALLY GOING TO HELP THIS GUY?
I TOLD HIM I'D LOOK INTO IT. I'VE GOT HIM STASHED AT A HOTEL.
WHICH MEANS YOU'RE GOING TO HELP HIM.
WHY DOES THIS BOTHER YOU SO MUCH?
I CAN'T BELIEVE YOU HAVE TO ASK.
IS IT BECAUSE HE RAPED A WOMAN?
SUTTON, I'VE KILLED WOMEN.
YES, BUT THE PEOPLE YOU KILLED... THEY... THEY...
DESERVED IT?

YES! EXACTLY. THEY DESERVED IT.

DIDN'T THEY?

THE PERSON HIRING ME OBVIOUSLY THOUGHT SO.

BUT *YOU* DIDN'T NECESSARILY THINK THEY DESERVED IT?

HONESTLY, I DIDN'T CARE.

AND... AND NOW?

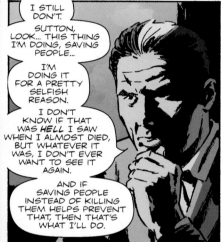

I STILL DON'T. SUTTON, LOOK... THIS THING I'M DOING, SAVING PEOPLE...

I'M DOING IT FOR A PRETTY SELFISH REASON.

I DON'T KNOW IF THAT WAS *HELL* I SAW WHEN I ALMOST DIED, BUT WHATEVER IT WAS, I DON'T EVER WANT TO SEE IT AGAIN.

AND IF SAVING PEOPLE INSTEAD OF KILLING THEM HELPS PREVENT THAT, THEN THAT'S WHAT I'LL DO.

I HAVE TO ADMIT I'M SURPRISED THAT YOU'RE REACTING THIS WAY.

YOU DON'T EVEN *LIKE* PEOPLE.

I THOUGHT THAT'S ONE OF THE THINGS WE HAD IN COMMON.

YEAH, I'M A MISANTHROPE. BUT YOU, YOU'RE A... A SOCIOPATH.

HOW COME LIFE WAS EASIER WHEN I WAS KILLING PEOPLE?

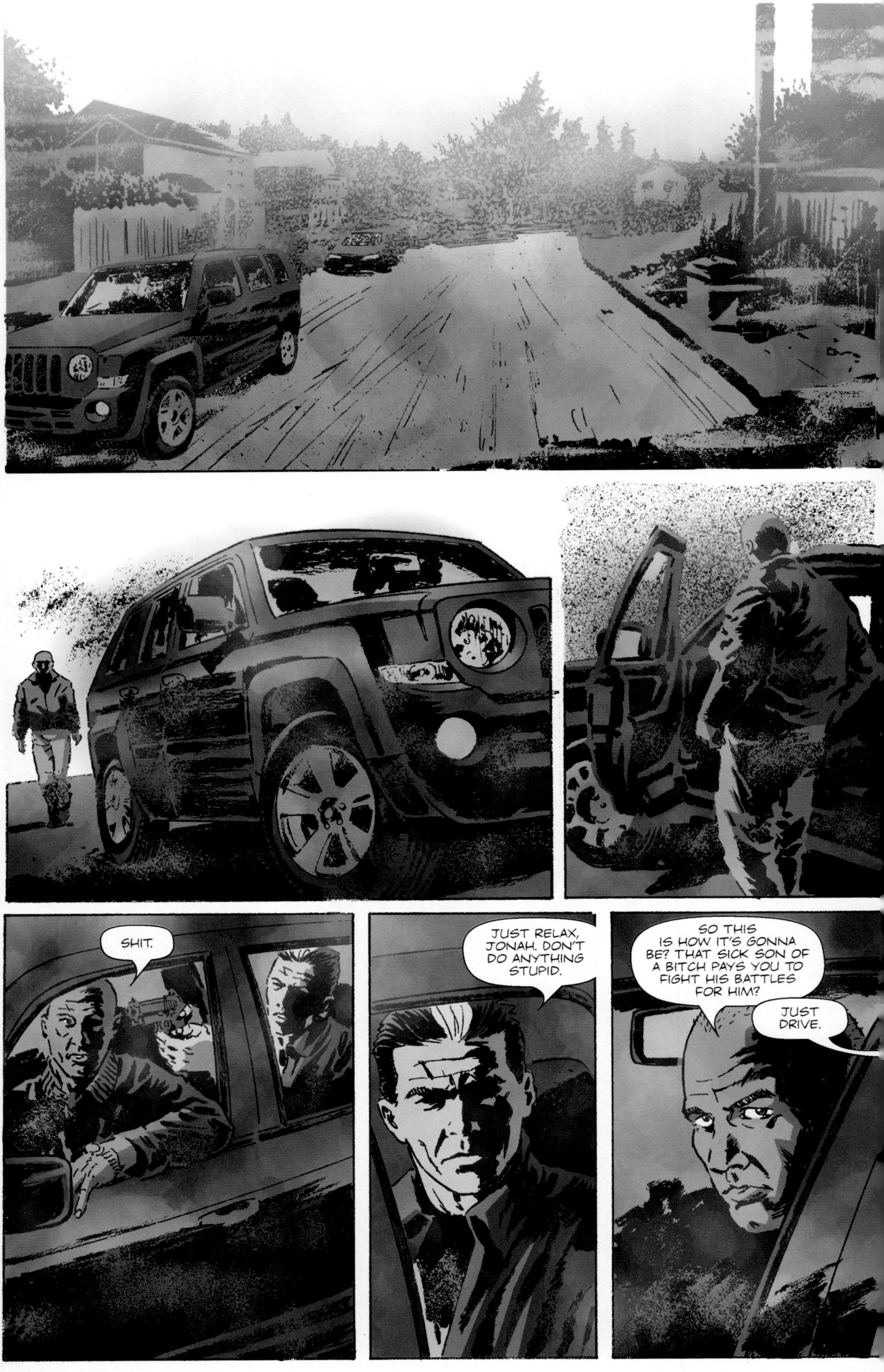
SHIT.
JUST RELAX, JONAH. DON'T DO ANYTHING STUPID.
SO THIS IS HOW IT'S GONNA BE? THAT SICK SON OF A BITCH PAYS YOU TO FIGHT HIS BATTLES FOR HIM?
JUST DRIVE.

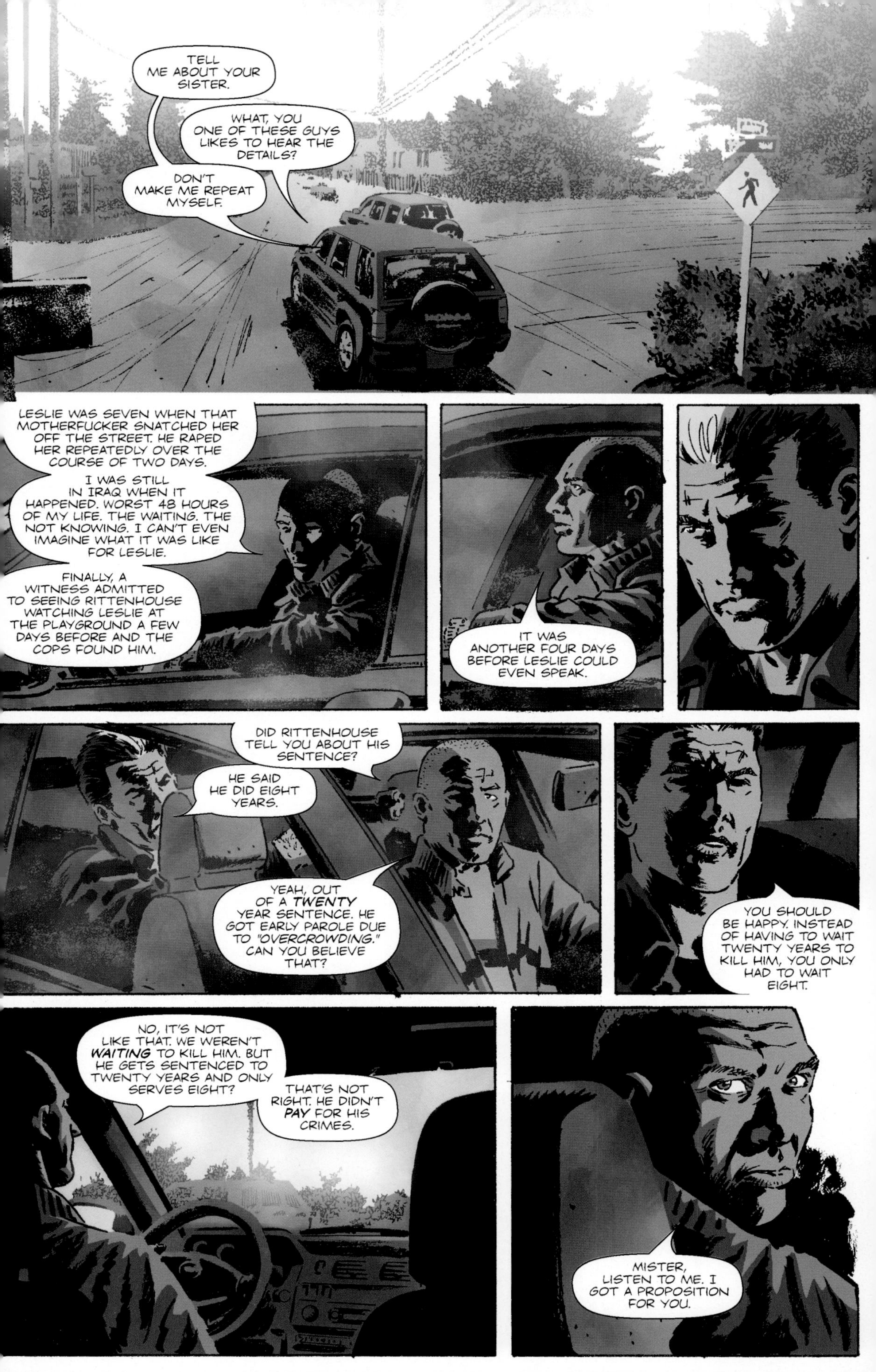
TELL ME ABOUT YOUR SISTER.
WHAT, YOU ONE OF THESE GUYS LIKES TO HEAR THE DETAILS?
DON'T MAKE ME REPEAT MYSELF.
LESLIE WAS SEVEN WHEN THAT MOTHERFUCKER SNATCHED HER OFF THE STREET. HE RAPED HER REPEATEDLY OVER THE COURSE OF TWO DAYS.
I WAS STILL IN IRAQ WHEN IT HAPPENED. WORST 48 HOURS OF MY LIFE. THE WAITING. THE NOT KNOWING. I CAN'T EVEN IMAGINE WHAT IT WAS LIKE FOR LESLIE.
FINALLY, A WITNESS ADMITTED TO SEEING RITTENHOUSE WATCHING LESLIE AT THE PLAYGROUND A FEW DAYS BEFORE AND THE COPS FOUND HIM.
IT WAS ANOTHER FOUR DAYS BEFORE LESLIE COULD EVEN SPEAK.
DID RITTENHOUSE TELL YOU ABOUT HIS SENTENCE?
HE SAID HE DID EIGHT YEARS.
YEAH, OUT OF A *TWENTY* YEAR SENTENCE. HE GOT EARLY PAROLE DUE TO *"OVERCROWDING."* CAN YOU BELIEVE THAT?
YOU SHOULD BE HAPPY. INSTEAD OF HAVING TO WAIT TWENTY YEARS TO KILL HIM, YOU ONLY HAD TO WAIT EIGHT.
NO, IT'S NOT LIKE THAT. WE WEREN'T *WAITING* TO KILL HIM. BUT HE GETS SENTENCED TO TWENTY YEARS AND ONLY SERVES EIGHT?
THAT'S NOT RIGHT. HE DIDN'T *PAY* FOR HIS CRIMES.
MISTER, LISTEN TO ME. I GOT A PROPOSITION FOR YOU.

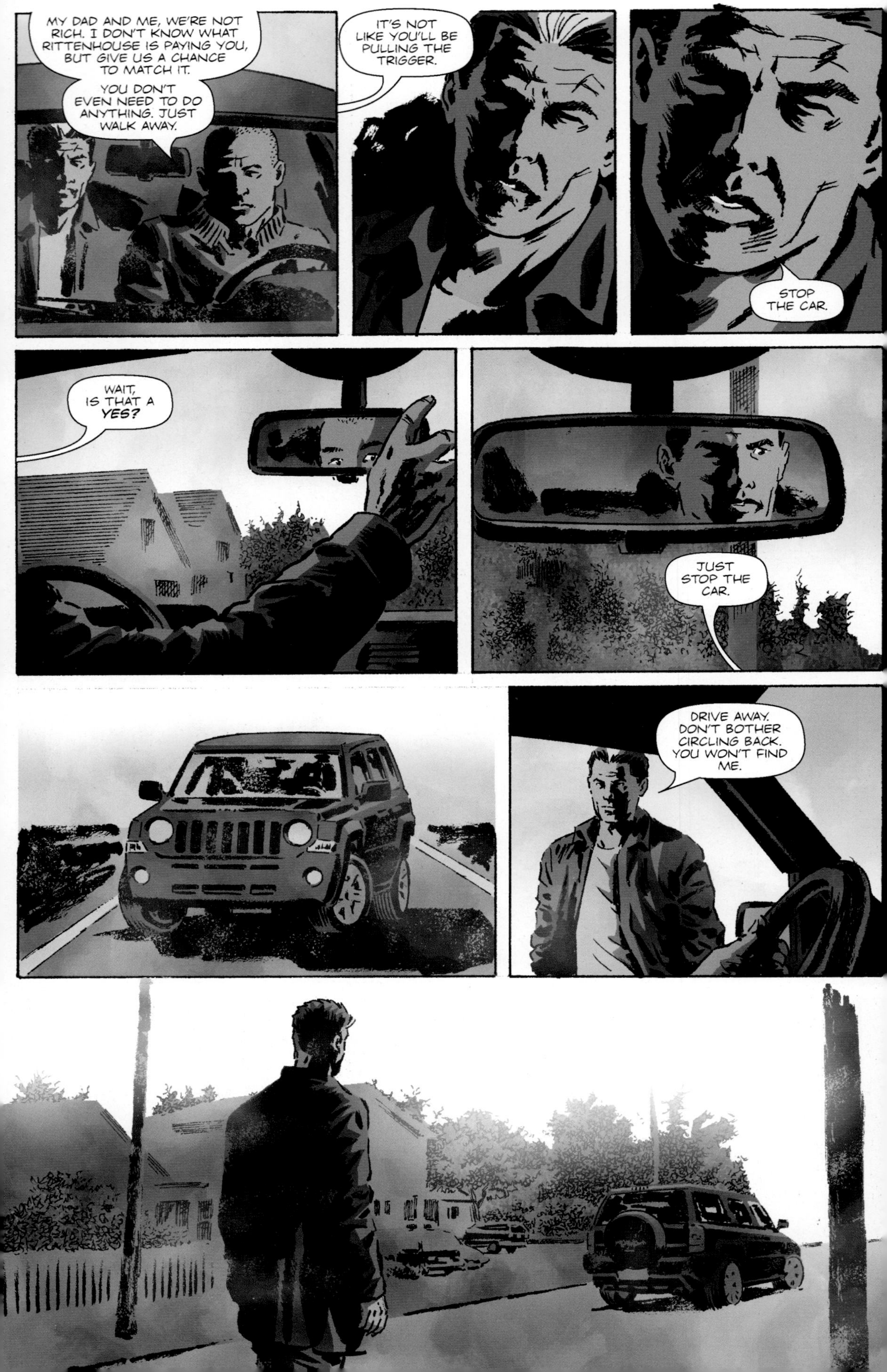
MY DAD AND ME, WE'RE NOT RICH. I DON'T KNOW WHAT RITTENHOUSE IS PAYING YOU, BUT GIVE US A CHANCE TO MATCH IT.
YOU DON'T EVEN NEED TO DO ANYTHING. JUST WALK AWAY.
IT'S NOT LIKE YOU'LL BE PULLING THE TRIGGER.
STOP THE CAR.
WAIT, IS THAT A *YES?*
JUST STOP THE CAR.
DRIVE AWAY. DON'T BOTHER CIRCLING BACK. YOU WON'T FIND ME.

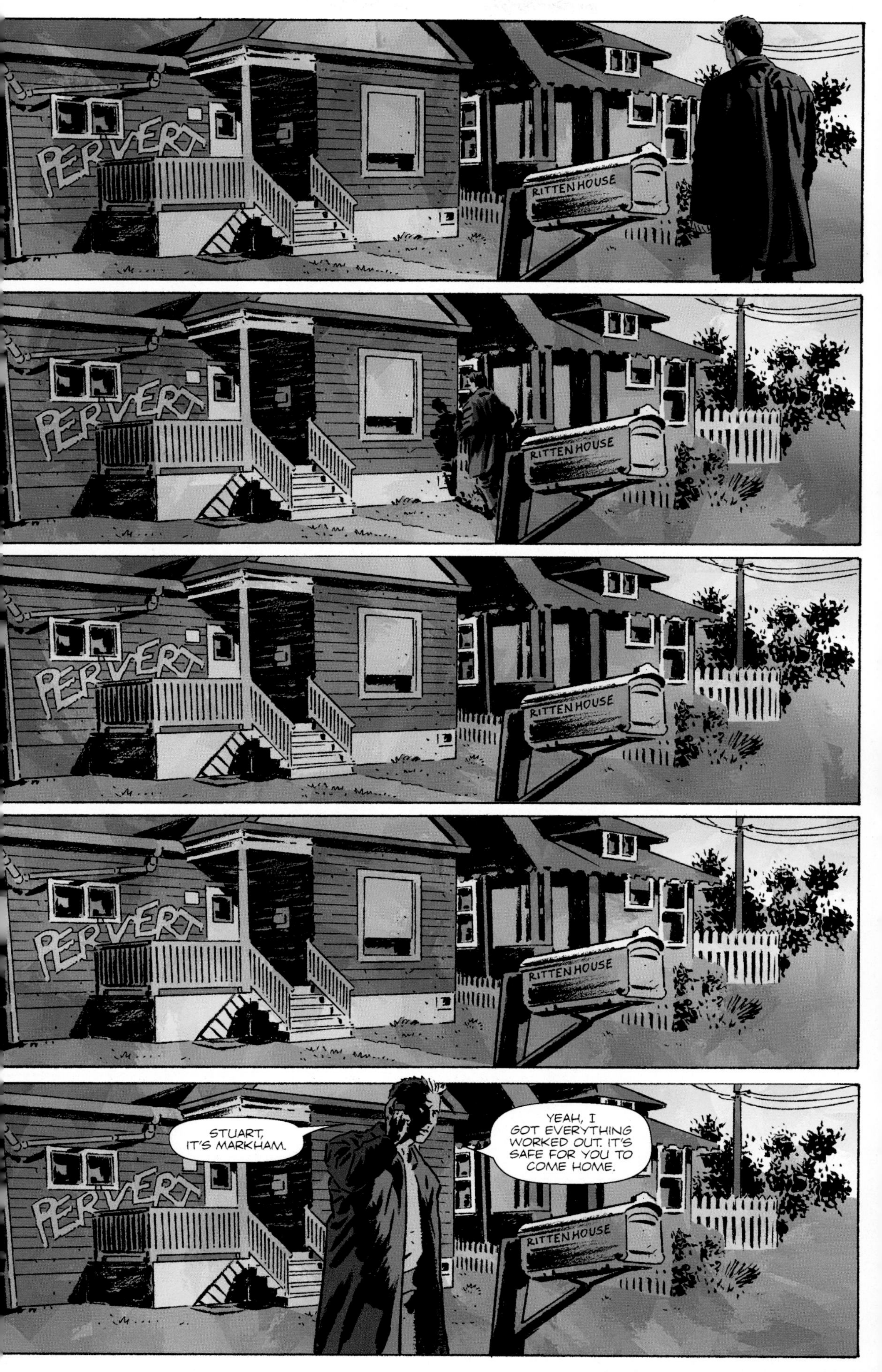
PERVERT
RITTENHOUSE
PERVERT
RITTENHOUSE
PERVERT
RITTENHOUSE
PERVERT
RITTENHOUSE
PERVERT
RITTENHOUSE
STUART, IT'S MARKHAM.
YEAH, I GOT EVERYTHING WORKED OUT. IT'S SAFE FOR YOU TO COME HOME.

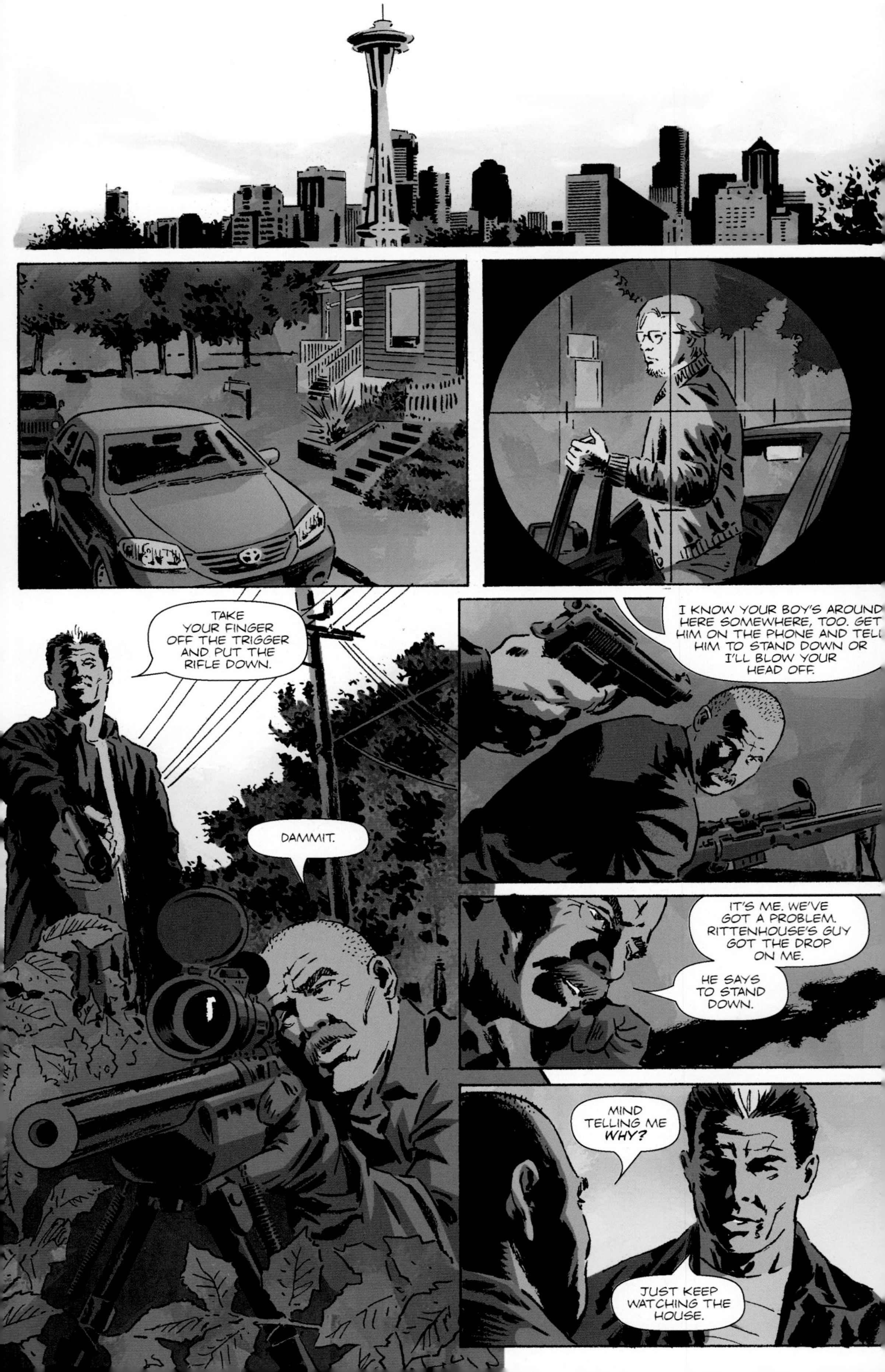
TAKE YOUR FINGER OFF THE TRIGGER AND PUT THE RIFLE DOWN.
I KNOW YOUR BOY'S AROUND HERE SOMEWHERE, TOO. GET HIM ON THE PHONE AND TELL HIM TO STAND DOWN OR I'LL BLOW YOUR HEAD OFF.
DAMMIT.
IT'S ME. WE'VE GOT A PROBLEM. RITTENHOUSE'S GUY GOT THE DROP ON ME.
HE SAYS TO STAND DOWN.
MIND TELLING ME *WHY?*
JUST KEEP WATCHING THE HOUSE.

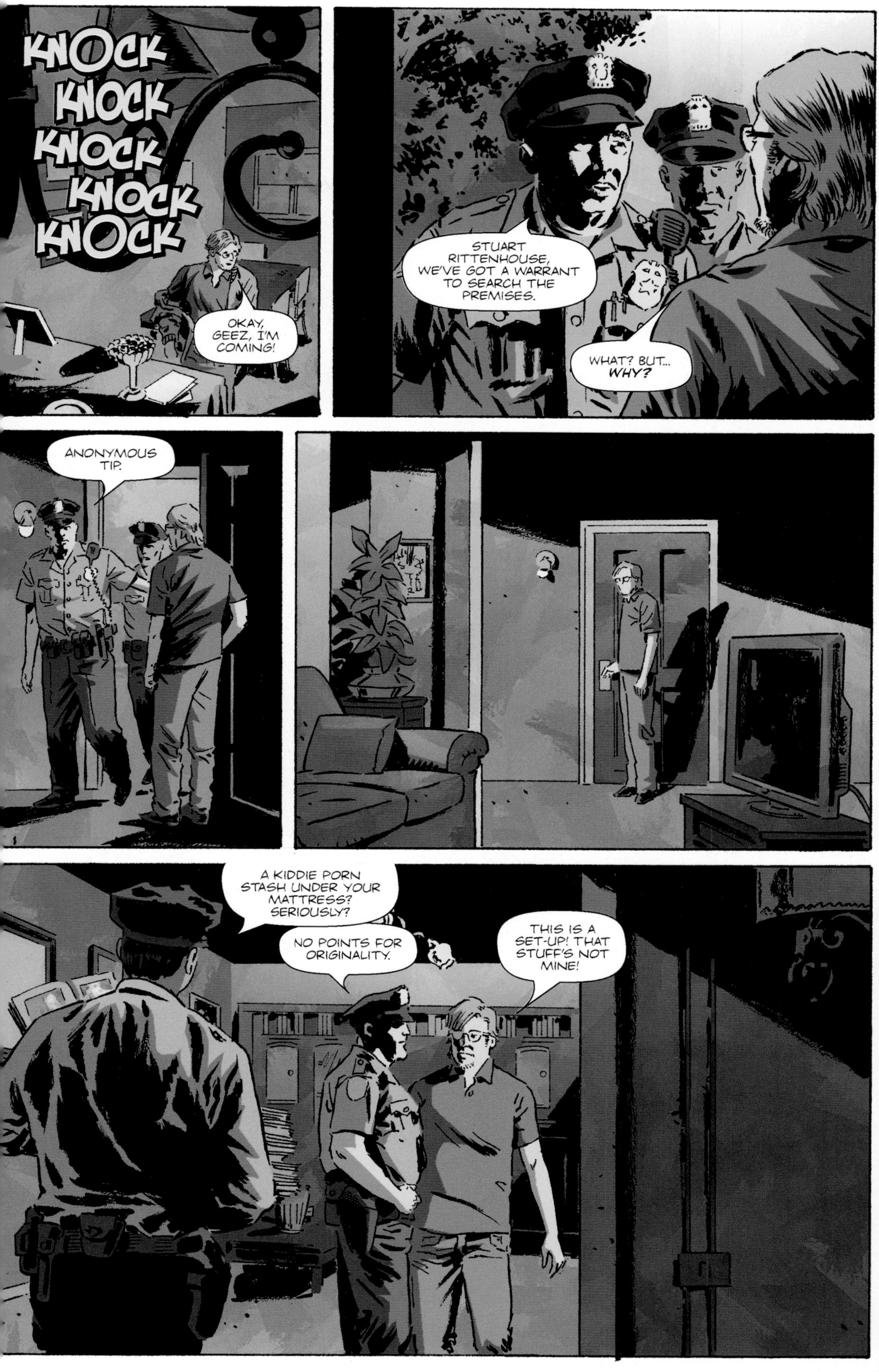
KNOCK KNOCK KNOCK KNOCK KNOCK
OKAY, GEEZ, I'M COMING!
STUART RITTENHOUSE, WE'VE GOT A WARRANT TO SEARCH THE PREMISES.
WHAT? BUT... *WHY?*
ANONYMOUS TIP.
A KIDDIE PORN STASH UNDER YOUR MATTRESS? SERIOUSLY?
NO POINTS FOR ORIGINALITY.
THIS IS A SET-UP! THAT STUFF'S NOT MINE!

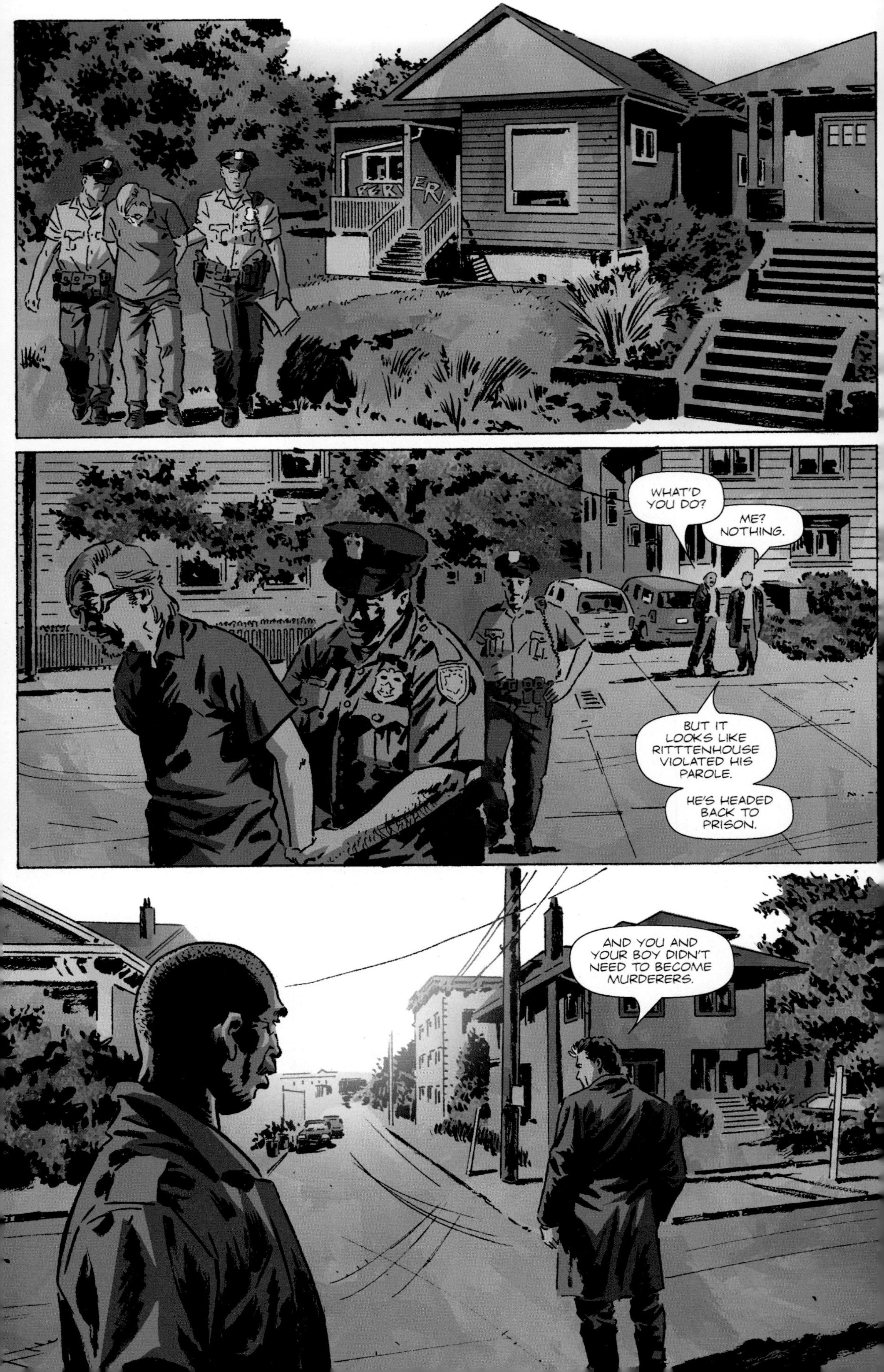
WHAT'D YOU DO?
ME? NOTHING.
BUT IT LOOKS LIKE RITTTENHOUSE VIOLATED HIS PAROLE.
HE'S HEADED BACK TO PRISON.
AND YOU AND YOUR BOY DIDN'T NEED TO BECOME MURDERERS.

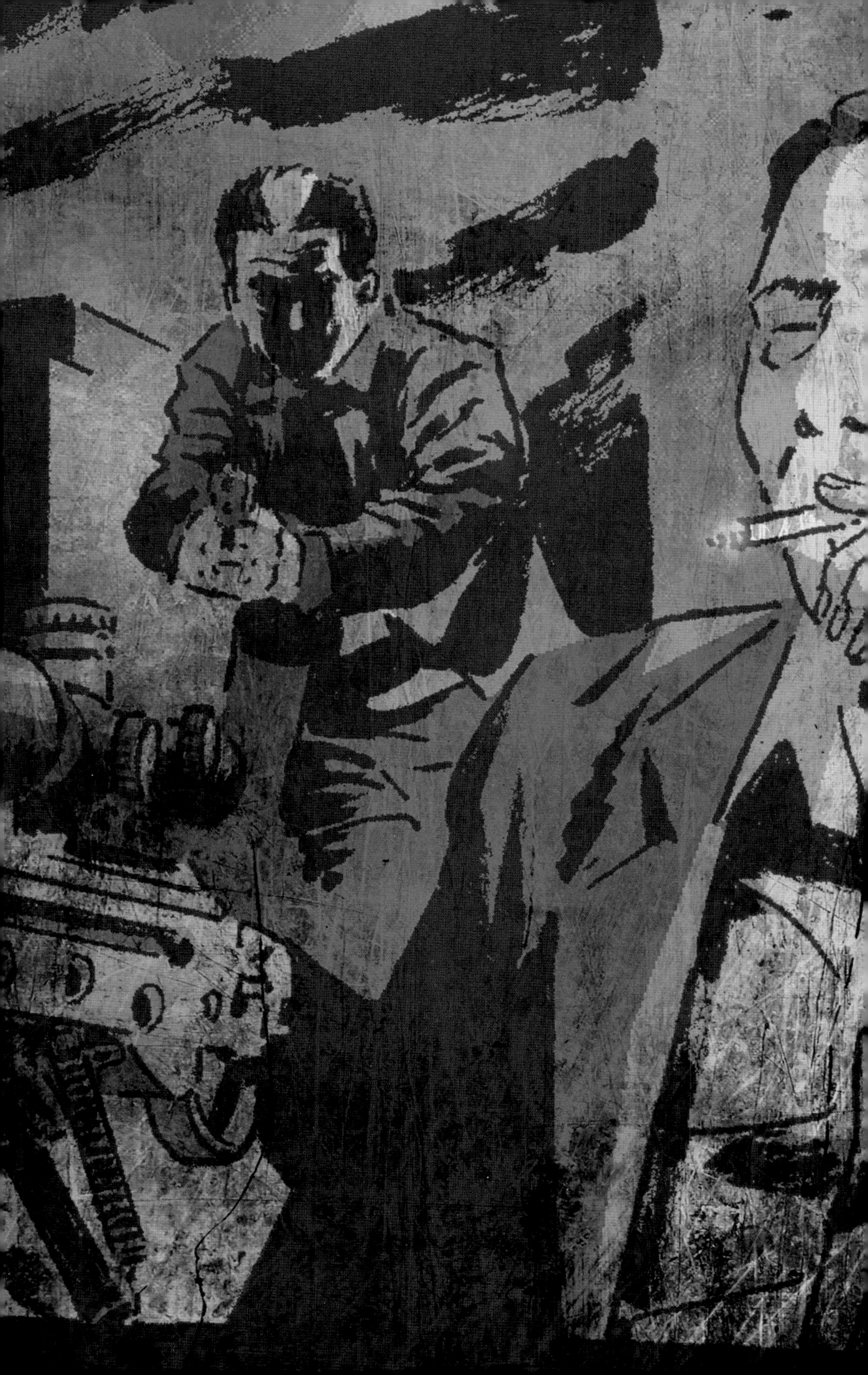

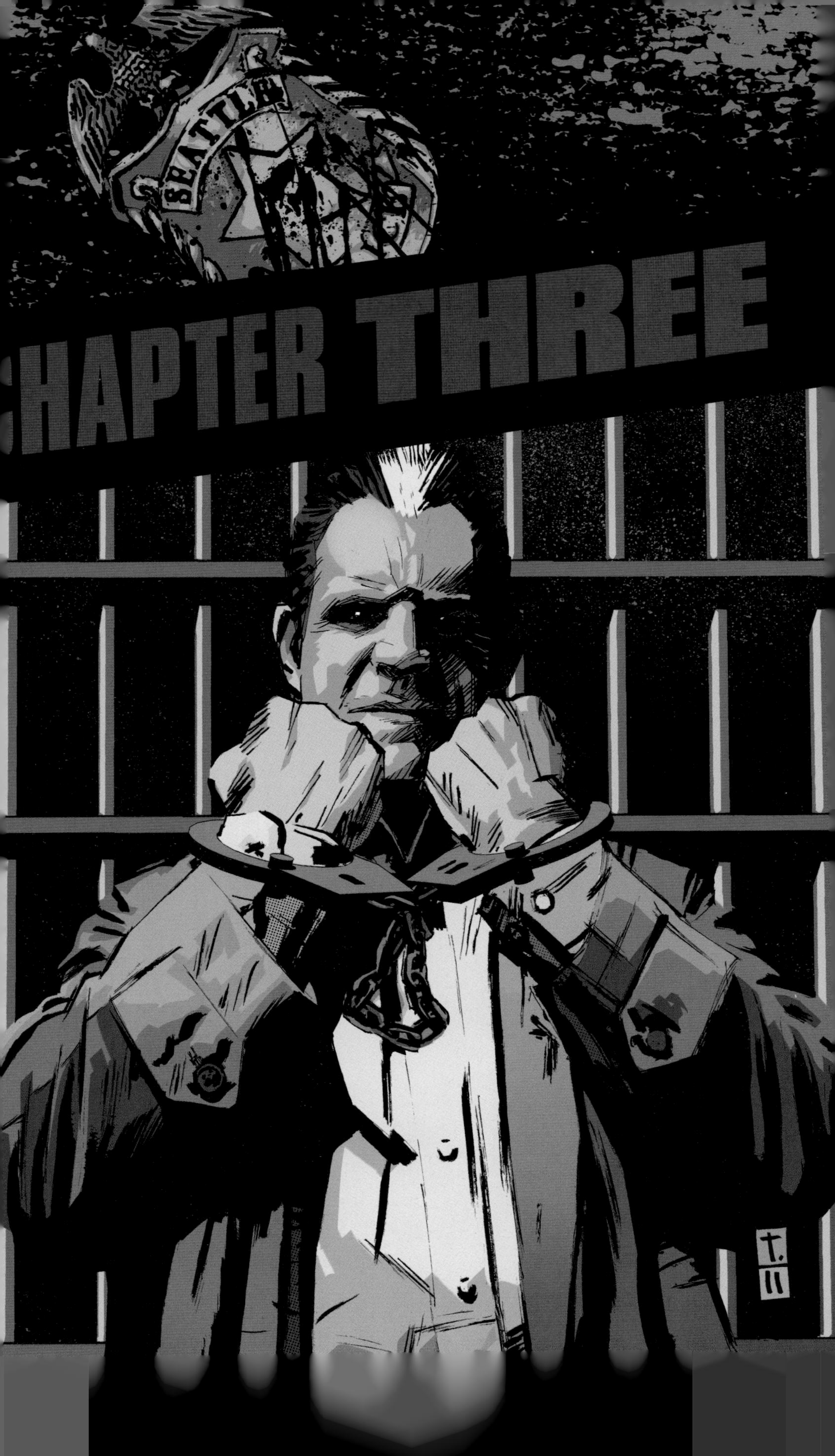
SEATTLE
CHAPTER THREE

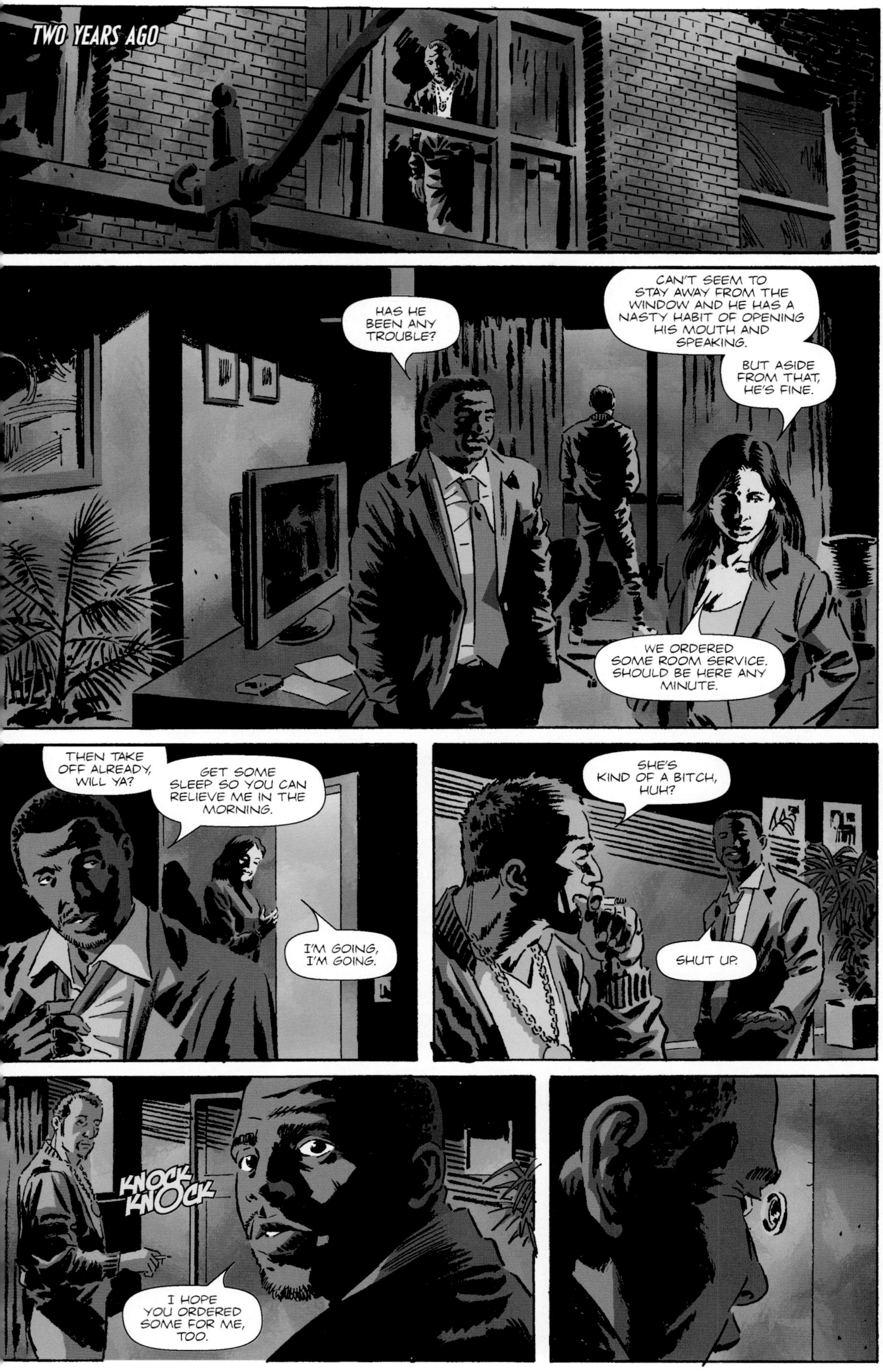
TWO YEARS AGO
HAS HE BEEN ANY TROUBLE?
CAN'T SEEM TO STAY AWAY FROM THE WINDOW AND HE HAS A NASTY HABIT OF OPENING HIS MOUTH AND SPEAKING.
BUT ASIDE FROM THAT, HE'S FINE.
WE ORDERED SOME ROOM SERVICE. SHOULD BE HERE ANY MINUTE.
THEN TAKE OFF ALREADY, WILL YA?
GET SOME SLEEP SO YOU CAN RELIEVE ME IN THE MORNING.
I'M GOING, I'M GOING.
SHE'S KIND OF A BITCH, HUH?
SHUT UP.
KNOCK KNOCK
I HOPE YOU ORDERED SOME FOR ME, TOO.

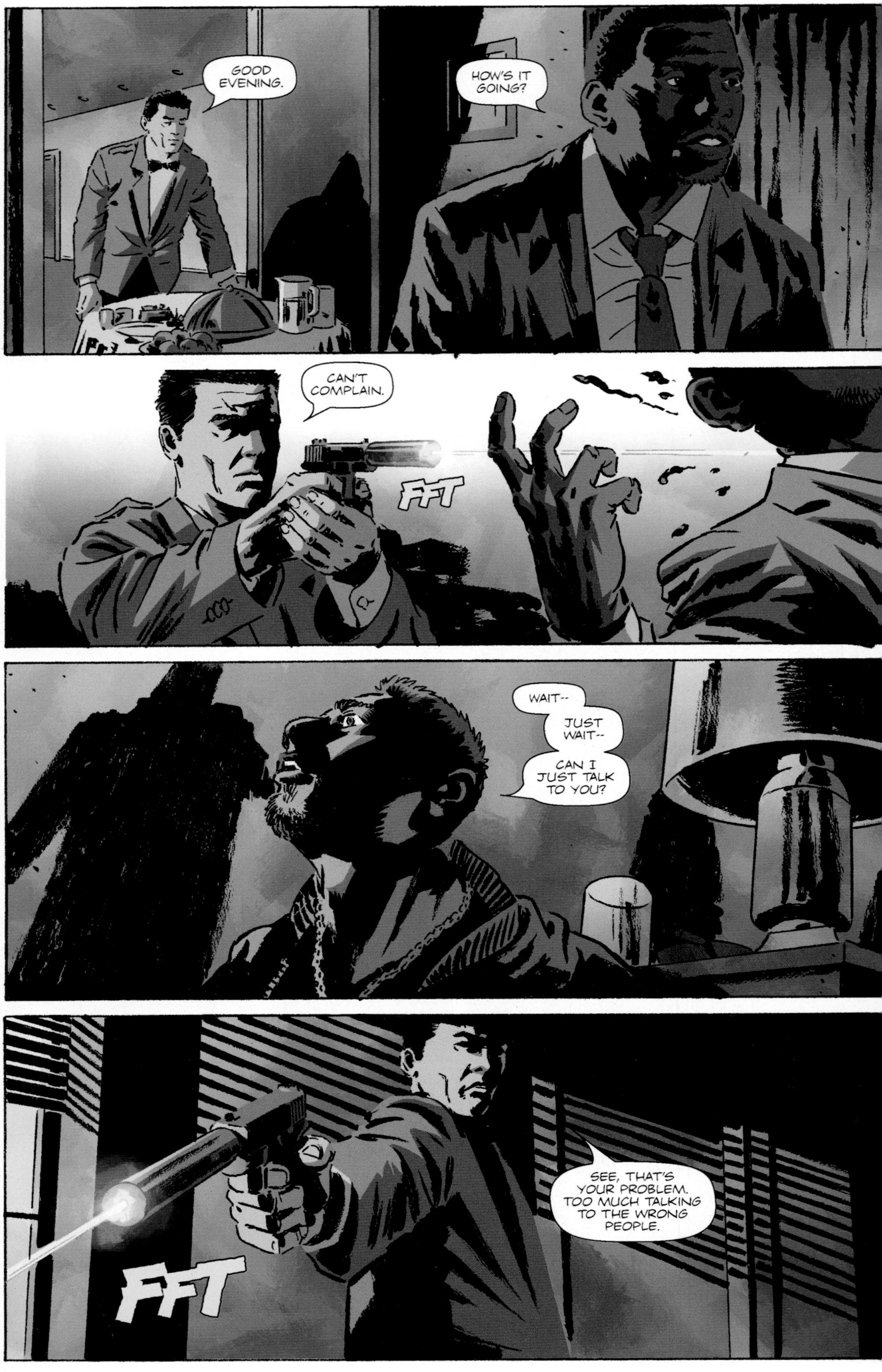
GOOD EVENING.
HOW'S IT GOING?
CAN'T COMPLAIN.
FFT
WAIT--
JUST WAIT--
CAN I JUST TALK TO YOU?
SEE, THAT'S YOUR PROBLEM. TOO MUCH TALKING TO THE WRONG PEOPLE.
FFT

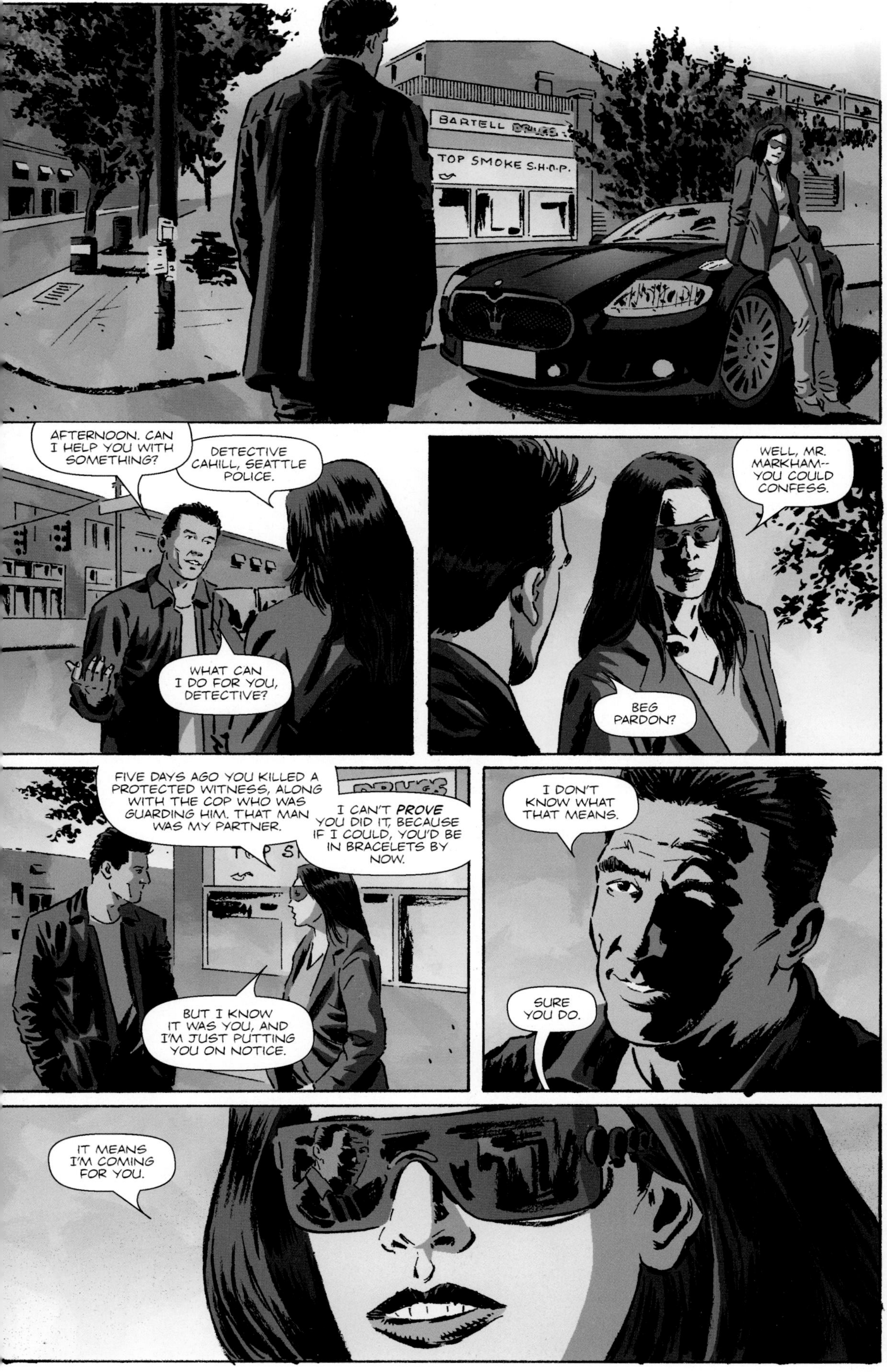
BARTELL DRUGS
TOP SMOKE S.H.O.P.
AFTERNOON. CAN I HELP YOU WITH SOMETHING?
DETECTIVE CAHILL, SEATTLE POLICE.
WHAT CAN I DO FOR YOU, DETECTIVE?
WELL, MR. MARKHAM-- YOU COULD CONFESS.
BEG PARDON?
FIVE DAYS AGO YOU KILLED A PROTECTED WITNESS, ALONG WITH THE COP WHO WAS GUARDING HIM. THAT MAN WAS MY PARTNER.
I CAN'T *PROVE* YOU DID IT, BECAUSE IF I COULD, YOU'D BE IN BRACELETS BY NOW.
BUT I KNOW IT WAS YOU, AND I'M JUST PUTTING YOU ON NOTICE.
I DON'T KNOW WHAT THAT MEANS.
SURE YOU DO.
IT MEANS I'M COMING FOR YOU.

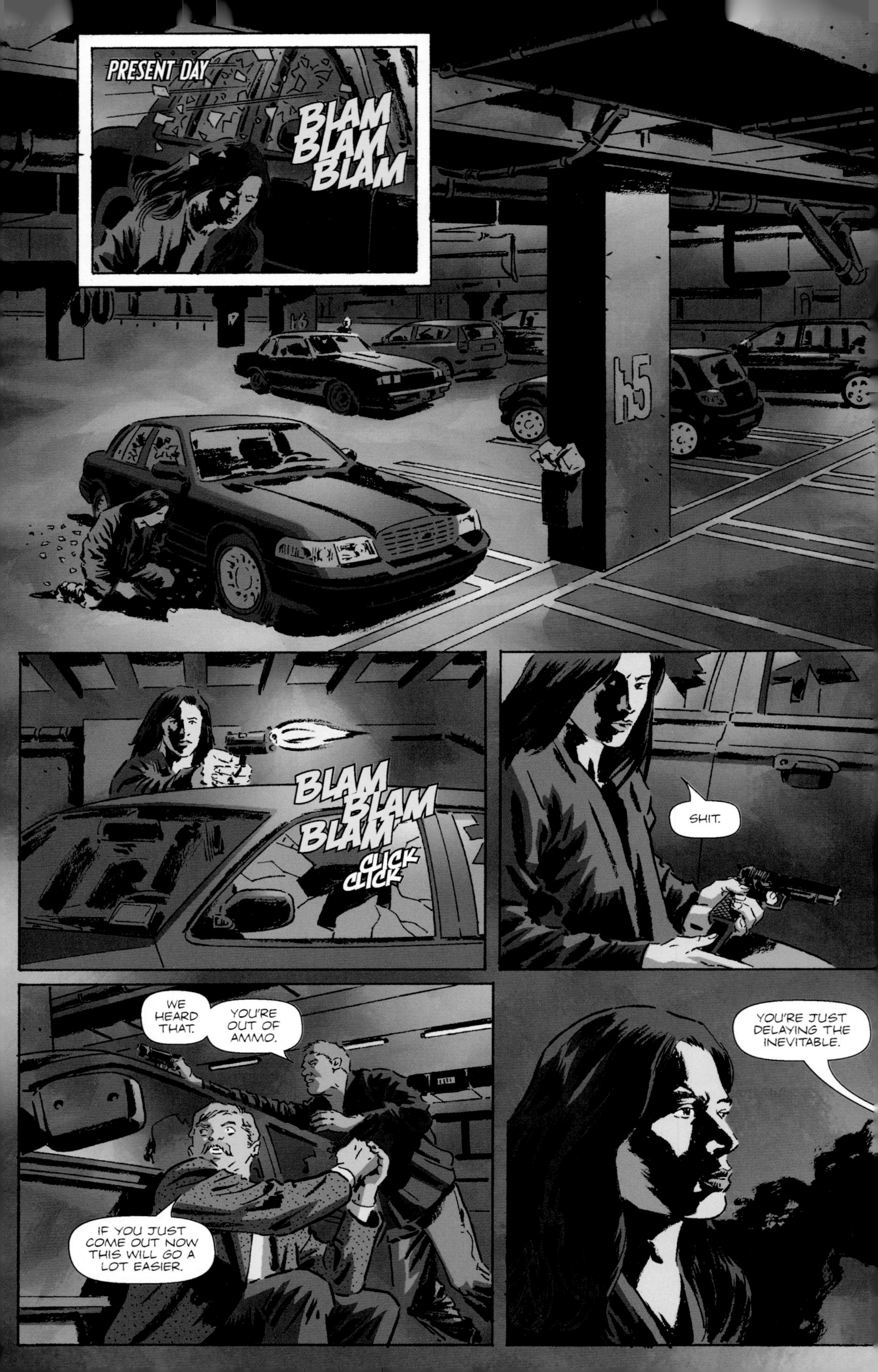
PRESENT DAY
BLAM BLAM BLAM
BLAM BLAM BLAM
CLICK CLICK
SHIT.
WE HEARD THAT.
YOU'RE OUT OF AMMO.
IF YOU JUST COME OUT NOW THIS WILL GO A LOT EASIER.
YOU'RE JUST DELAYING THE INEVITABLE.

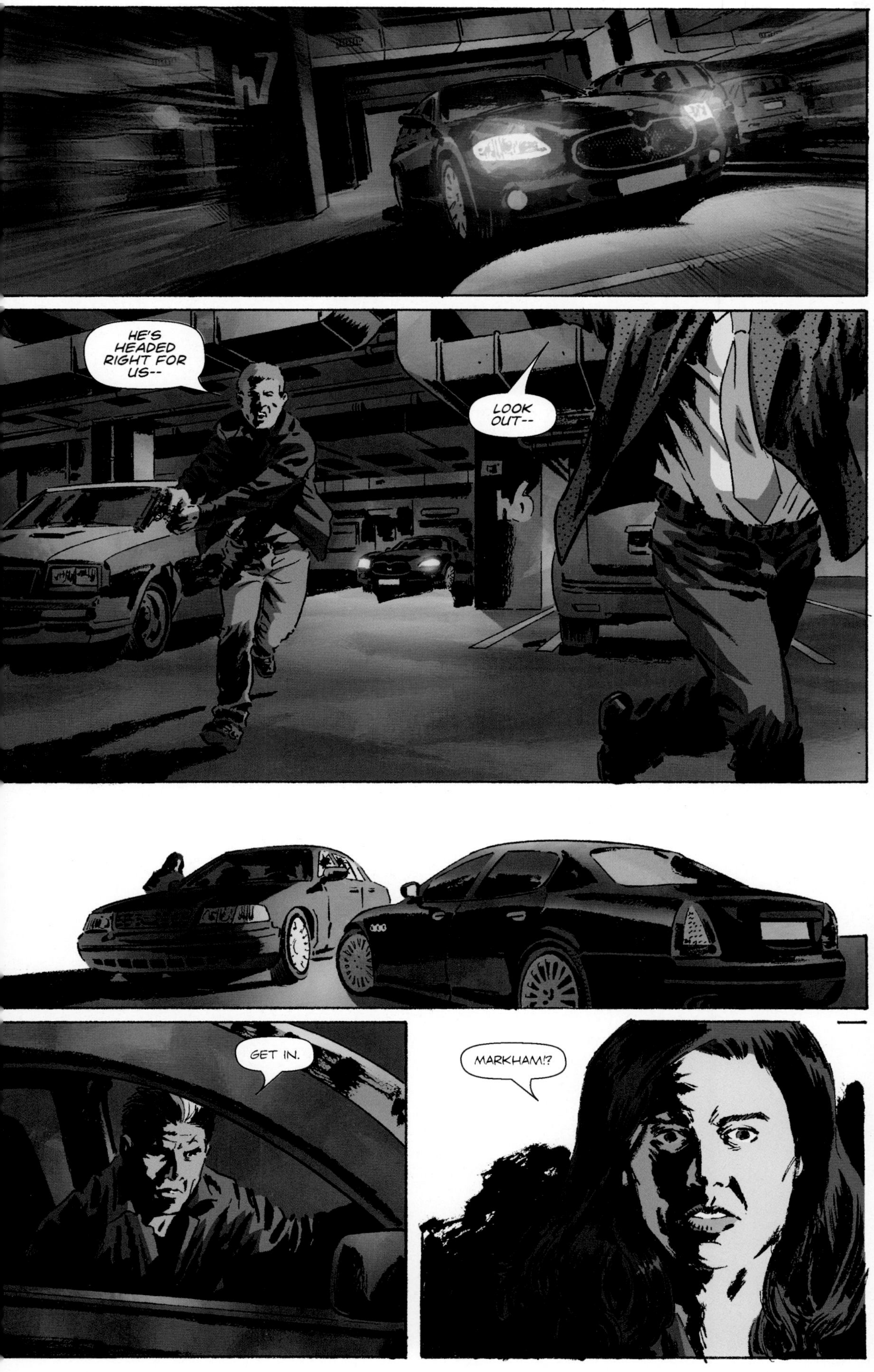
HE'S HEADED RIGHT FOR US--
LOOK OUT--
GET IN.
MARKHAM!?

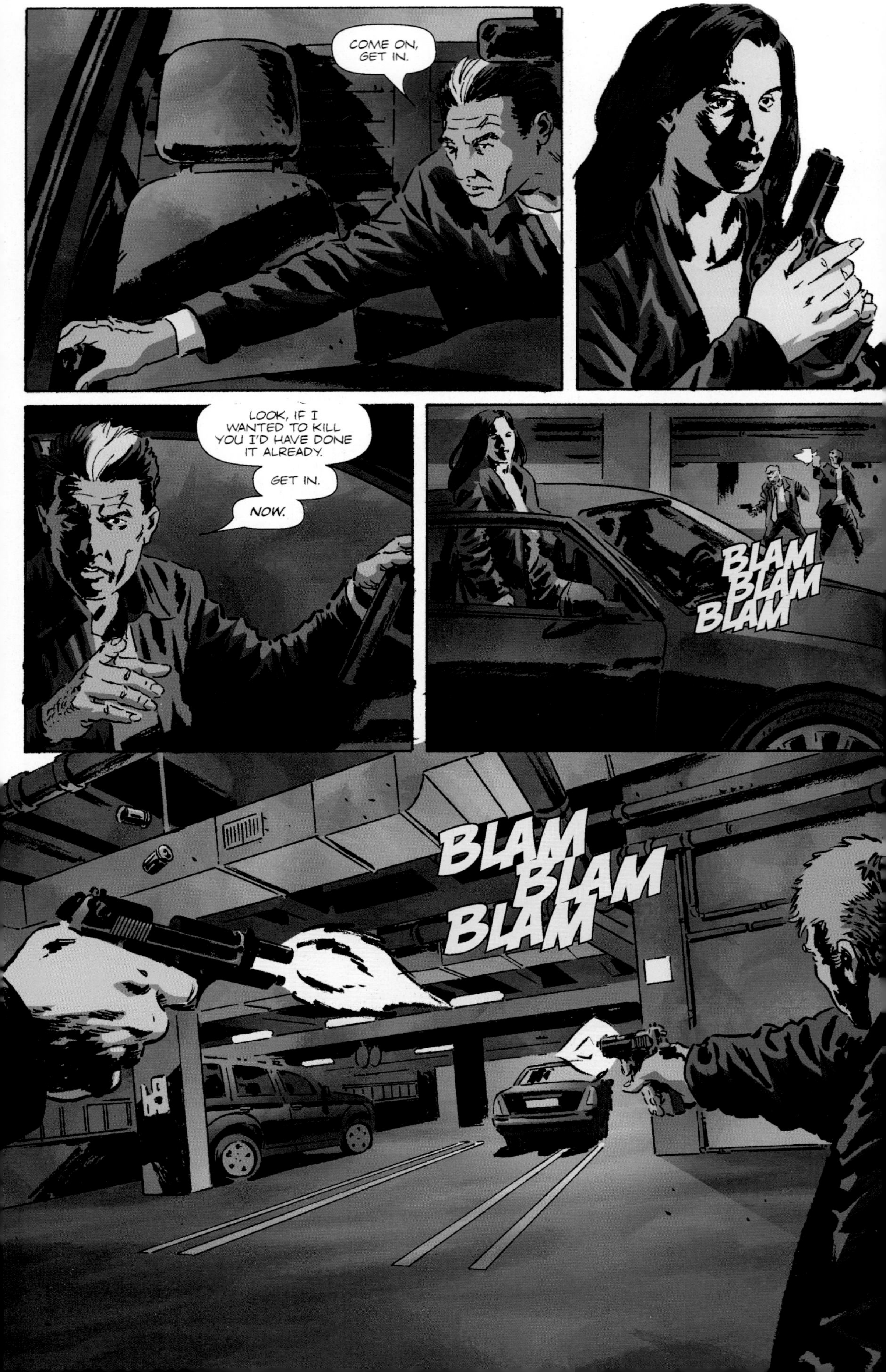
COME ON, GET IN.
LOOK, IF I WANTED TO KILL YOU I'D HAVE DONE IT ALREADY.
GET IN.
NOW.
BLAM BLAM BLAM
BLAM BLAM BLAM

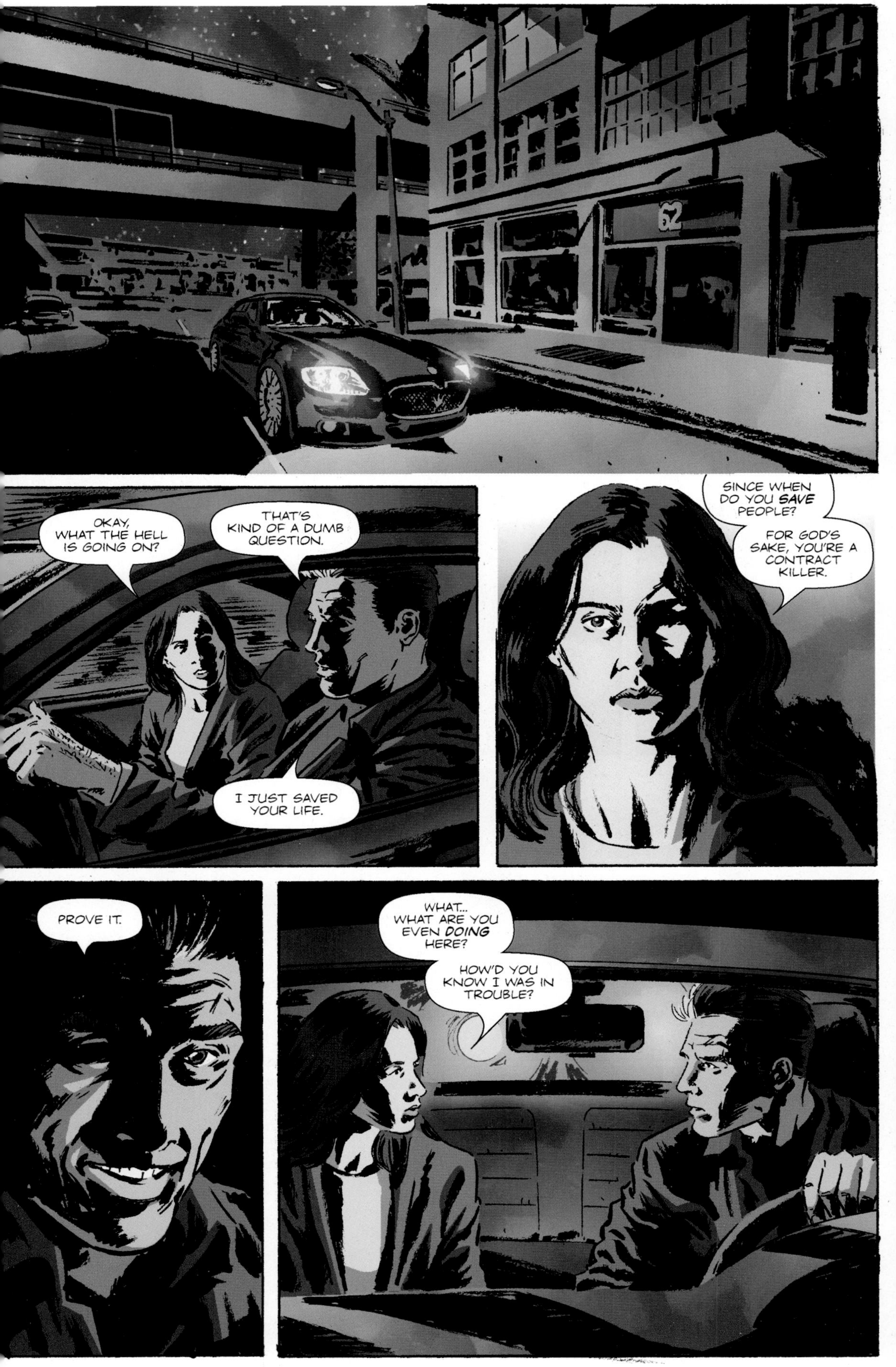
OKAY, WHAT THE HELL IS GOING ON?
THAT'S KIND OF A DUMB QUESTION.
I JUST SAVED YOUR LIFE.
SINCE WHEN DO YOU SAVE PEOPLE?
FOR GOD'S SAKE, YOU'RE A CONTRACT KILLER.
PROVE IT.
WHAT... WHAT ARE YOU EVEN DOING HERE?
HOW'D YOU KNOW I WAS IN TROUBLE?

SOMEONE'S BEEN ASKING AROUND, MAKING NOISES ABOUT PUTTING OUT A CONTRACT ON YOU.

GUESS YOU PISSED SOMEONE OFF.

YEAH, WELL, I'M A COP. KINDA COMES WITH THE TERRITORY.

SO WHERE DO YOU WANT ME TO DROP YOU? POLICE HEADQUARTERS?

YOU GOTTA BE KIDDING ME.

LOOK, YOU GOTTA TRUST SOMEONE, RIGHT?

AND I JUST SAVED YOUR LIFE.

FINE. BUT YOU CAN'T TAKE ME TO POLICE HEADQUARTERS BECAUSE THE GUYS WHO WANT ME DEAD ARE COPS.

OH, GREAT.

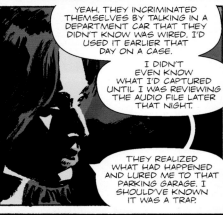

YEAH. THEY INCRIMINATED THEMSELVES BY TALKING IN A DEPARTMENT CAR THAT THEY DIDN'T KNOW WAS WIRED. I'D USED IT EARLIER THAT DAY ON A CASE.

I DIDN'T EVEN KNOW WHAT I'D CAPTURED UNTIL I WAS REVIEWING THE AUDIO FILE LATER THAT NIGHT.

THEY REALIZED WHAT HAD HAPPENED AND LURED ME TO THAT PARKING GARAGE. I SHOULD'VE KNOWN IT WAS A TRAP.

THE AUDIO FILE. WHERE IS IT NOW?

I DIDN'T WANT TO KEEP IT ON ME IN CASE THEY GOT TO ME, SO I STASHED IT IN THE WOMEN'S BATHROOM ON THE THIRD FLOOR OF POLICE HEADQUARTERS.

FANTASTIC.

WE'RE GOING TO MY PLACE. WE NEED TO REGROUP.

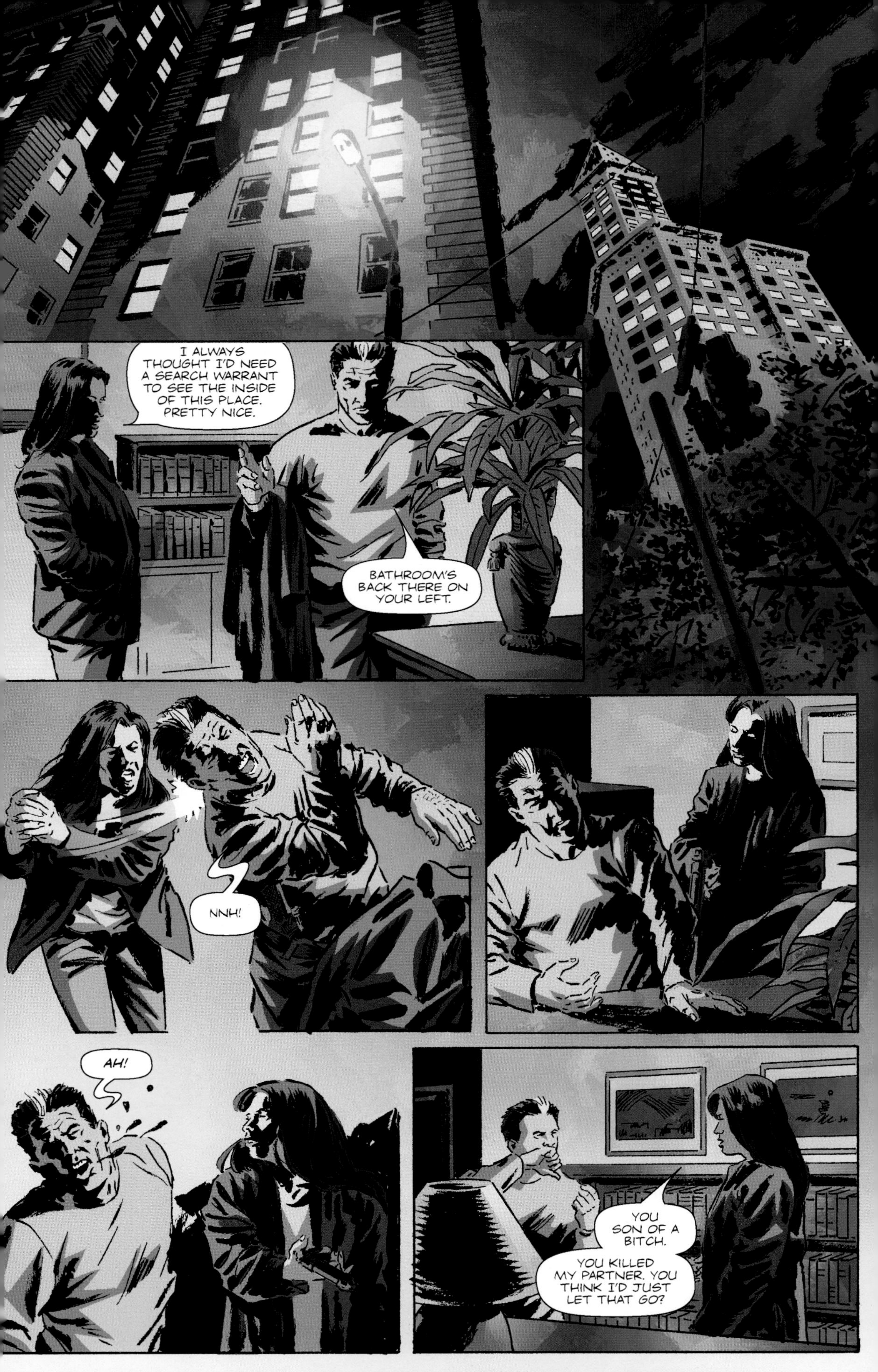
I ALWAYS THOUGHT I'D NEED A SEARCH WARRANT TO SEE THE INSIDE OF THIS PLACE. PRETTY NICE.
BATHROOM'S BACK THERE ON YOUR LEFT.
NNH!
AH!
YOU SON OF A BITCH.
YOU KILLED MY PARTNER. YOU THINK I'D JUST LET THAT GO?

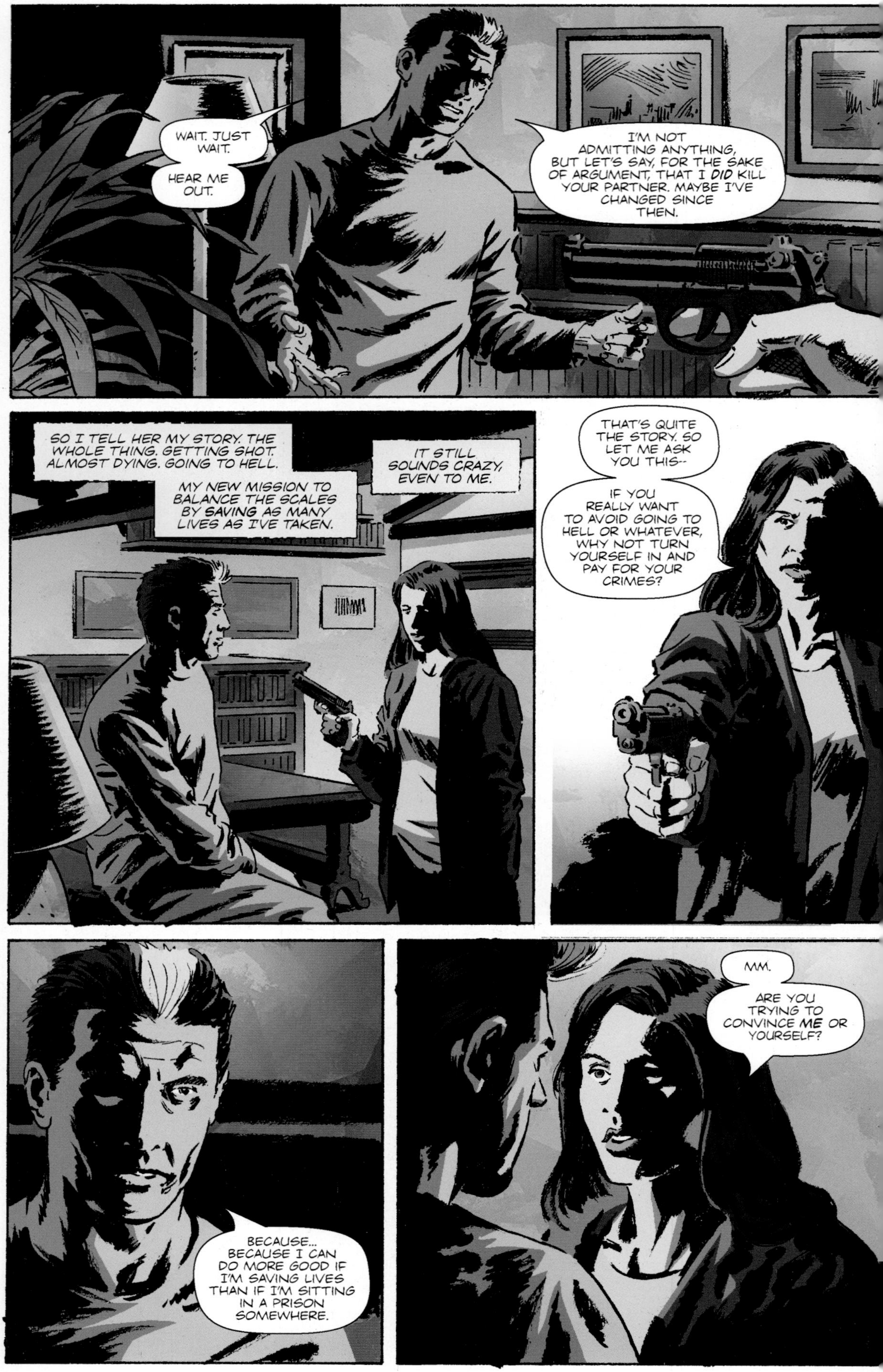
WAIT. JUST WAIT.
HEAR ME OUT.
I'M NOT ADMITTING ANYTHING, BUT LET'S SAY, FOR THE SAKE OF ARGUMENT, THAT I *DID* KILL YOUR PARTNER. MAYBE I'VE CHANGED SINCE THEN.
SO I TELL HER MY STORY. THE WHOLE THING. GETTING SHOT. ALMOST DYING. GOING TO HELL.
MY NEW MISSION TO BALANCE THE SCALES BY **SAVING** AS MANY LIVES AS I'VE TAKEN.
IT STILL SOUNDS CRAZY, EVEN TO ME.
THAT'S QUITE THE STORY. SO LET ME ASK YOU THIS--
IF YOU REALLY WANT TO AVOID GOING TO HELL OR WHATEVER, WHY NOT TURN YOURSELF IN AND PAY FOR YOUR CRIMES?
BECAUSE... BECAUSE I CAN DO MORE GOOD IF I'M SAVING LIVES THAN IF I'M SITTING IN A PRISON SOMEWHERE.
MM.
ARE YOU TRYING TO CONVINCE ***ME*** OR YOURSELF?

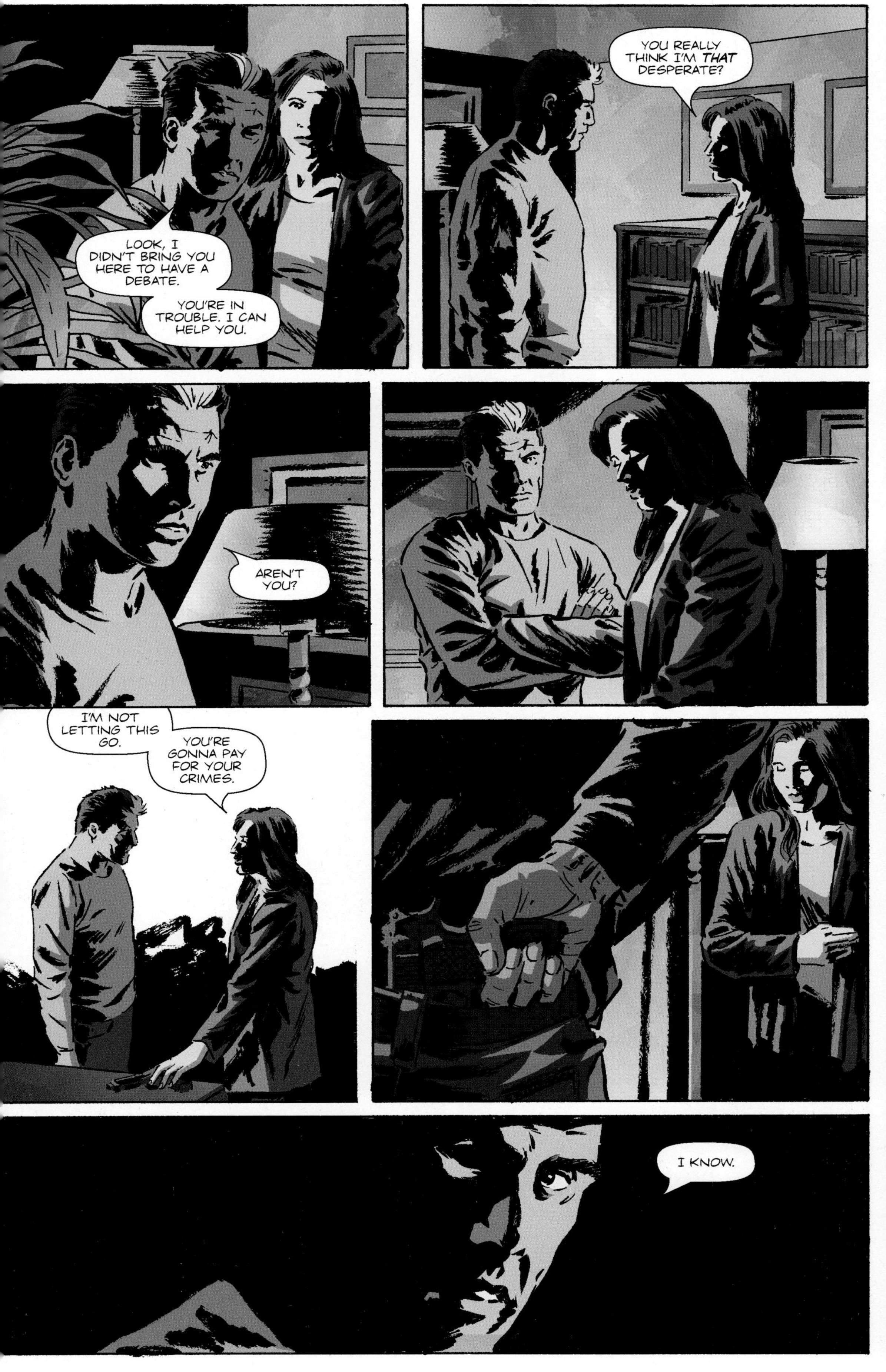
LOOK, I DIDN'T BRING YOU HERE TO HAVE A DEBATE.
YOU'RE IN TROUBLE. I CAN HELP YOU.
YOU REALLY THINK I'M *THAT* DESPERATE?
AREN'T YOU?
I'M NOT LETTING THIS GO.
YOU'RE GONNA PAY FOR YOUR CRIMES.
I KNOW.

SO YOU MUST KNOW THEY'RE PROBABLY GOING TO COME AFTER YOU.

AND YET HERE YOU ARE, STILL LIVING IN THIS SAME APARTMENT.

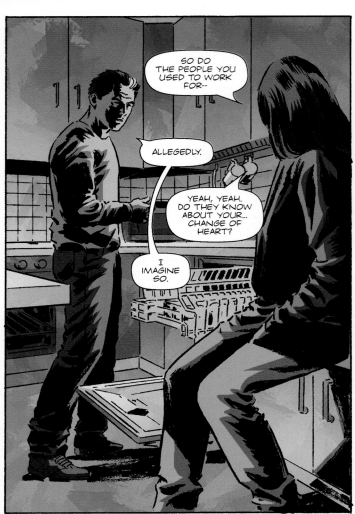

SO DO THE PEOPLE YOU USED TO WORK FOR--

ALLEGEDLY.

YEAH, YEAH. DO THEY KNOW ABOUT YOUR... CHANGE OF HEART?

I IMAGINE SO.

HAVE YOU SEEN MY VIEW?

OH, OF COURSE. MISTER TOUGH GUY. TOO TOUGH TO SHOW CONCERN.

WAIT A SECOND... ARE YOU WORRIED ABOUT ME?

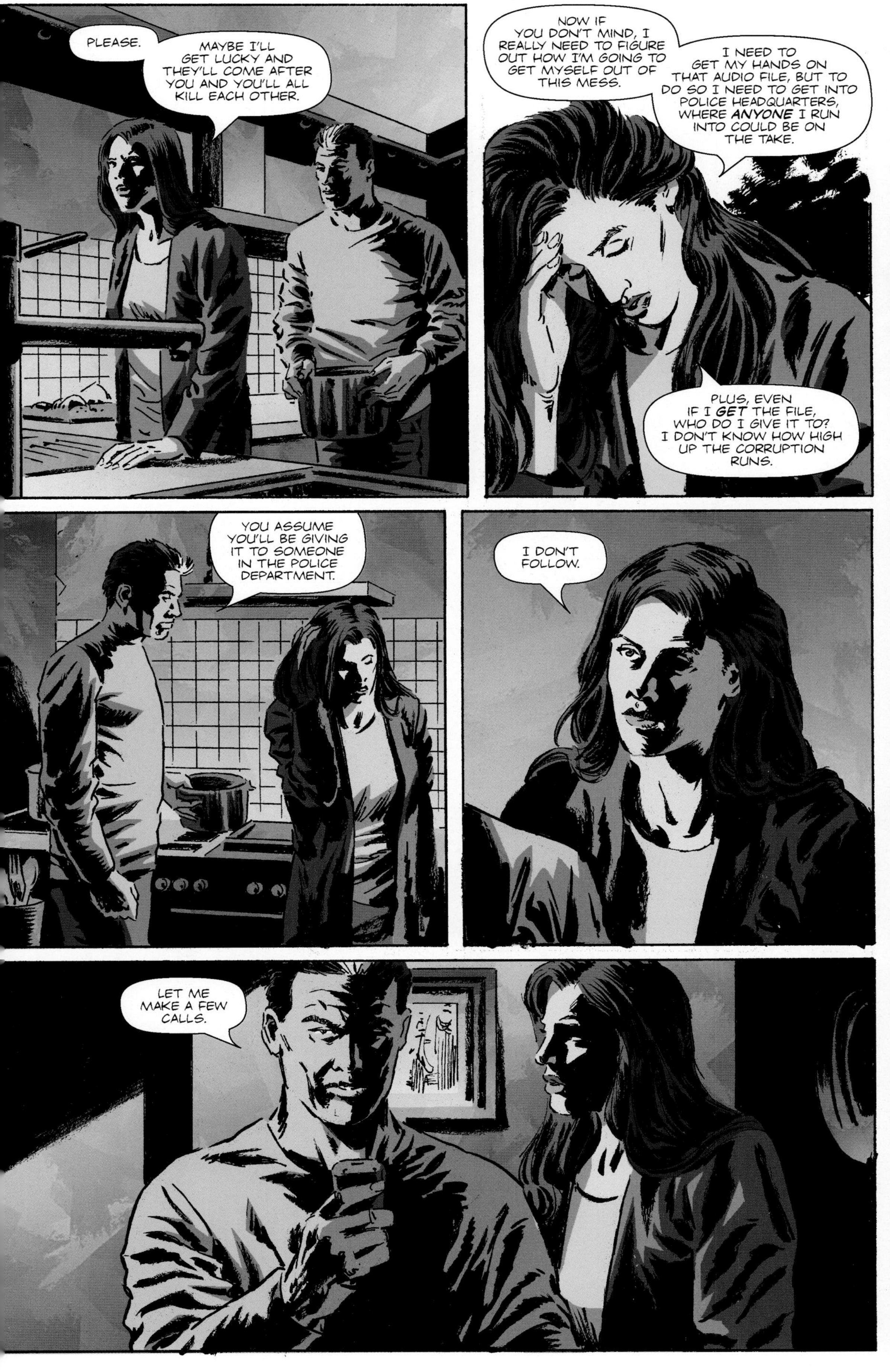
PLEASE.
MAYBE I'LL GET LUCKY AND THEY'LL COME AFTER YOU AND YOU'LL ALL KILL EACH OTHER.
NOW IF YOU DON'T MIND, I REALLY NEED TO FIGURE OUT HOW I'M GOING TO GET MYSELF OUT OF THIS MESS.
I NEED TO GET MY HANDS ON THAT AUDIO FILE, BUT TO DO SO I NEED TO GET INTO POLICE HEADQUARTERS, WHERE ***ANYONE*** I RUN INTO COULD BE ON THE TAKE.
PLUS, EVEN IF I ***GET*** THE FILE, WHO DO I GIVE IT TO? I DON'T KNOW HOW HIGH UP THE CORRUPTION RUNS.
YOU ASSUME YOU'LL BE GIVING IT TO SOMEONE IN THE POLICE DEPARTMENT.
I DON'T FOLLOW.
LET ME MAKE A FEW CALLS.

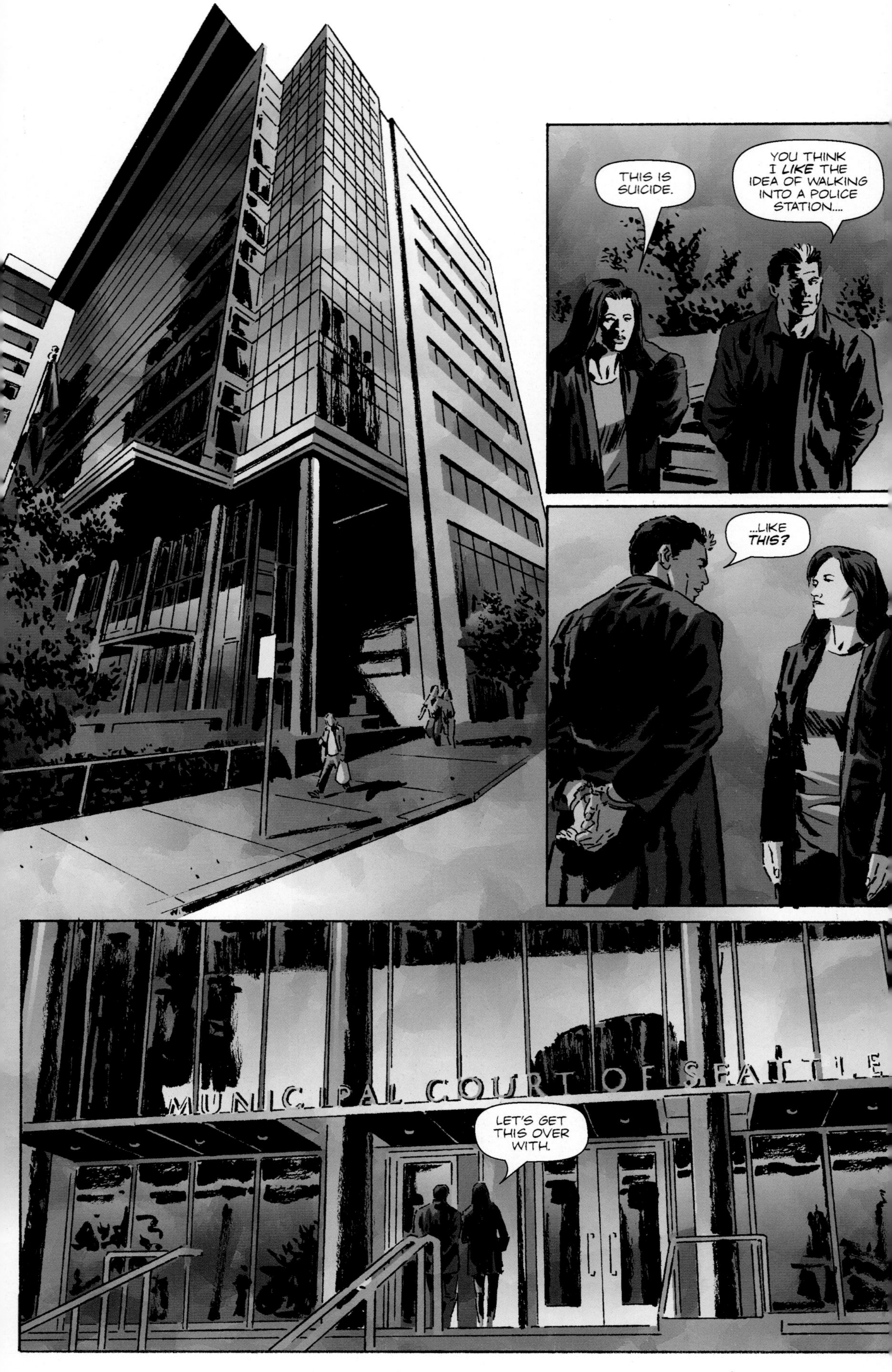
THIS IS SUICIDE.
YOU THINK I *LIKE* THE IDEA OF WALKING INTO A POLICE STATION....
...LIKE *THIS?*
MUNICIPAL COURT OF SEATTLE
LET'S GET THIS OVER WITH.

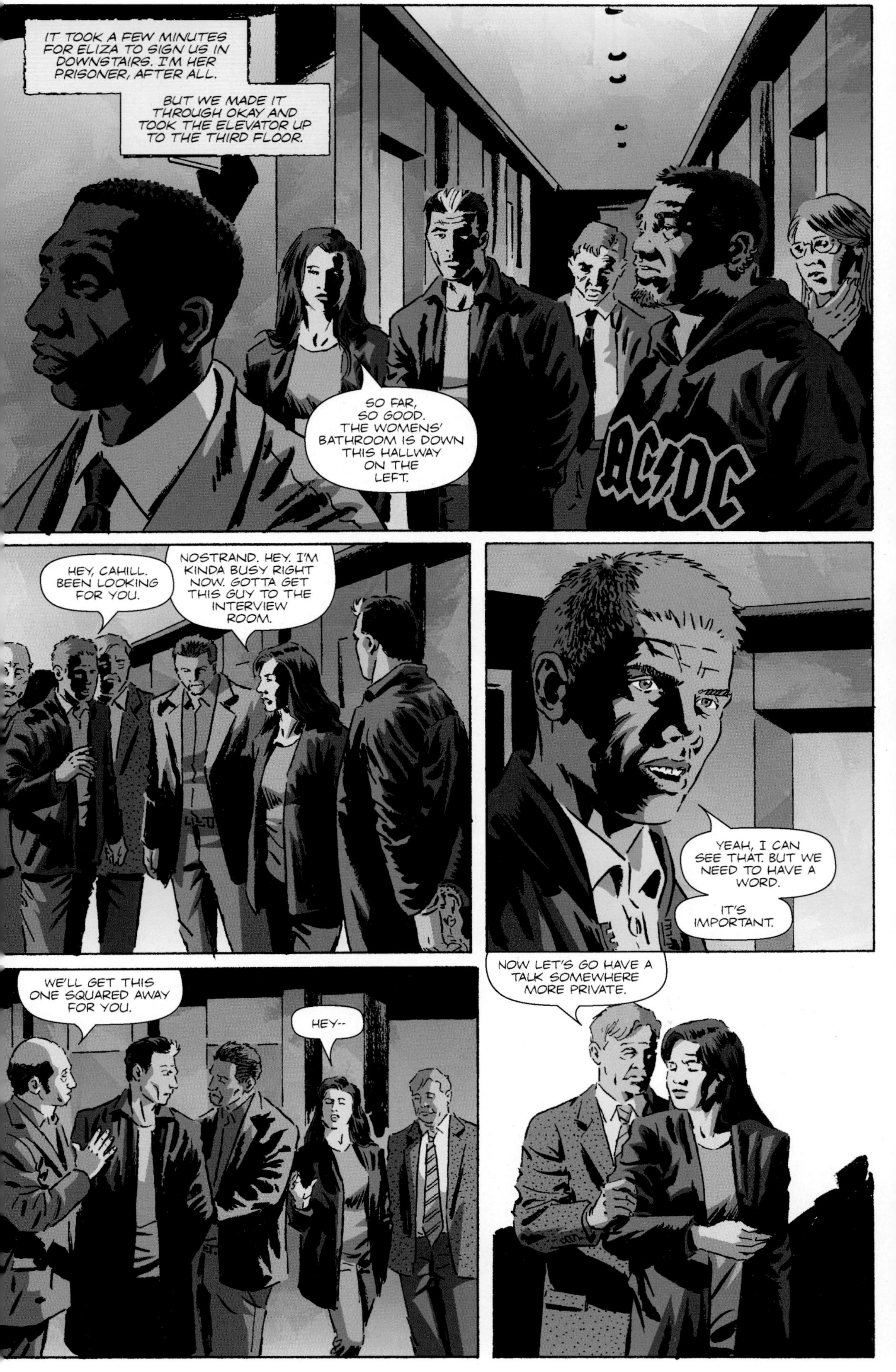
IT TOOK A FEW MINUTES FOR ELIZA TO SIGN US IN DOWNSTAIRS. I'M HER PRISONER, AFTER ALL.
BUT WE MADE IT THROUGH OKAY AND TOOK THE ELEVATOR UP TO THE THIRD FLOOR.
SO FAR, SO GOOD. THE WOMENS' BATHROOM IS DOWN THIS HALLWAY ON THE LEFT.
AC/DC
HEY, CAHILL. BEEN LOOKING FOR YOU.
NOSTRAND. HEY. I'M KINDA BUSY RIGHT NOW. GOTTA GET THIS GUY TO THE INTERVIEW ROOM.
YEAH, I CAN SEE THAT. BUT WE NEED TO HAVE A WORD.
IT'S IMPORTANT.
WE'LL GET THIS ONE SQUARED AWAY FOR YOU.
HEY--
NOW LET'S GO HAVE A TALK SOMEWHERE MORE PRIVATE.

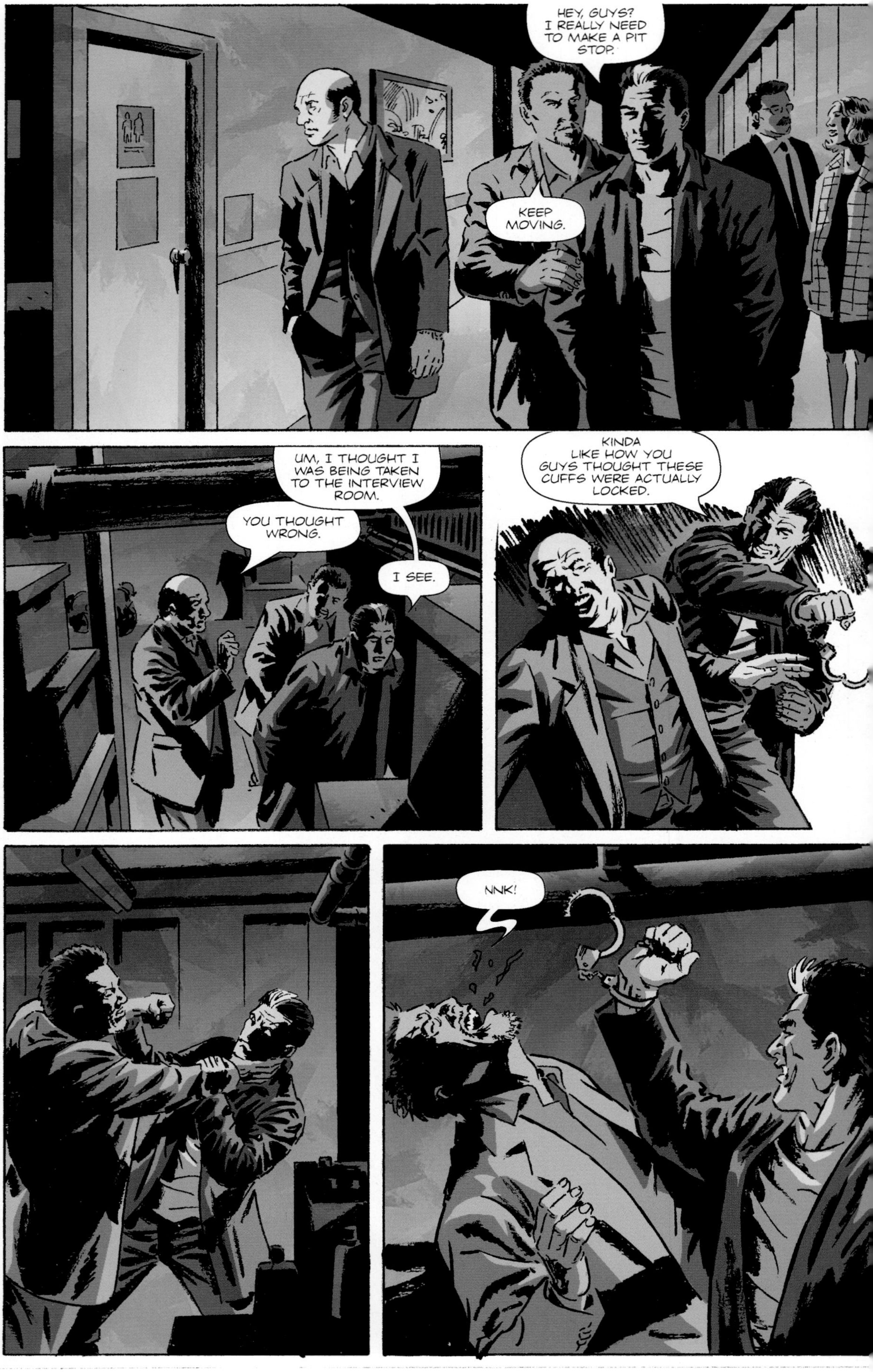
HEY, GUYS? I REALLY NEED TO MAKE A PIT STOP.
KEEP MOVING.
UM, I THOUGHT I WAS BEING TAKEN TO THE INTERVIEW ROOM.
YOU THOUGHT WRONG.
I SEE.
KINDA LIKE HOW YOU GUYS THOUGHT THESE CUFFS WERE ACTUALLY LOCKED.
NNK!

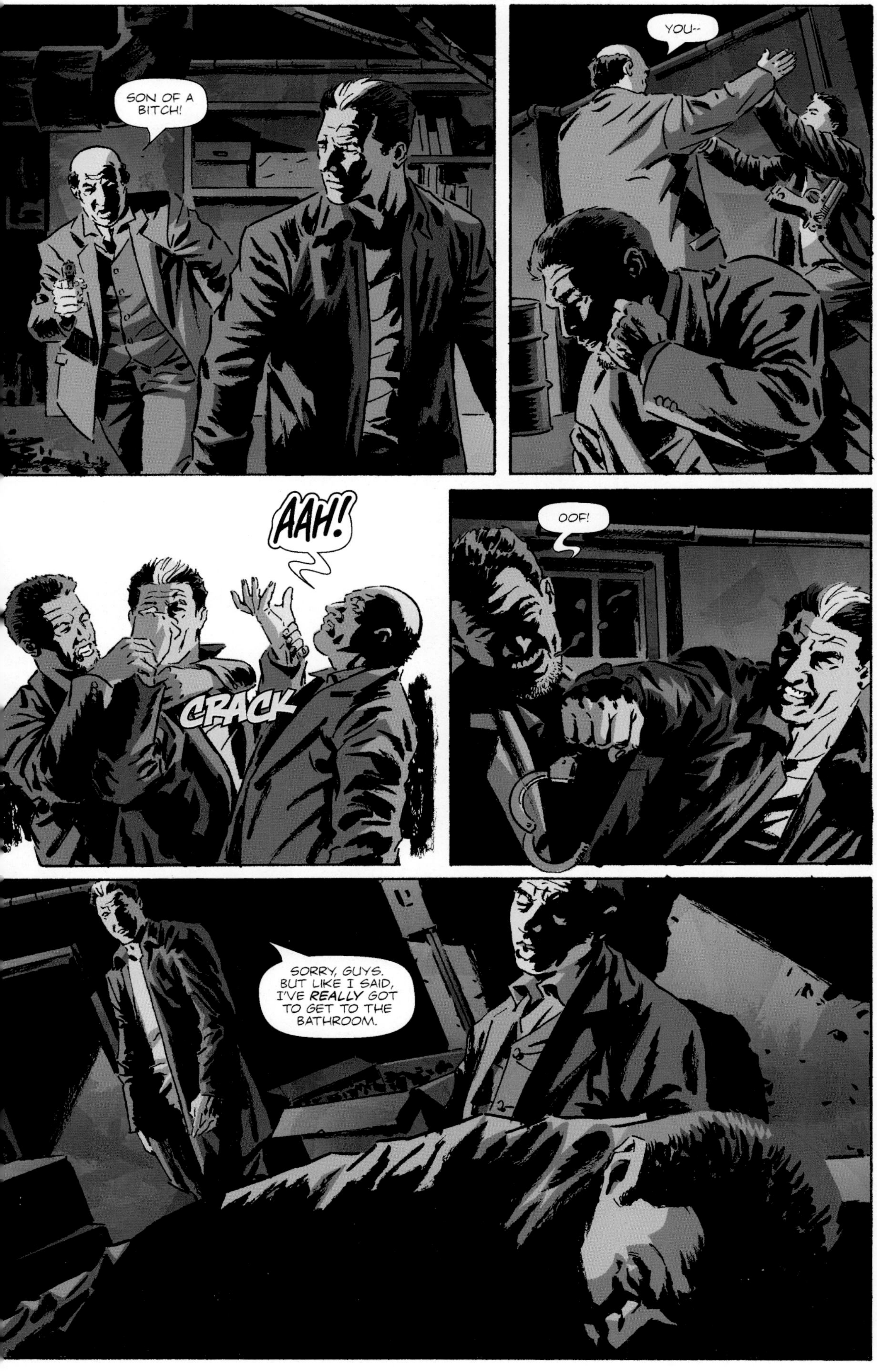
SON OF A BITCH!
YOU--
AAH!
CRACK
OOF!
SORRY, GUYS. BUT LIKE I SAID, I'VE **REALLY** GOT TO GET TO THE BATHROOM.

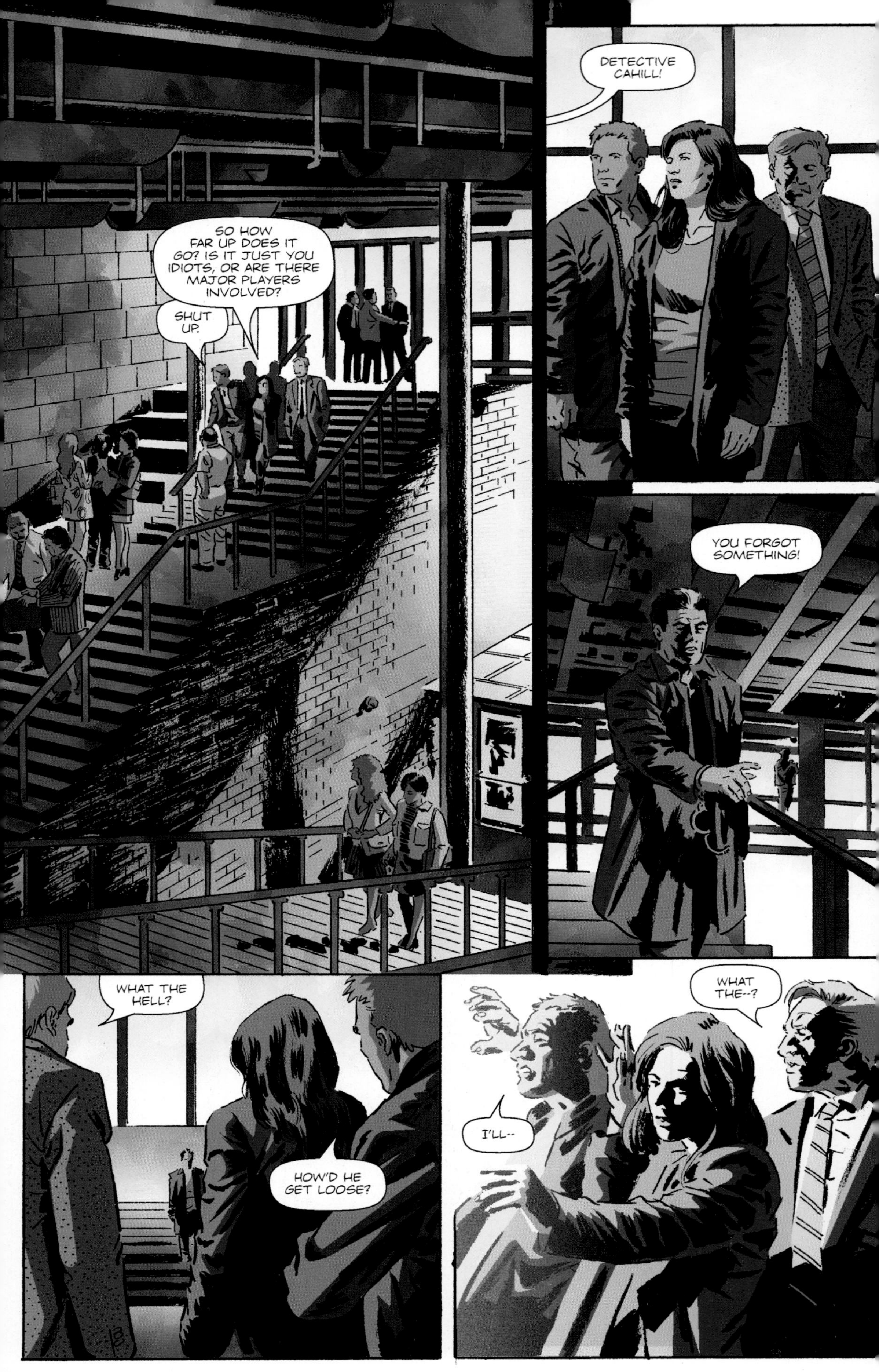
SO HOW FAR UP DOES IT GO? IS IT JUST YOU IDIOTS, OR ARE THERE MAJOR PLAYERS INVOLVED?
SHUT UP.
DETECTIVE CAHILL!
YOU FORGOT SOMETHING!
WHAT THE HELL?
HOW'D HE GET LOOSE?
WHAT THE--?
I'LL--

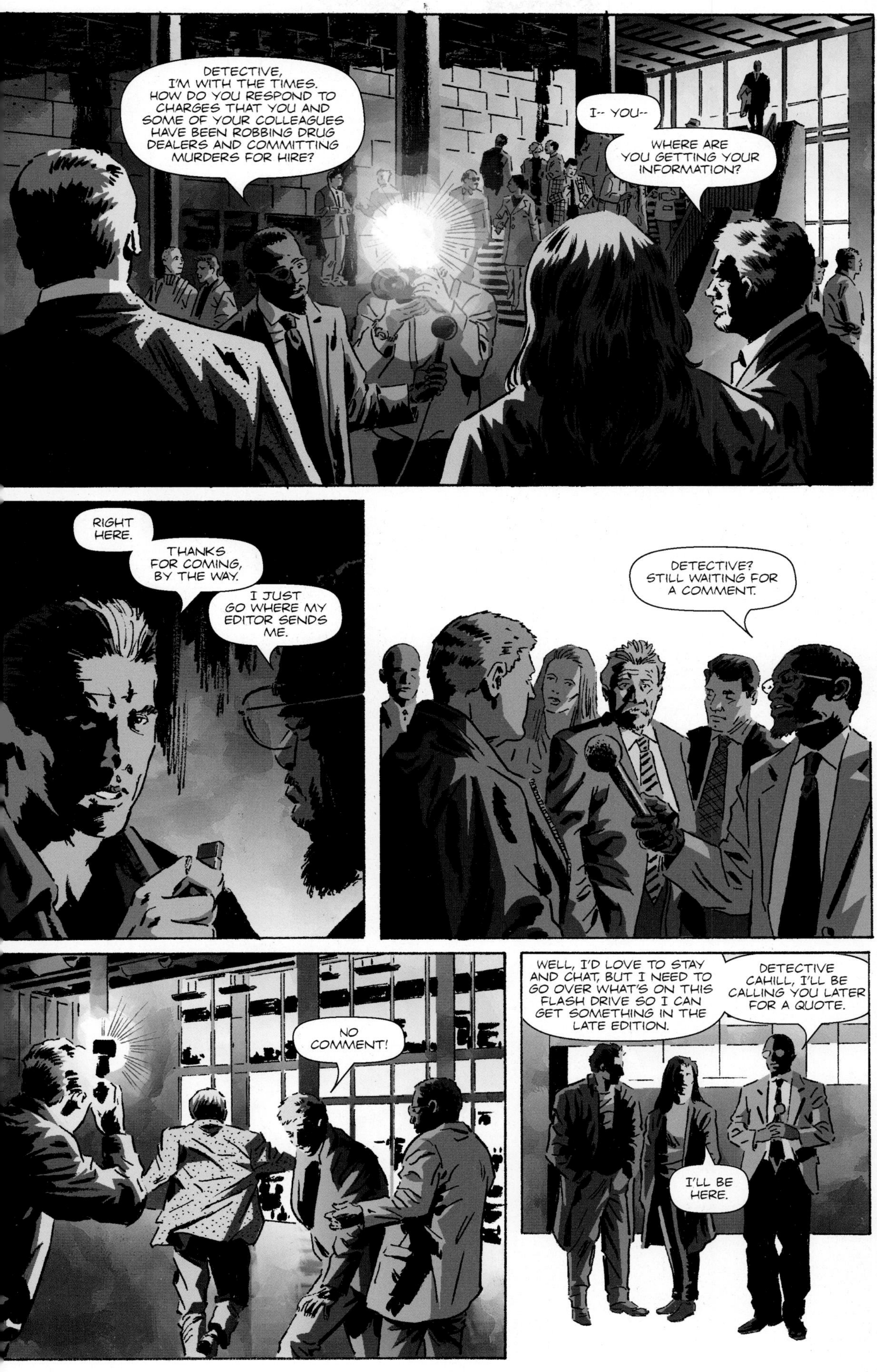
DETECTIVE, I'M WITH THE TIMES. HOW DO YOU RESPOND TO CHARGES THAT YOU AND SOME OF YOUR COLLEAGUES HAVE BEEN ROBBING DRUG DEALERS AND COMMITTING MURDERS FOR HIRE?
I-- YOU--
WHERE ARE YOU GETTING YOUR INFORMATION?
RIGHT HERE.
THANKS FOR COMING, BY THE WAY.
I JUST GO WHERE MY EDITOR SENDS ME.
DETECTIVE? STILL WAITING FOR A COMMENT.
NO COMMENT!
WELL, I'D LOVE TO STAY AND CHAT, BUT I NEED TO GO OVER WHAT'S ON THIS FLASH DRIVE SO I CAN GET SOMETHING IN THE LATE EDITION.
DETECTIVE CAHILL, I'LL BE CALLING YOU LATER FOR A QUOTE.
I'LL BE HERE.

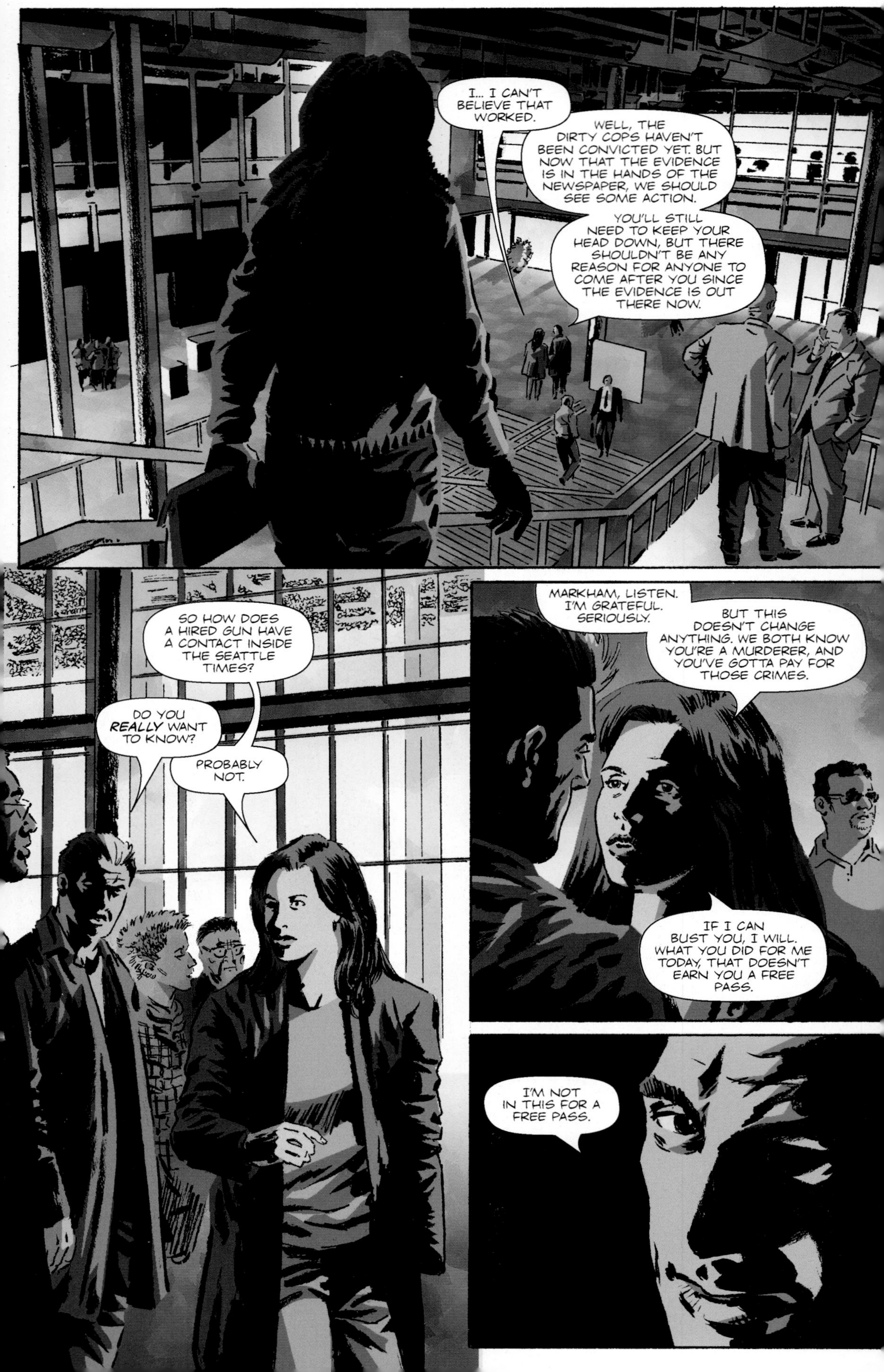
I... I CAN'T BELIEVE THAT WORKED.
WELL, THE DIRTY COPS HAVEN'T BEEN CONVICTED YET. BUT NOW THAT THE EVIDENCE IS IN THE HANDS OF THE NEWSPAPER, WE SHOULD SEE SOME ACTION.
YOU'LL STILL NEED TO KEEP YOUR HEAD DOWN, BUT THERE SHOULDN'T BE ANY REASON FOR ANYONE TO COME AFTER YOU SINCE THE EVIDENCE IS OUT THERE NOW.
SO HOW DOES A HIRED GUN HAVE A CONTACT INSIDE THE SEATTLE TIMES?
DO YOU *REALLY* WANT TO KNOW?
PROBABLY NOT.
MARKHAM, LISTEN. I'M GRATEFUL. SERIOUSLY.
BUT THIS DOESN'T CHANGE ANYTHING. WE BOTH KNOW YOU'RE A MURDERER, AND YOU'VE GOTTA PAY FOR THOSE CRIMES.
IF I CAN BUST YOU, I WILL. WHAT YOU DID FOR ME TODAY, THAT DOESN'T EARN YOU A FREE PASS.
I'M NOT IN THIS FOR A FREE PASS.

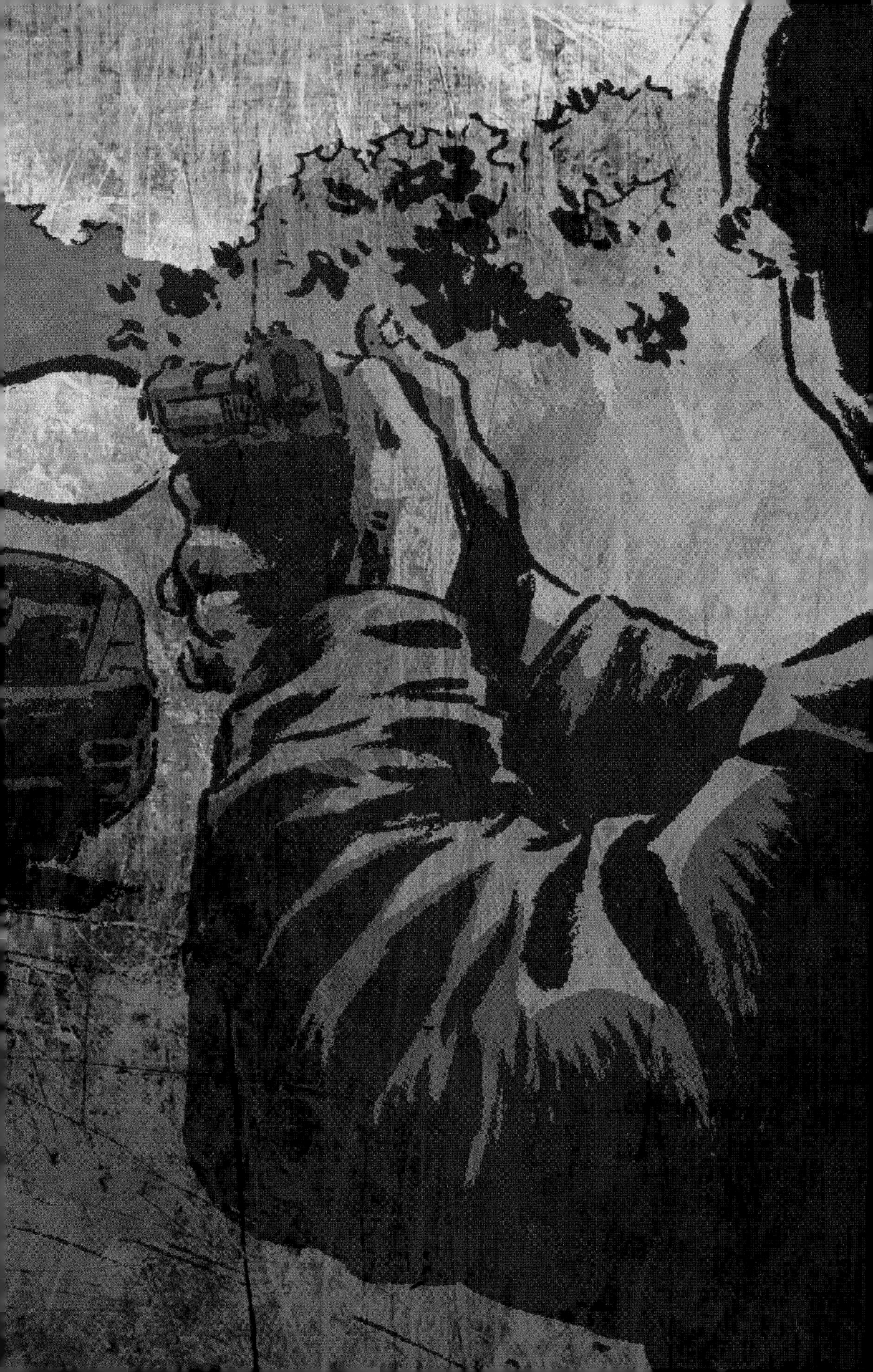

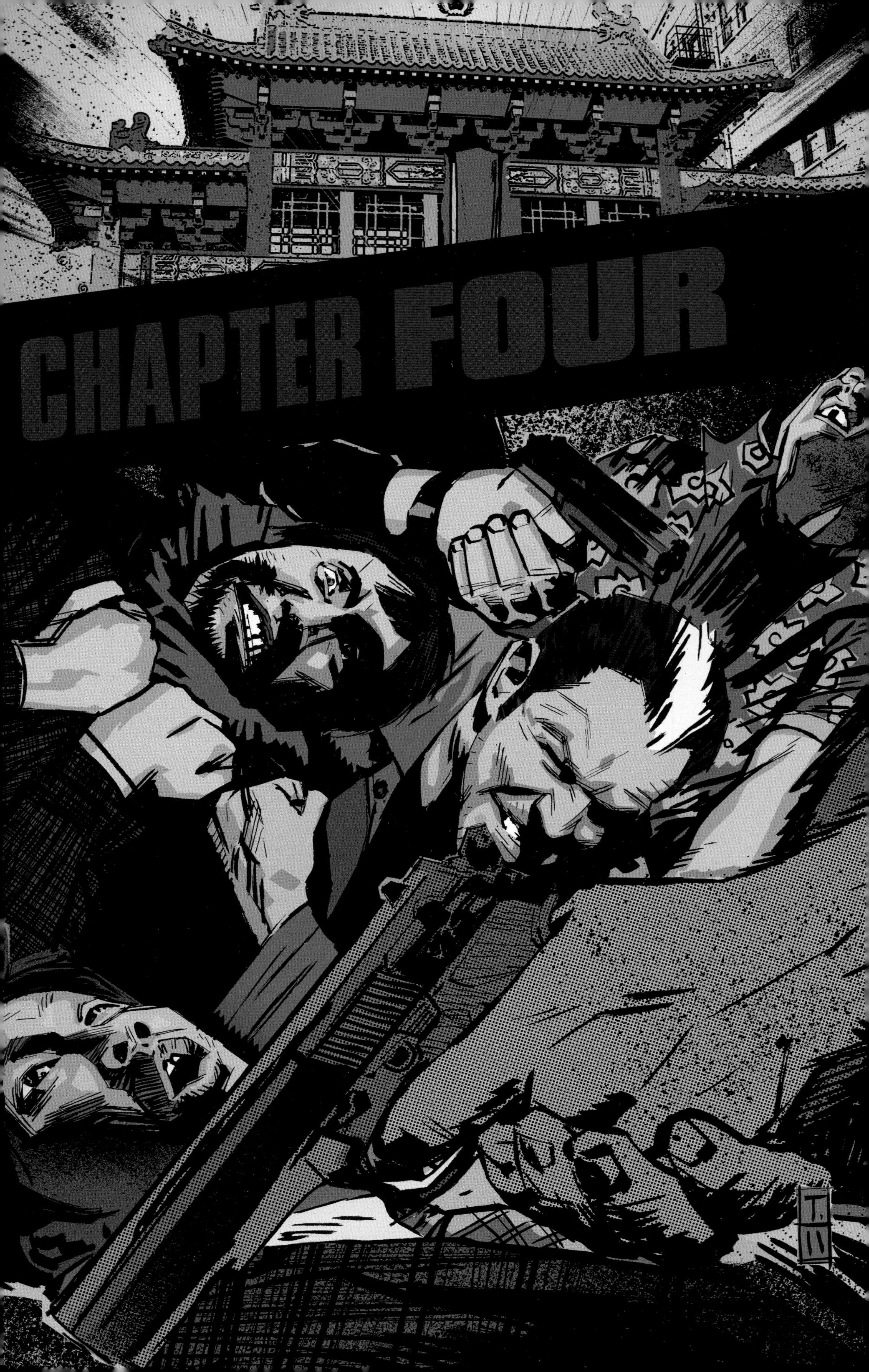
CHAPTER FOUR

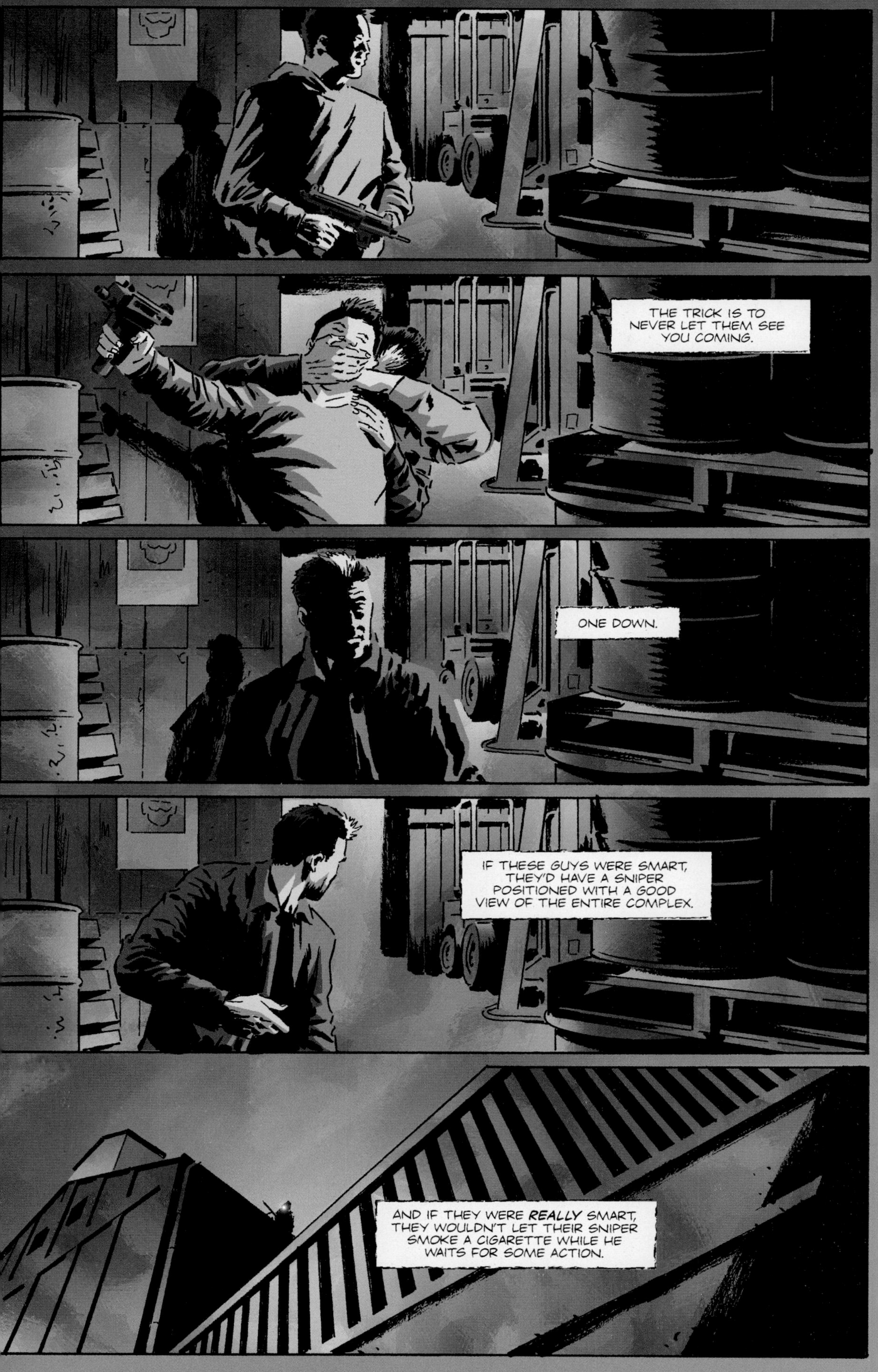
THE TRICK IS TO NEVER LET THEM SEE YOU COMING.
ONE DOWN.
IF THESE GUYS WERE SMART, THEY'D HAVE A SNIPER POSITIONED WITH A GOOD VIEW OF THE ENTIRE COMPLEX.
AND IF THEY WERE *REALLY* SMART, THEY WOULDN'T LET THEIR SNIPER SMOKE A CIGARETTE WHILE HE WAITS FOR SOME ACTION.

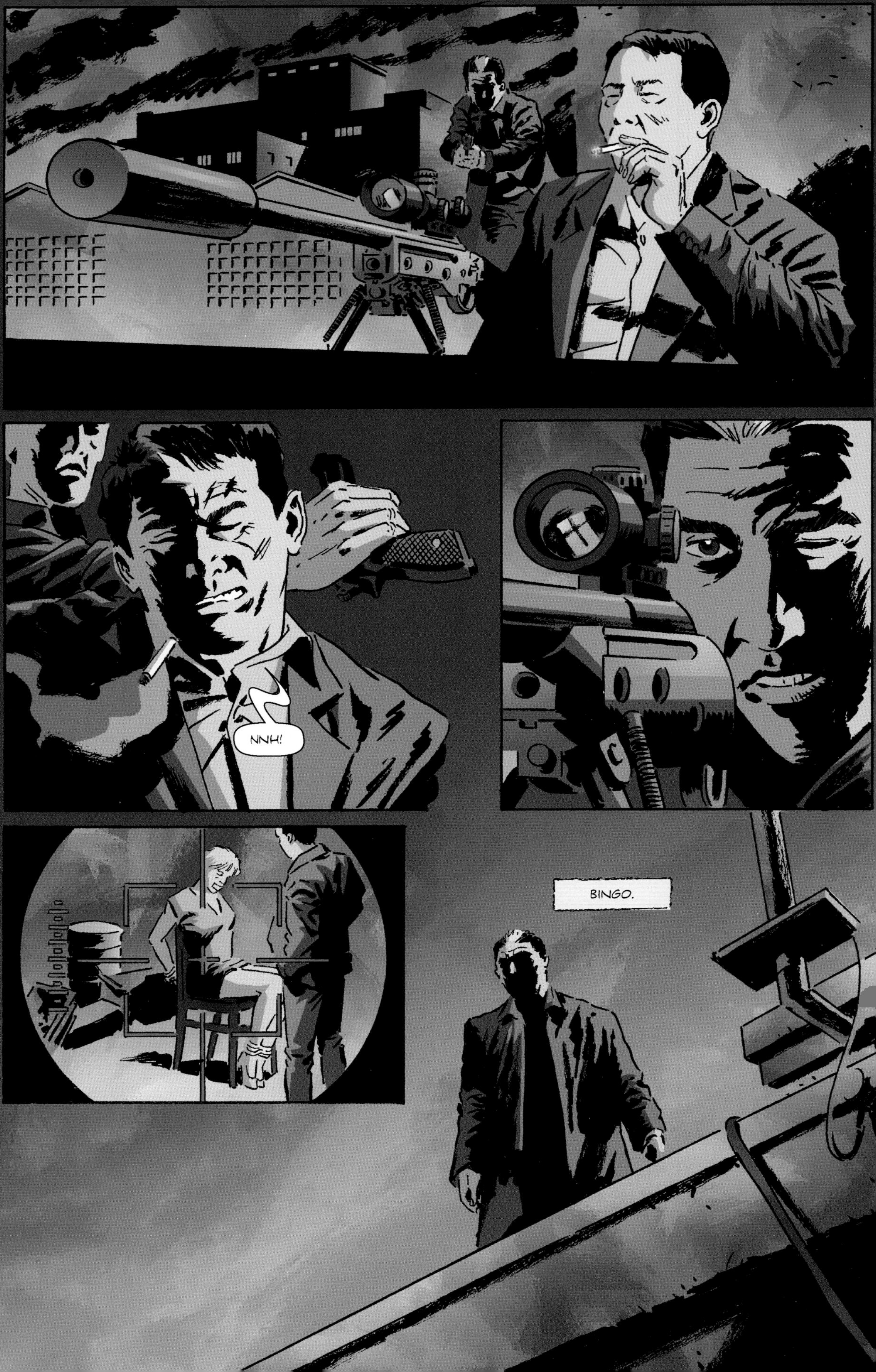
NNH!
BINGO.

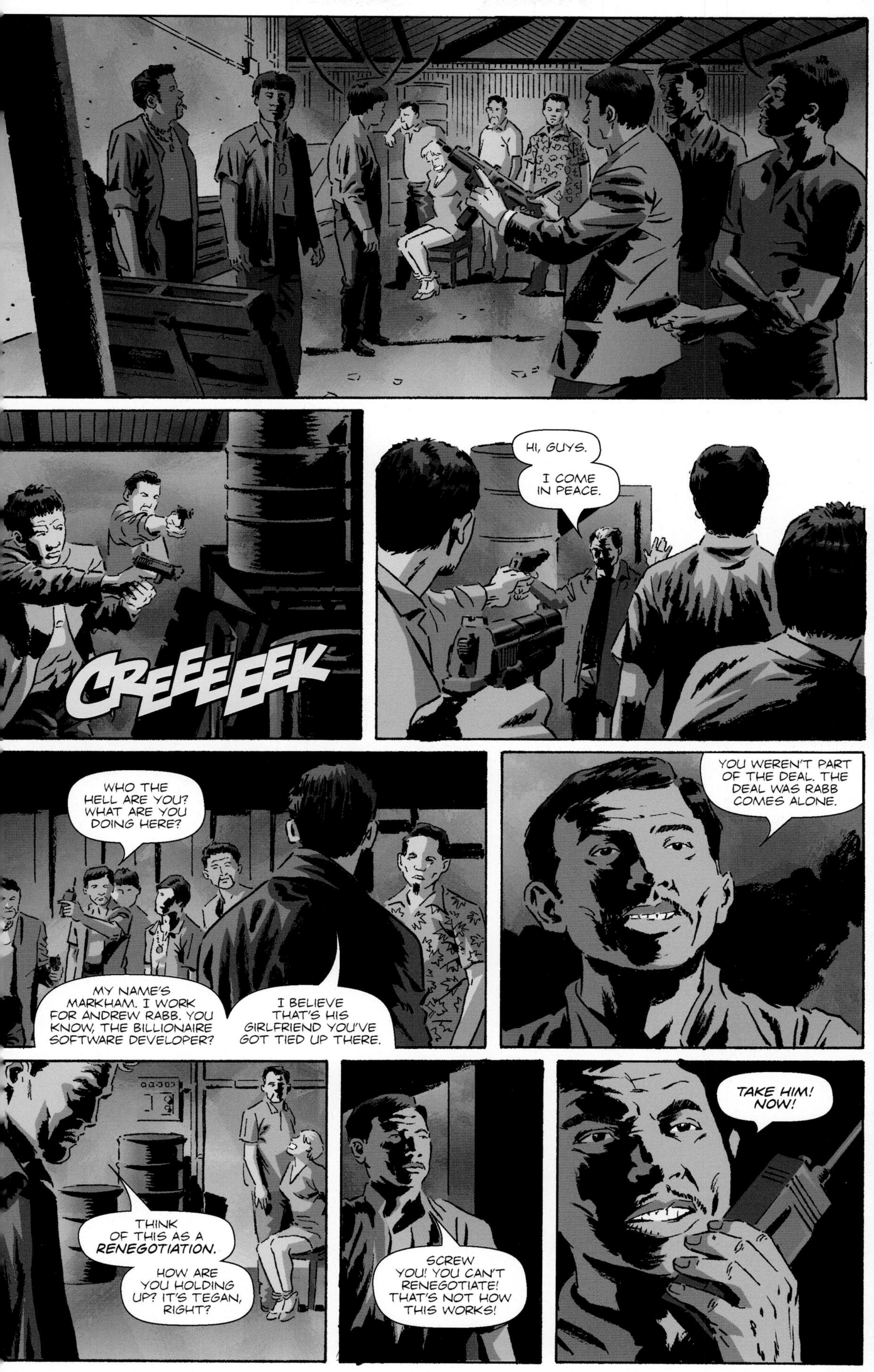
CREEEEEK
HI, GUYS.
I COME IN PEACE.
WHO THE HELL ARE YOU? WHAT ARE YOU DOING HERE?
MY NAME'S MARKHAM. I WORK FOR ANDREW RABB. YOU KNOW, THE BILLIONAIRE SOFTWARE DEVELOPER?
I BELIEVE THAT'S HIS GIRLFRIEND YOU'VE GOT TIED UP THERE.
YOU WEREN'T PART OF THE DEAL. THE DEAL WAS RABB COMES ALONE.
THINK OF THIS AS A RENEGOTIATION.
HOW ARE YOU HOLDING UP? IT'S TEGAN, RIGHT?
SCREW YOU! YOU CAN'T RENEGOTIATE! THAT'S NOT HOW THIS WORKS!
TAKE HIM! NOW!

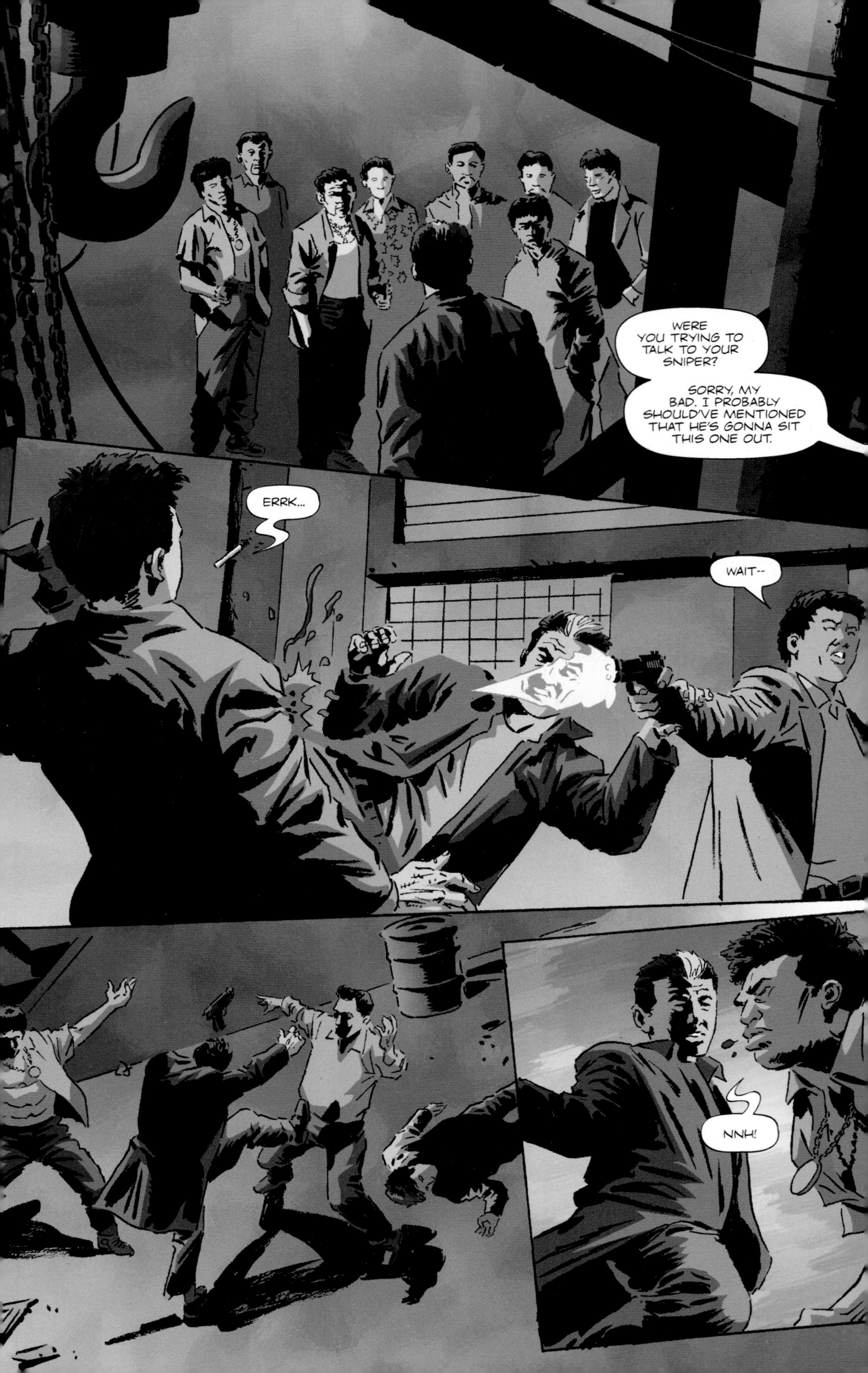
WERE YOU TRYING TO TALK TO YOUR SNIPER?
SORRY, MY BAD. I PROBABLY SHOULD'VE MENTIONED THAT HE'S GONNA SIT THIS ONE OUT.
ERRK...
WAIT--
NNH!

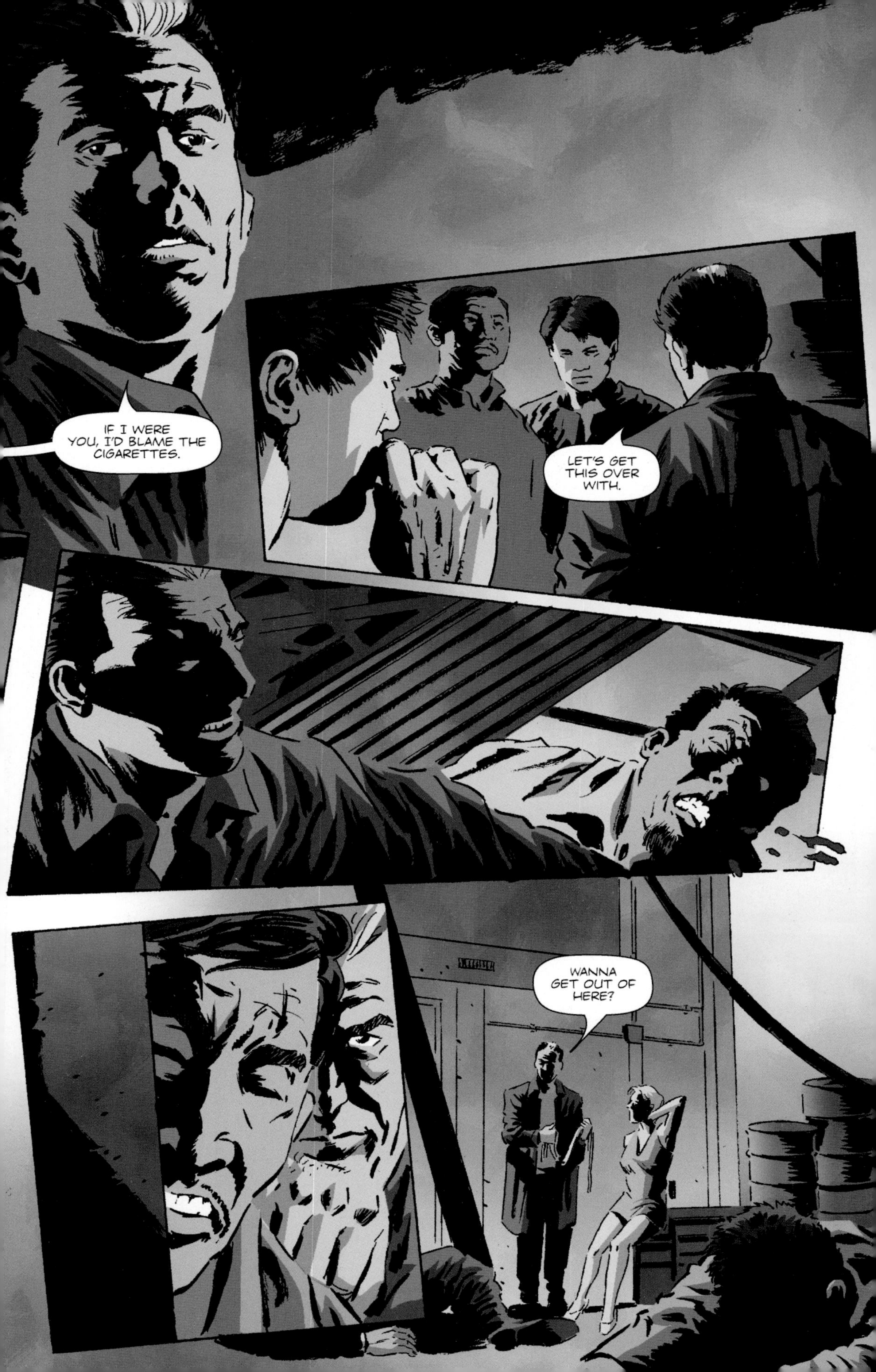
IF I WERE YOU, I'D BLAME THE CIGARETTES.
LET'S GET THIS OVER WITH.
WANNA GET OUT OF HERE?

OH, THANK GOD YOU'RE ALL RIGHT!

I WAS SO SCARED!

MR. MARKHAM, I CAN'T THANK YOU ENOUGH.

THIS IS JUST A SHORT-TERM FIX. I CAN'T BE YOUR BODYGUARD PERMANENTLY. SINCE THE TRIADS THOUGHT YOU WERE A GOOD TARGET FOR RANSOM, THEY MAY TRY AGAIN.

≶SIGH≶

YOU'RE RIGHT. I NEVER SHOULD'VE GONE INTO BUSINESS WITH THEM.

WAIT-- WHAT?

YOU'RE IN BUSINESS WITH THEM?

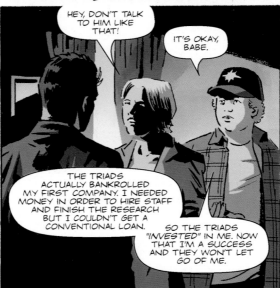

HEY, DON'T TALK TO HIM LIKE THAT!

IT'S OKAY, BABE.

THE TRIADS ACTUALLY BANKROLLED MY FIRST COMPANY. I NEEDED MONEY IN ORDER TO HIRE STAFF AND FINISH THE RESEARCH BUT I COULDN'T GET A CONVENTIONAL LOAN.

SO THE TRIADS "INVESTED" IN ME. NOW THAT I'M A SUCCESS AND THEY WON'T LET GO OF ME.

≶SIGH≶

WHY DIDN'T YOU TELL ME THIS BEFORE?

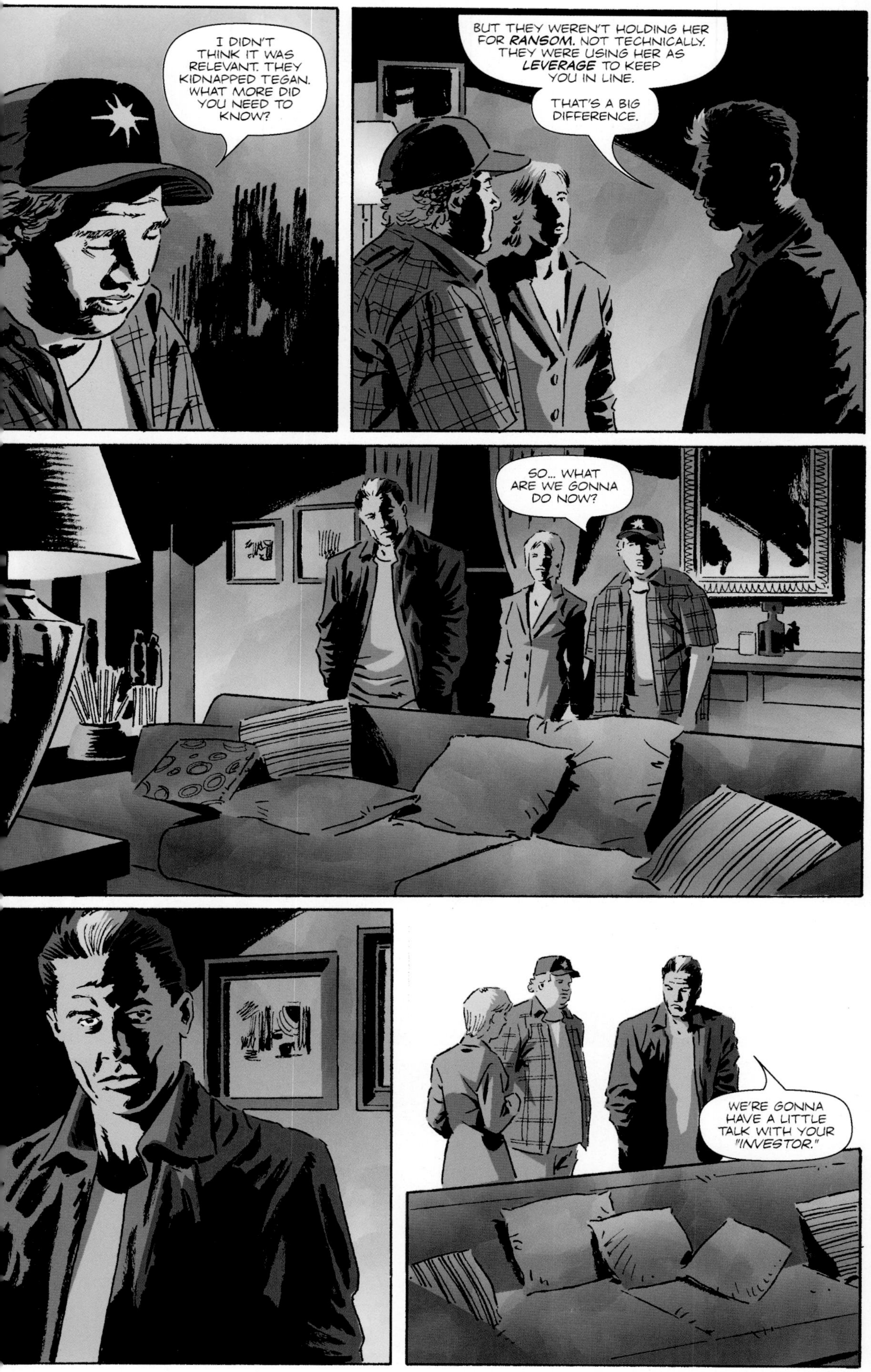

I DIDN'T THINK IT WAS RELEVANT. THEY KIDNAPPED TEGAN. WHAT MORE DID YOU NEED TO KNOW?
BUT THEY WEREN'T HOLDING HER FOR ***RANSOM.*** NOT TECHNICALLY. THEY WERE USING HER AS ***LEVERAGE*** TO KEEP YOU IN LINE.
THAT'S A BIG DIFFERENCE.
SO... WHAT ARE WE GONNA DO NOW?
WE'RE GONNA HAVE A LITTLE TALK WITH YOUR *"INVESTOR."*

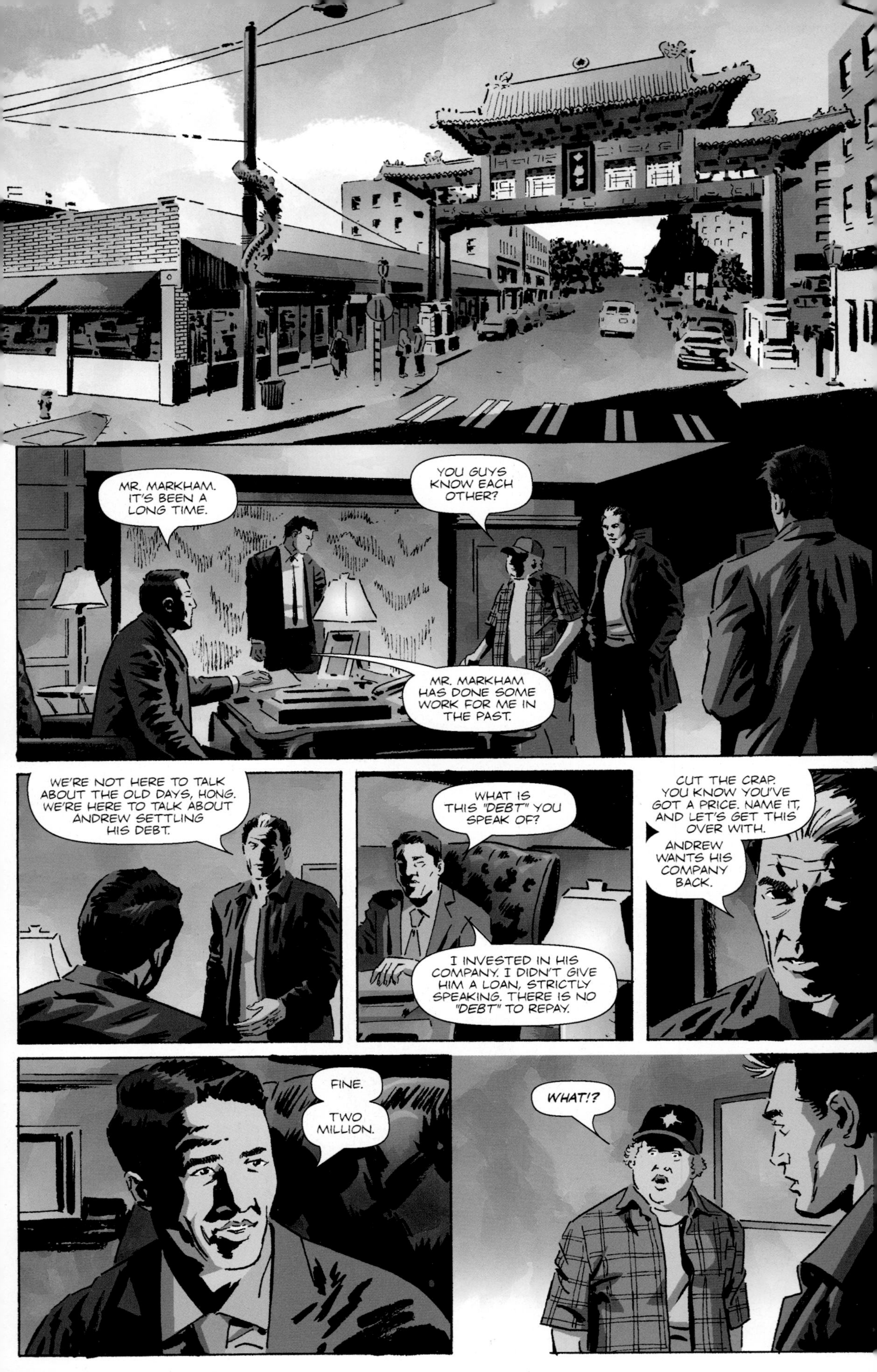
MR. MARKHAM. IT'S BEEN A LONG TIME.
YOU GUYS KNOW EACH OTHER?
MR. MARKHAM HAS DONE SOME WORK FOR ME IN THE PAST.
WE'RE NOT HERE TO TALK ABOUT THE OLD DAYS, HONG. WE'RE HERE TO TALK ABOUT ANDREW SETTLING HIS DEBT.
WHAT IS THIS "DEBT" YOU SPEAK OF?
I INVESTED IN HIS COMPANY. I DIDN'T GIVE HIM A LOAN, STRICTLY SPEAKING. THERE IS NO "DEBT" TO REPAY.
CUT THE CRAP. YOU KNOW YOU'VE GOT A PRICE. NAME IT, AND LET'S GET THIS OVER WITH.
ANDREW WANTS HIS COMPANY BACK.
FINE.
TWO MILLION.
WHAT!?

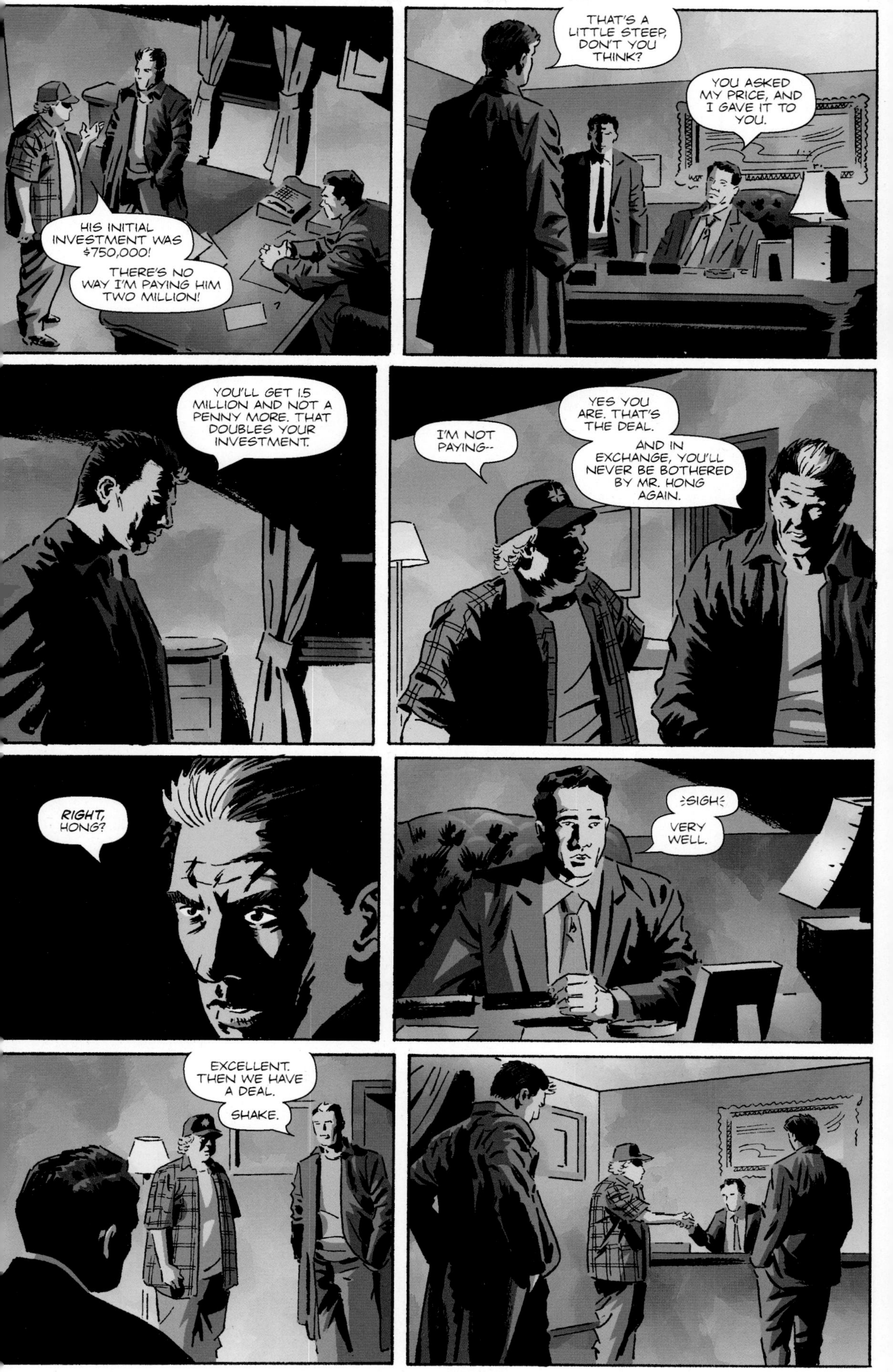
HIS INITIAL INVESTMENT WAS $750,000!
THERE'S NO WAY I'M PAYING HIM TWO MILLION!
THAT'S A LITTLE STEEP, DON'T YOU THINK?
YOU ASKED MY PRICE, AND I GAVE IT TO YOU.
YOU'LL GET 1.5 MILLION AND NOT A PENNY MORE. THAT DOUBLES YOUR INVESTMENT.
I'M NOT PAYING--
YES YOU ARE. THAT'S THE DEAL.
AND IN EXCHANGE, YOU'LL NEVER BE BOTHERED BY MR. HONG AGAIN.
RIGHT, HONG?
SIGH
VERY WELL.
EXCELLENT. THEN WE HAVE A DEAL.
SHAKE.

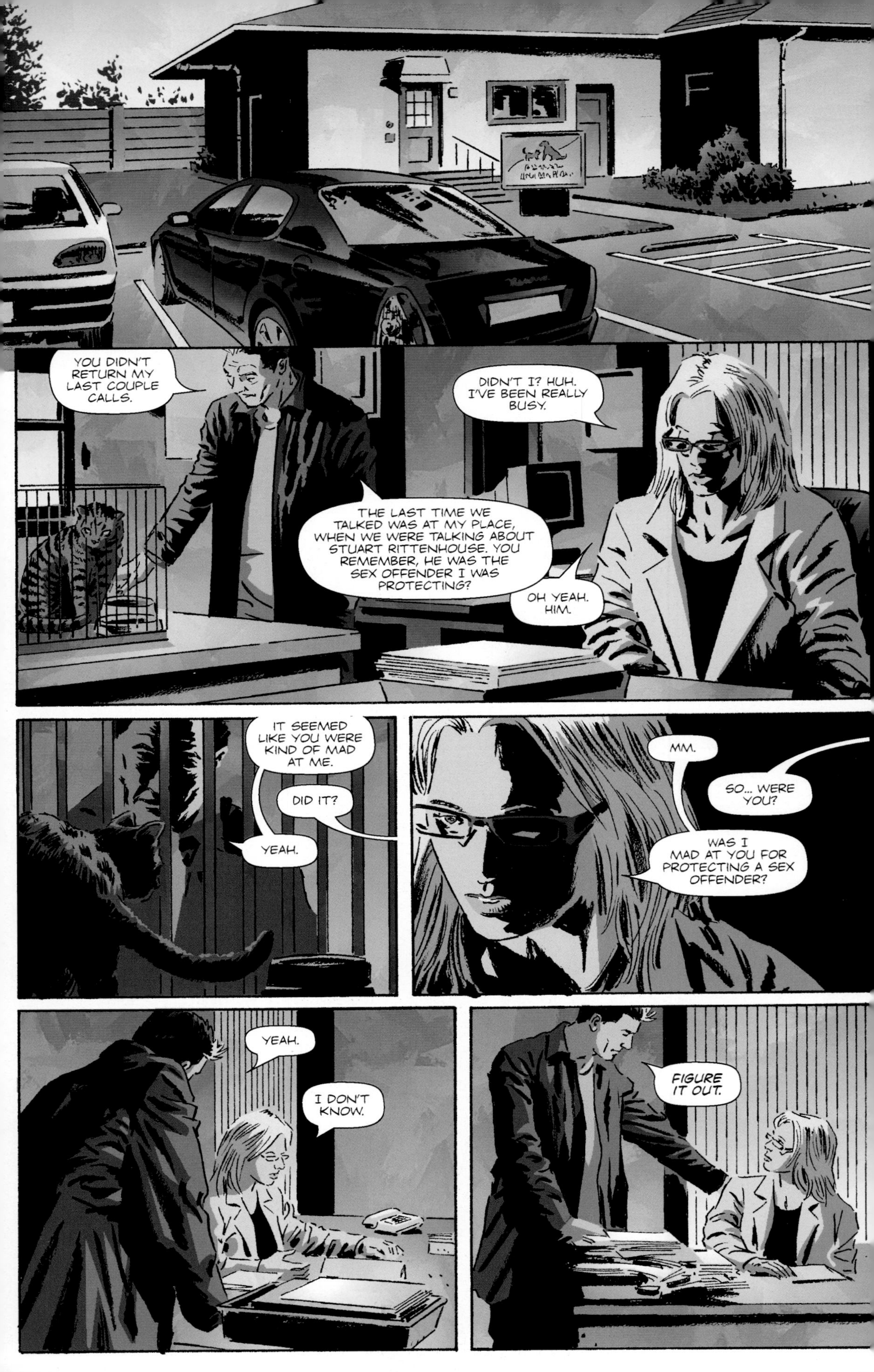
YOU DIDN'T RETURN MY LAST COUPLE CALLS.
DIDN'T I? HUH. I'VE BEEN REALLY BUSY.
THE LAST TIME WE TALKED WAS AT MY PLACE, WHEN WE WERE TALKING ABOUT STUART RITTENHOUSE. YOU REMEMBER, HE WAS THE SEX OFFENDER I WAS PROTECTING?
OH YEAH. HIM.
IT SEEMED LIKE YOU WERE KIND OF MAD AT ME.
DID IT?
YEAH.
MM.
SO... WERE YOU?
WAS I MAD AT YOU FOR PROTECTING A SEX OFFENDER?
YEAH.
I DON'T KNOW.
FIGURE IT OUT.

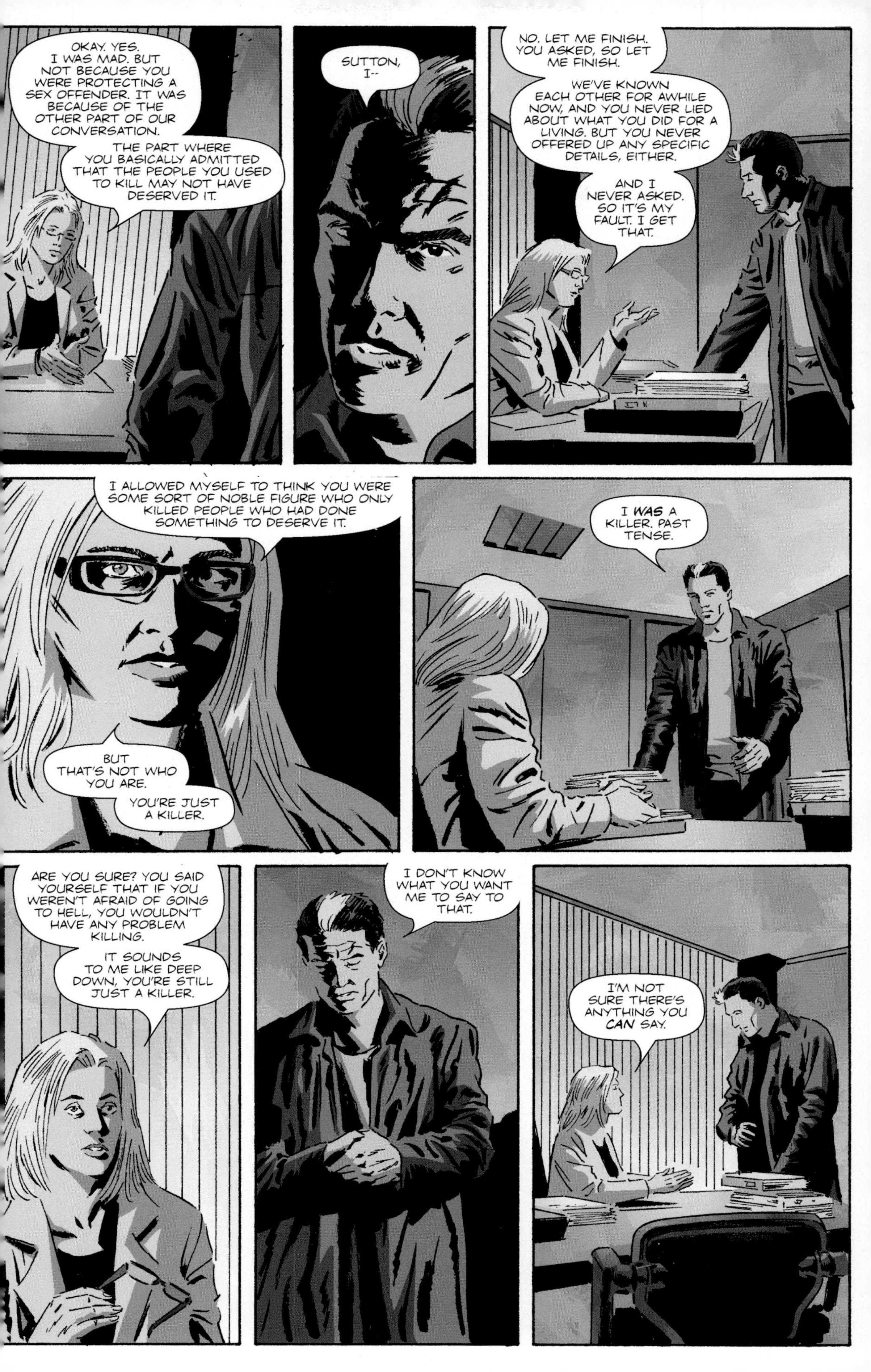
OKAY. YES. I WAS MAD. BUT NOT BECAUSE YOU WERE PROTECTING A SEX OFFENDER. IT WAS BECAUSE OF THE OTHER PART OF OUR CONVERSATION.
THE PART WHERE YOU BASICALLY ADMITTED THAT THE PEOPLE YOU USED TO KILL MAY NOT HAVE DESERVED IT.
SUTTON, I--
NO. LET ME FINISH. YOU ASKED, SO LET ME FINISH.
WE'VE KNOWN EACH OTHER FOR AWHILE NOW, AND YOU NEVER LIED ABOUT WHAT YOU DID FOR A LIVING. BUT YOU NEVER OFFERED UP ANY SPECIFIC DETAILS, EITHER.
AND I NEVER ASKED. SO IT'S MY FAULT. I GET THAT.
I ALLOWED MYSELF TO THINK YOU WERE SOME SORT OF NOBLE FIGURE WHO ONLY KILLED PEOPLE WHO HAD DONE SOMETHING TO DESERVE IT.
BUT THAT'S NOT WHO YOU ARE.
YOU'RE JUST A KILLER.
I WAS A KILLER. PAST TENSE.
ARE YOU SURE? YOU SAID YOURSELF THAT IF YOU WEREN'T AFRAID OF GOING TO HELL, YOU WOULDN'T HAVE ANY PROBLEM KILLING.
IT SOUNDS TO ME LIKE DEEP DOWN, YOU'RE STILL JUST A KILLER.
I DON'T KNOW WHAT YOU WANT ME TO SAY TO THAT.
I'M NOT SURE THERE'S ANYTHING YOU CAN SAY.

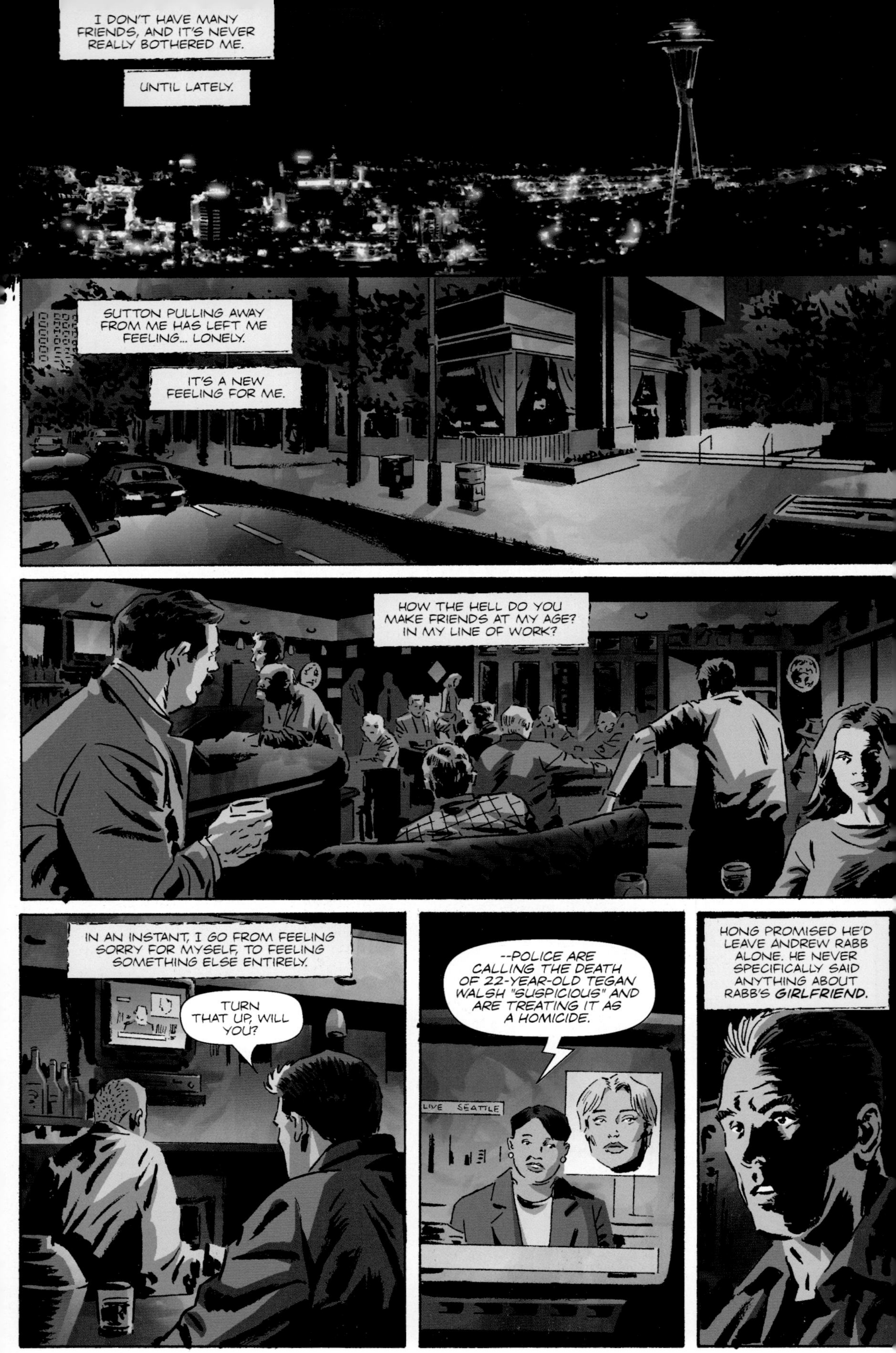
I DON'T HAVE MANY FRIENDS, AND IT'S NEVER REALLY BOTHERED ME.
UNTIL LATELY.
SUTTON PULLING AWAY FROM ME HAS LEFT ME FEELING... LONELY.
IT'S A NEW FEELING FOR ME.
HOW THE HELL DO YOU MAKE FRIENDS AT MY AGE? IN MY LINE OF WORK?
IN AN INSTANT, I GO FROM FEELING SORRY FOR MYSELF, TO FEELING SOMETHING ELSE ENTIRELY.
TURN THAT UP, WILL YOU?
--POLICE ARE CALLING THE DEATH OF 22-YEAR-OLD TEGAN WALSH "SUSPICIOUS" AND ARE TREATING IT AS A HOMICIDE.
LIVE SEATTLE
HONG PROMISED HE'D LEAVE ANDREW RABB ALONE. HE NEVER SPECIFICALLY SAID ANYTHING ABOUT RABB'S GIRLFRIEND.

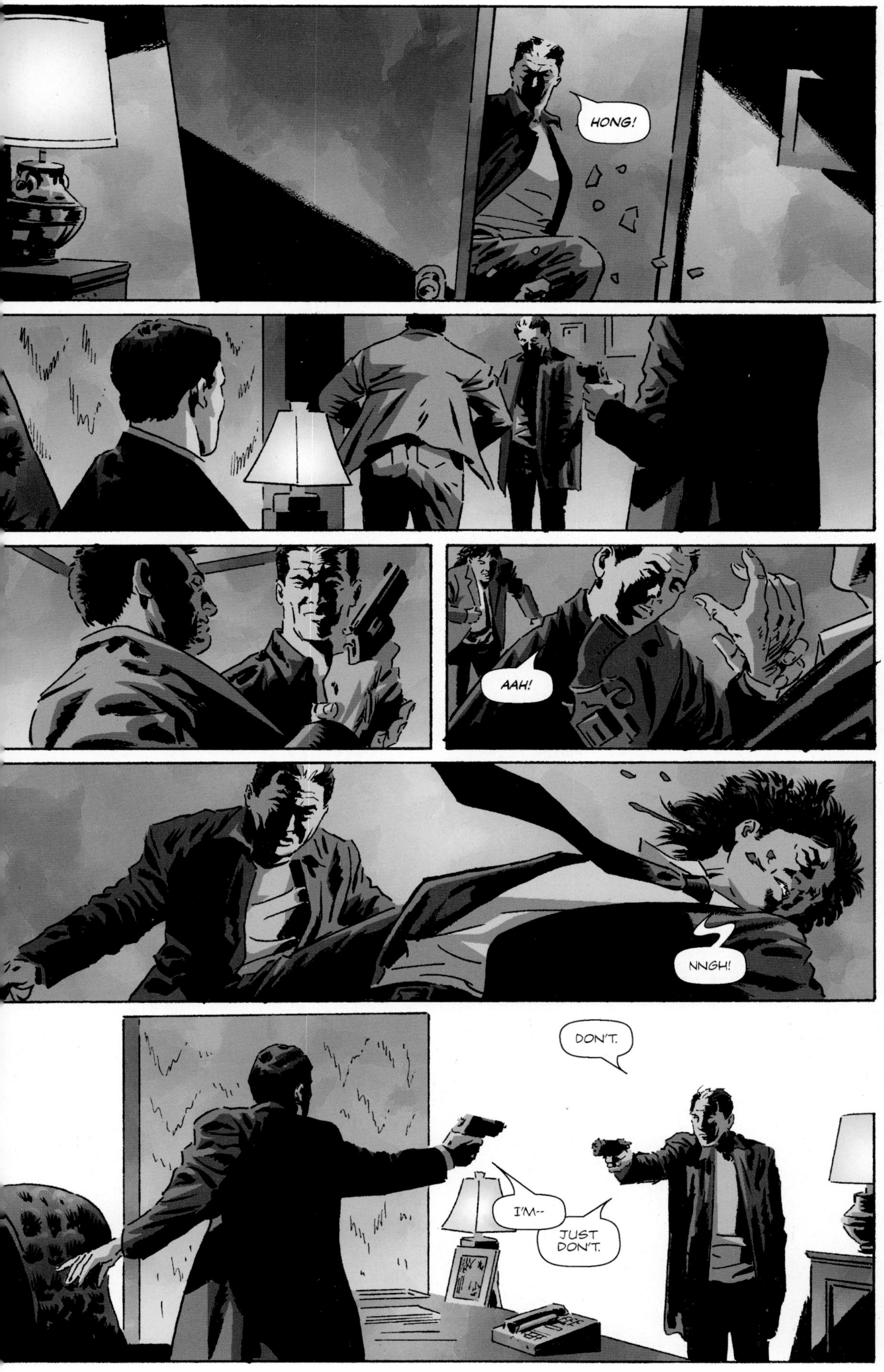
HONG!
AAH!
NNGH!
DON'T.
I'M--
JUST DON'T.

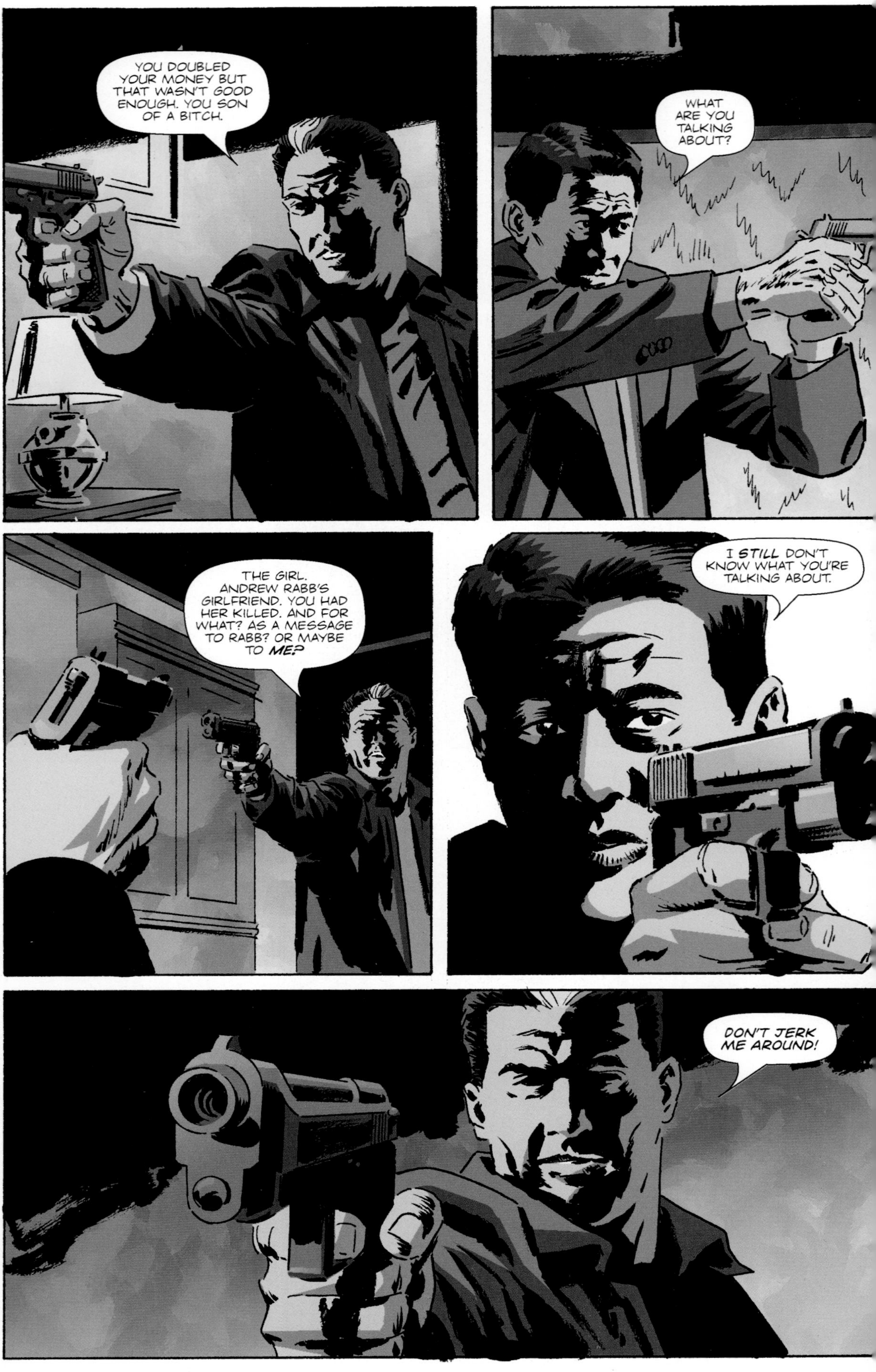
YOU DOUBLED YOUR MONEY BUT THAT WASN'T GOOD ENOUGH. YOU SON OF A BITCH.
WHAT ARE YOU TALKING ABOUT?
THE GIRL. ANDREW RABB'S GIRLFRIEND. YOU HAD HER KILLED. AND FOR WHAT? AS A MESSAGE TO RABB? OR MAYBE TO *ME?*
I *STILL* DON'T KNOW WHAT YOU'RE TALKING ABOUT.
DON'T JERK ME AROUND!

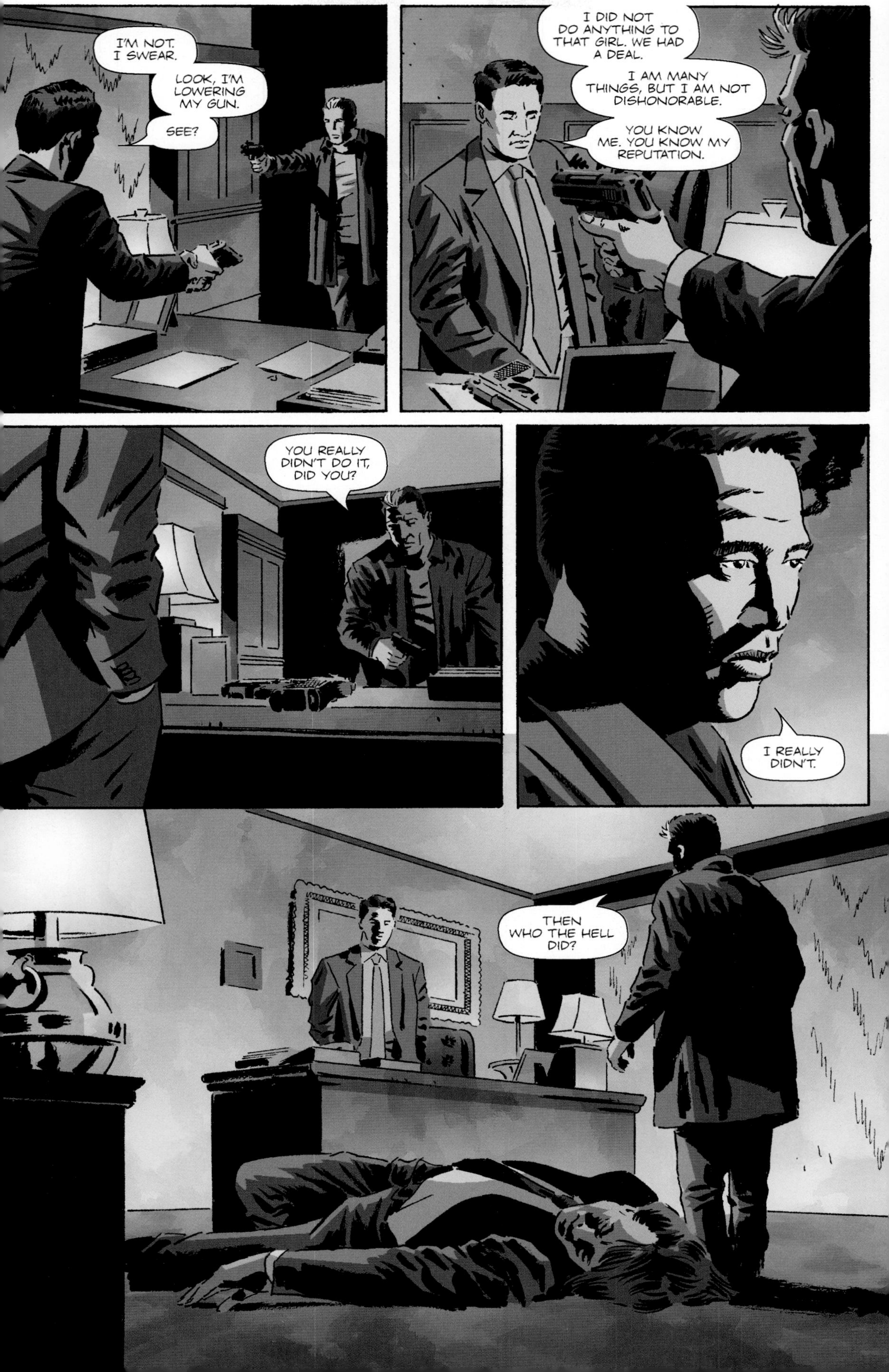
I'M NOT. I SWEAR.
LOOK, I'M LOWERING MY GUN.
SEE?
I DID NOT DO ANYTHING TO THAT GIRL. WE HAD A DEAL.
I AM MANY THINGS, BUT I AM NOT DISHONORABLE.
YOU KNOW ME. YOU KNOW MY REPUTATION.
YOU REALLY DIDN'T DO IT, DID YOU?
I REALLY DIDN'T.
THEN WHO THE HELL DID?

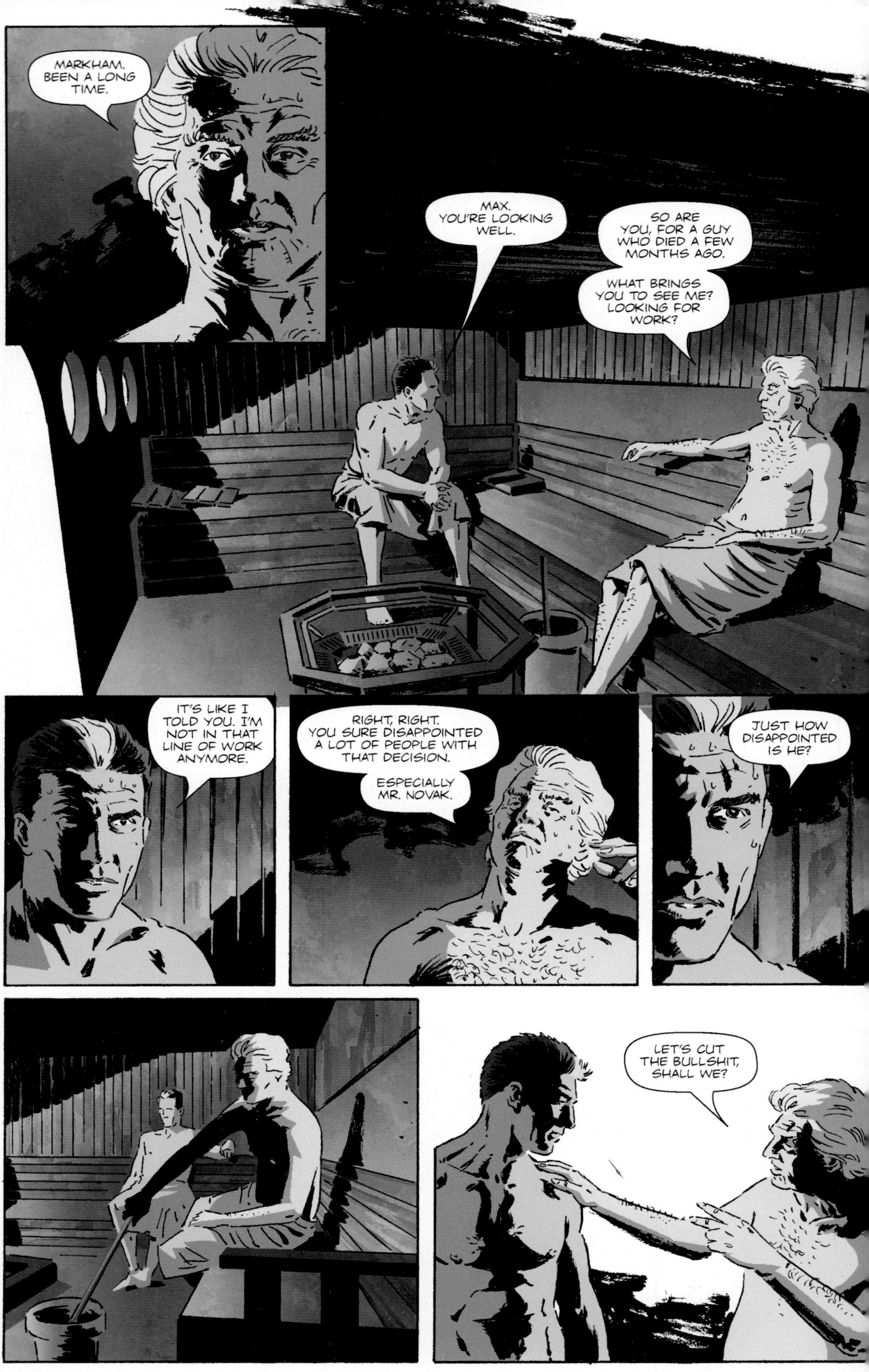
MARKHAM. BEEN A LONG TIME.
MAX. YOU'RE LOOKING WELL.
SO ARE YOU, FOR A GUY WHO DIED A FEW MONTHS AGO.
WHAT BRINGS YOU TO SEE ME? LOOKING FOR WORK?
IT'S LIKE I TOLD YOU. I'M NOT IN THAT LINE OF WORK ANYMORE.
RIGHT, RIGHT. YOU SURE DISAPPOINTED A LOT OF PEOPLE WITH THAT DECISION.
ESPECIALLY MR. NOVAK.
JUST HOW DISAPPOINTED IS HE?
LET'S CUT THE BULLSHIT, SHALL WE?

YEAH, LET'S.

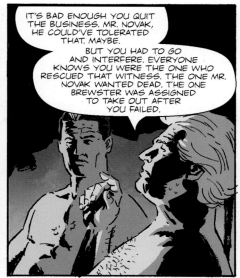

IT'S BAD ENOUGH YOU QUIT THE BUSINESS. MR. NOVAK, HE COULD'VE TOLERATED THAT. MAYBE.

BUT YOU HAD TO GO AND INTERFERE. EVERYONE KNOWS YOU WERE THE ONE WHO RESCUED THAT WITNESS. THE ONE MR. NOVAK WANTED DEAD. THE ONE BREWSTER WAS ASSIGNED TO TAKE OUT AFTER YOU FAILED.

EVERYONE?

YEAH. EVERYONE.

INCLUDING BREWSTER.

SHIT.

THAT'S RIGHT. BREWSTER DIDN'T DIE, DESPITE THE FACT THAT YOU SHOT HIM IN THE HEAD.

HE'S FULLY RECOVERED.

AND I IMAGINE HE'S PRETTY PISSED AT YOU.

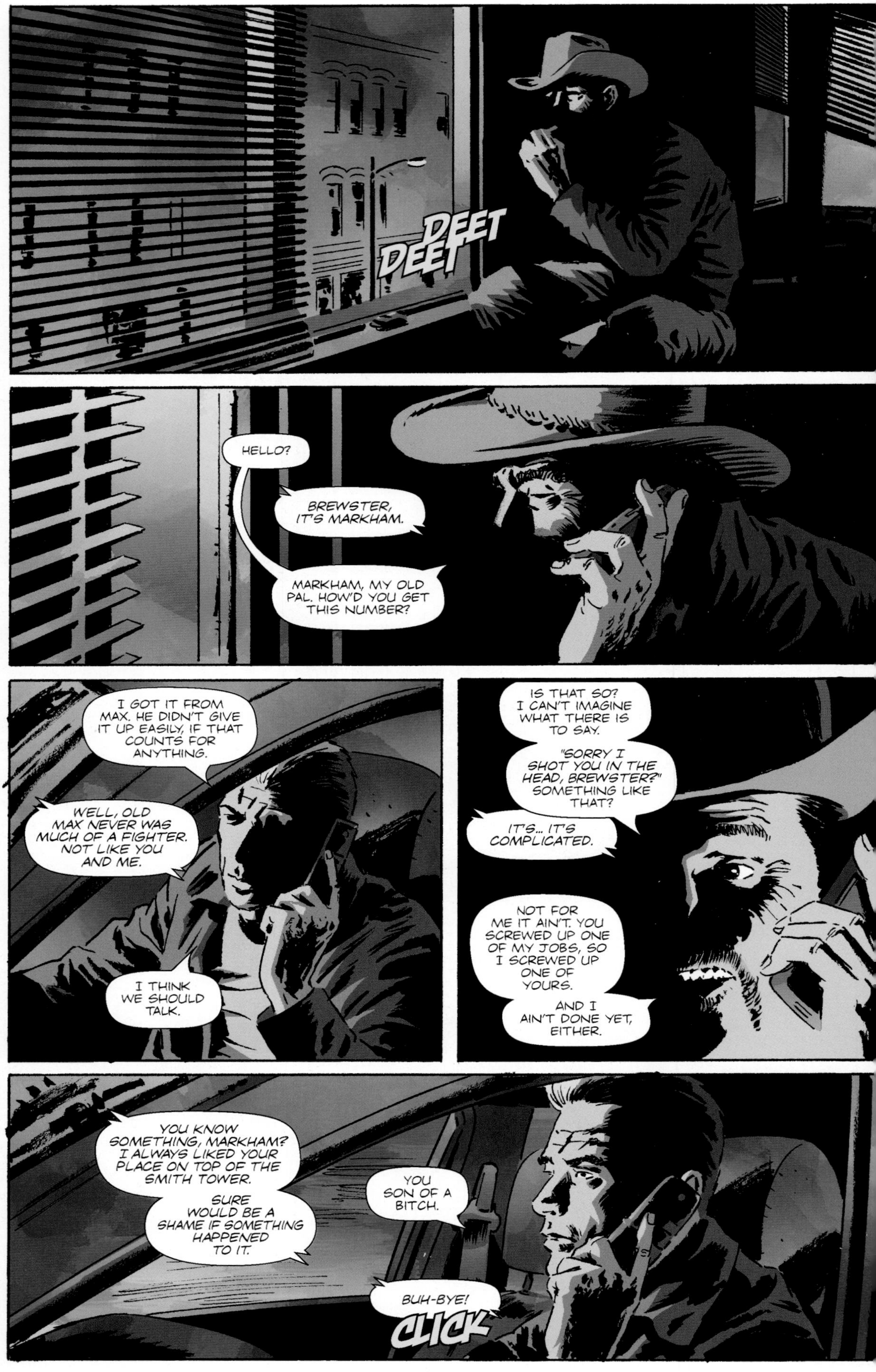
DEET DEET
HELLO?
BREWSTER, IT'S MARKHAM.
MARKHAM, MY OLD PAL. HOW'D YOU GET THIS NUMBER?
I GOT IT FROM MAX. HE DIDN'T GIVE IT UP EASILY, IF THAT COUNTS FOR ANYTHING.
WELL, OLD MAX NEVER WAS MUCH OF A FIGHTER. NOT LIKE YOU AND ME.
I THINK WE SHOULD TALK.
IS THAT SO? I CAN'T IMAGINE WHAT THERE IS TO SAY.
"SORRY I SHOT YOU IN THE HEAD, BREWSTER?" SOMETHING LIKE THAT?
IT'S... IT'S COMPLICATED.
NOT FOR ME IT AIN'T. YOU SCREWED UP ONE OF MY JOBS, SO I SCREWED UP ONE OF YOURS.
AND I AIN'T DONE YET, EITHER.
YOU KNOW SOMETHING, MARKHAM? I ALWAYS LIKED YOUR PLACE ON TOP OF THE SMITH TOWER.
SURE WOULD BE A SHAME IF SOMETHING HAPPENED TO IT.
YOU SON OF A BITCH.
BUH-BYE!
CLICK

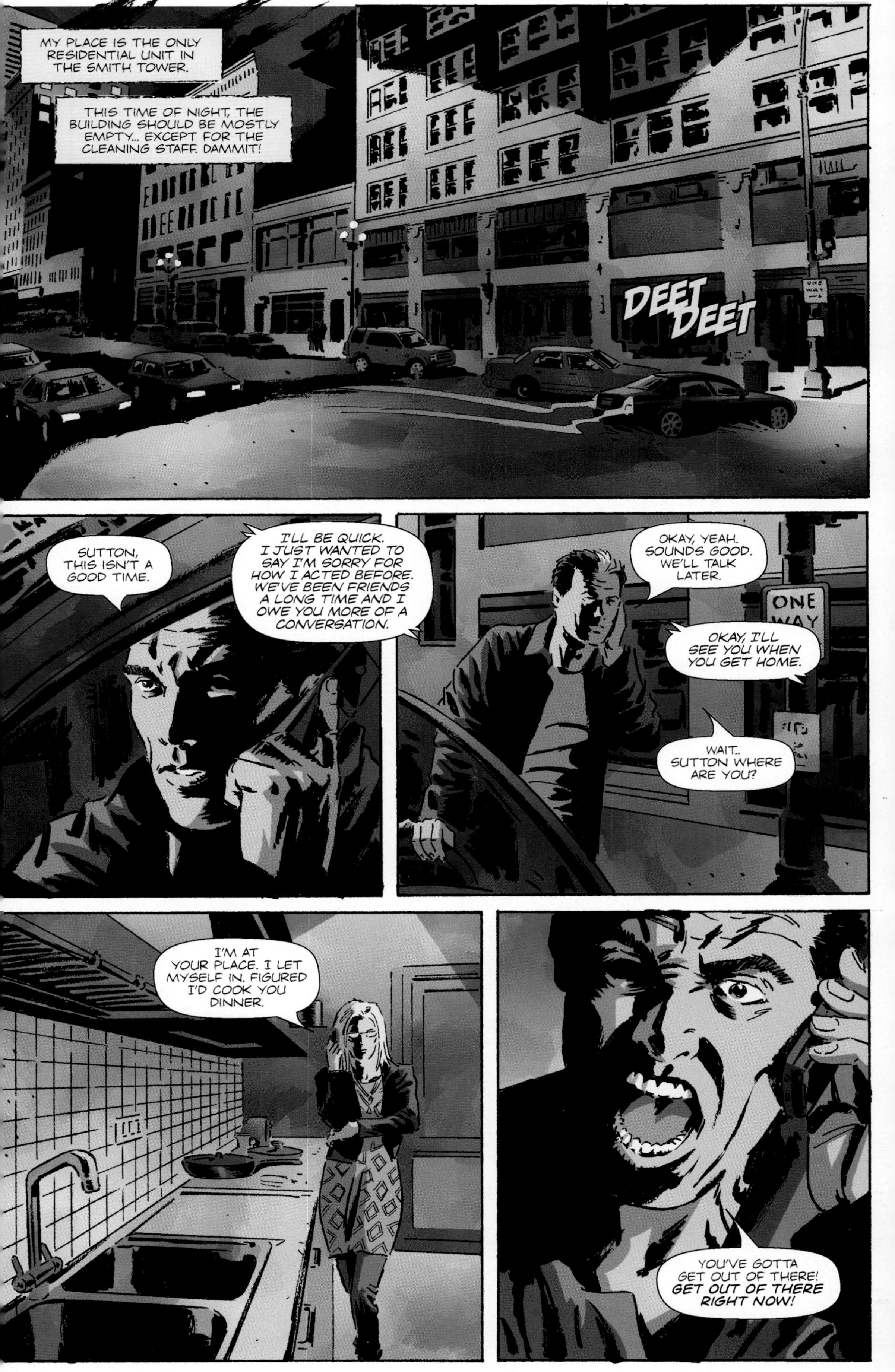

MY PLACE IS THE ONLY RESIDENTIAL UNIT IN THE SMITH TOWER.
THIS TIME OF NIGHT, THE BUILDING SHOULD BE MOSTLY EMPTY... EXCEPT FOR THE CLEANING STAFF. DAMMIT!
DEET DEET
SUTTON, THIS ISN'T A GOOD TIME.
I'LL BE QUICK. I JUST WANTED TO SAY I'M SORRY FOR HOW I ACTED BEFORE. WE'VE BEEN FRIENDS A LONG TIME AND I OWE YOU MORE OF A CONVERSATION.
OKAY, YEAH. SOUNDS GOOD. WE'LL TALK LATER.
ONE WAY
OKAY, I'LL SEE YOU WHEN YOU GET HOME.
WAIT.. SUTTON WHERE ARE YOU?
I'M AT YOUR PLACE. I LET MYSELF IN. FIGURED I'D COOK YOU DINNER.
YOU'VE GOTTA GET OUT OF THERE! GET OUT OF THERE RIGHT NOW!

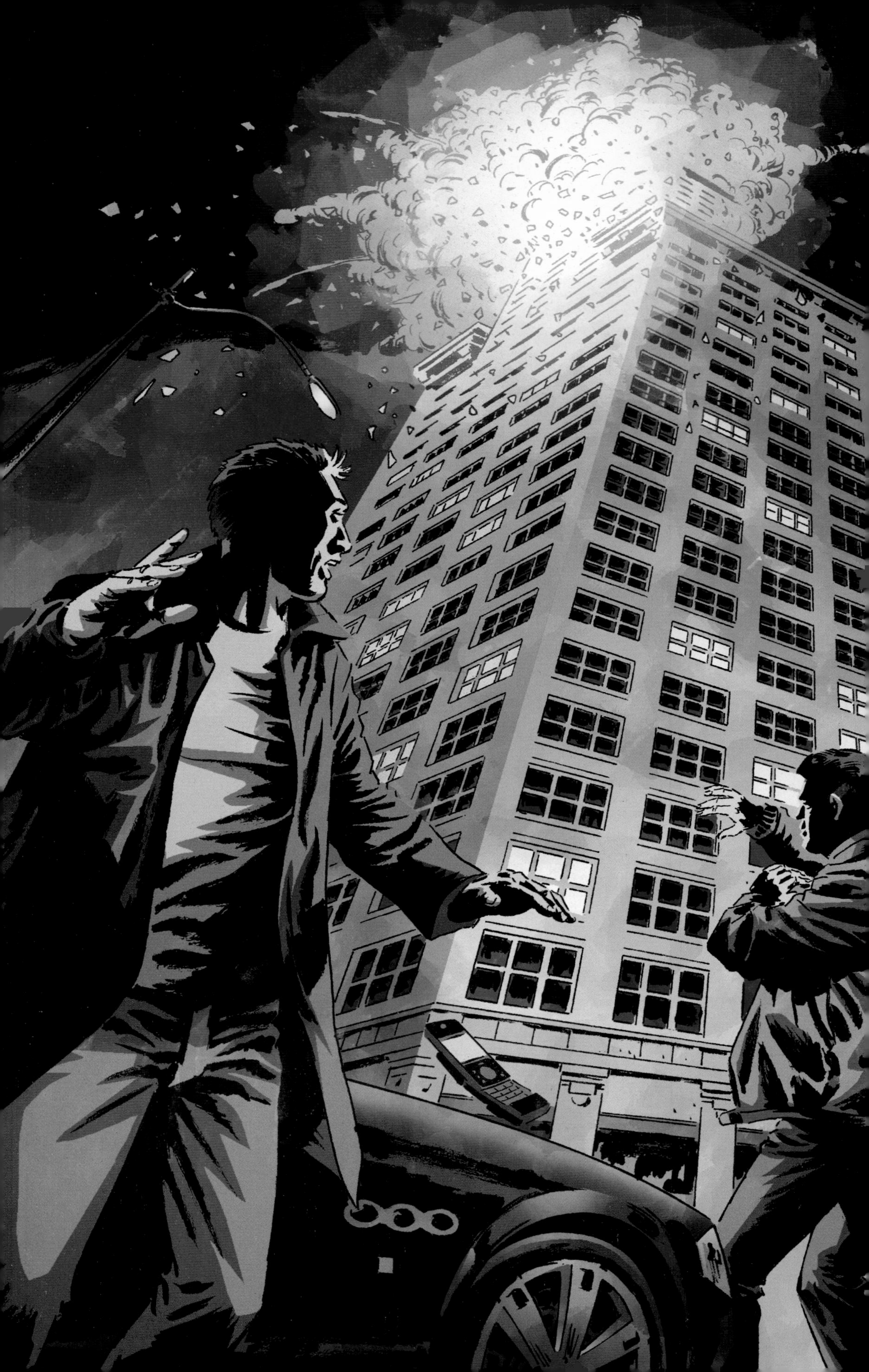

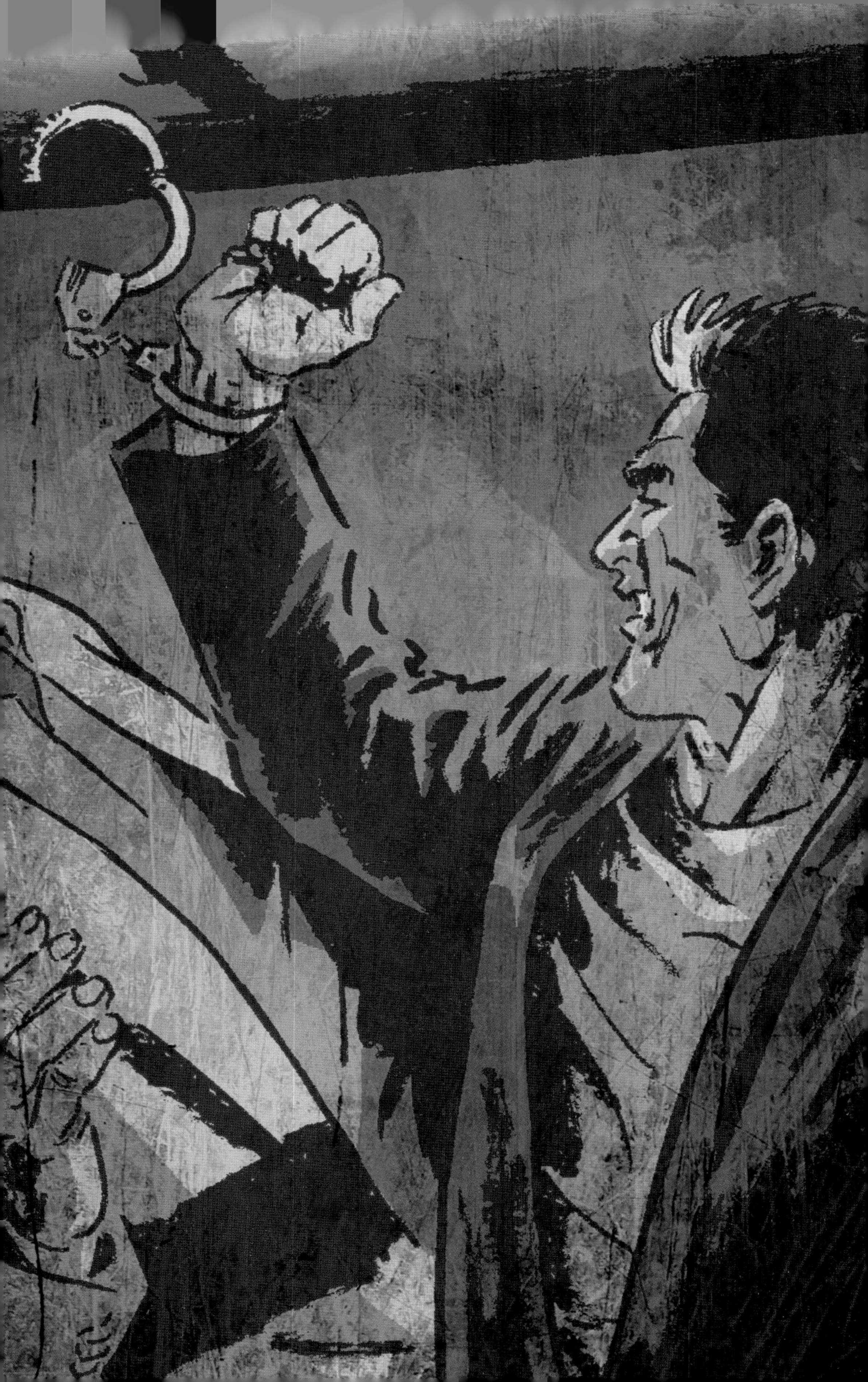

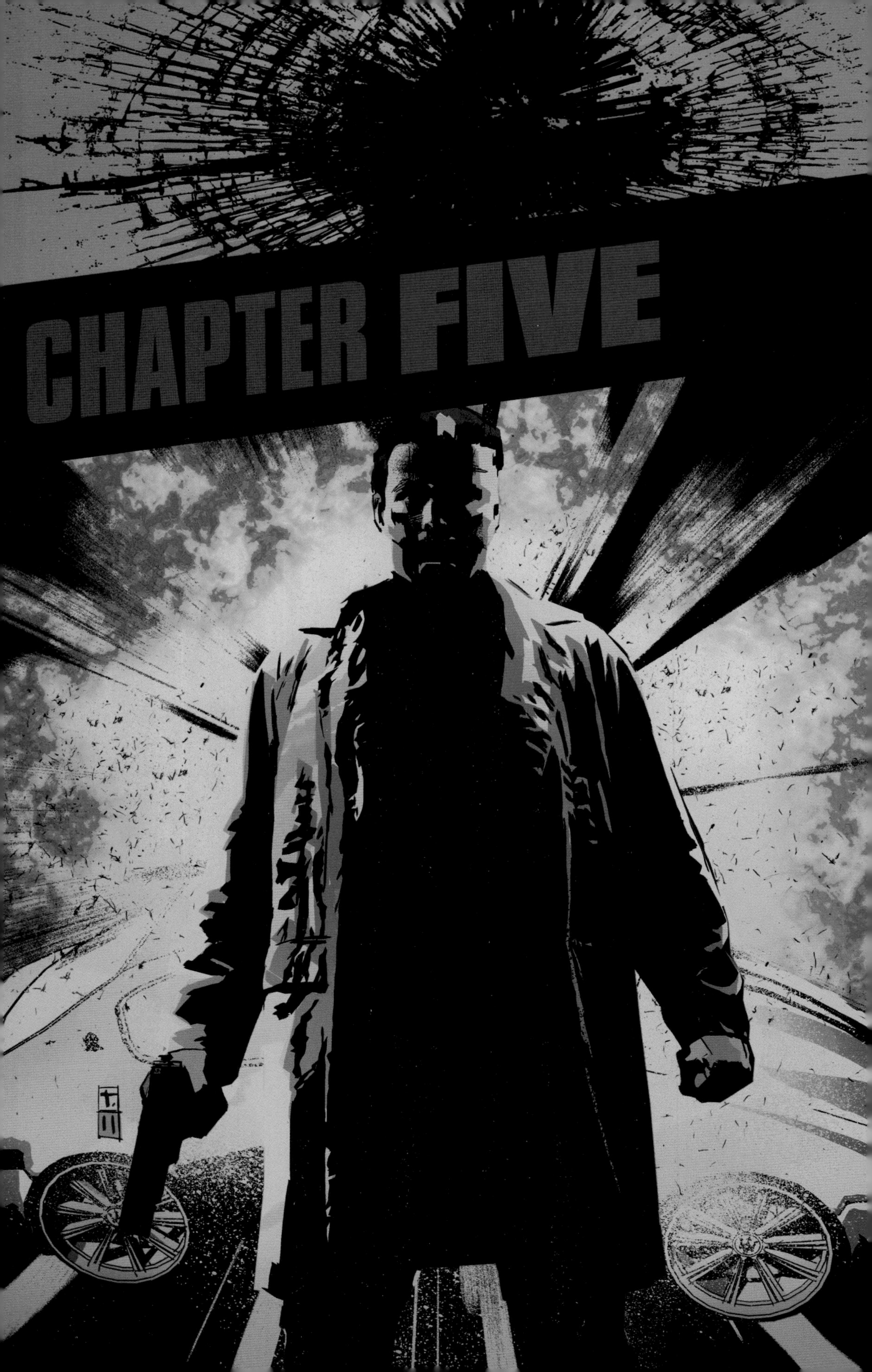
CHAPTER FIVE

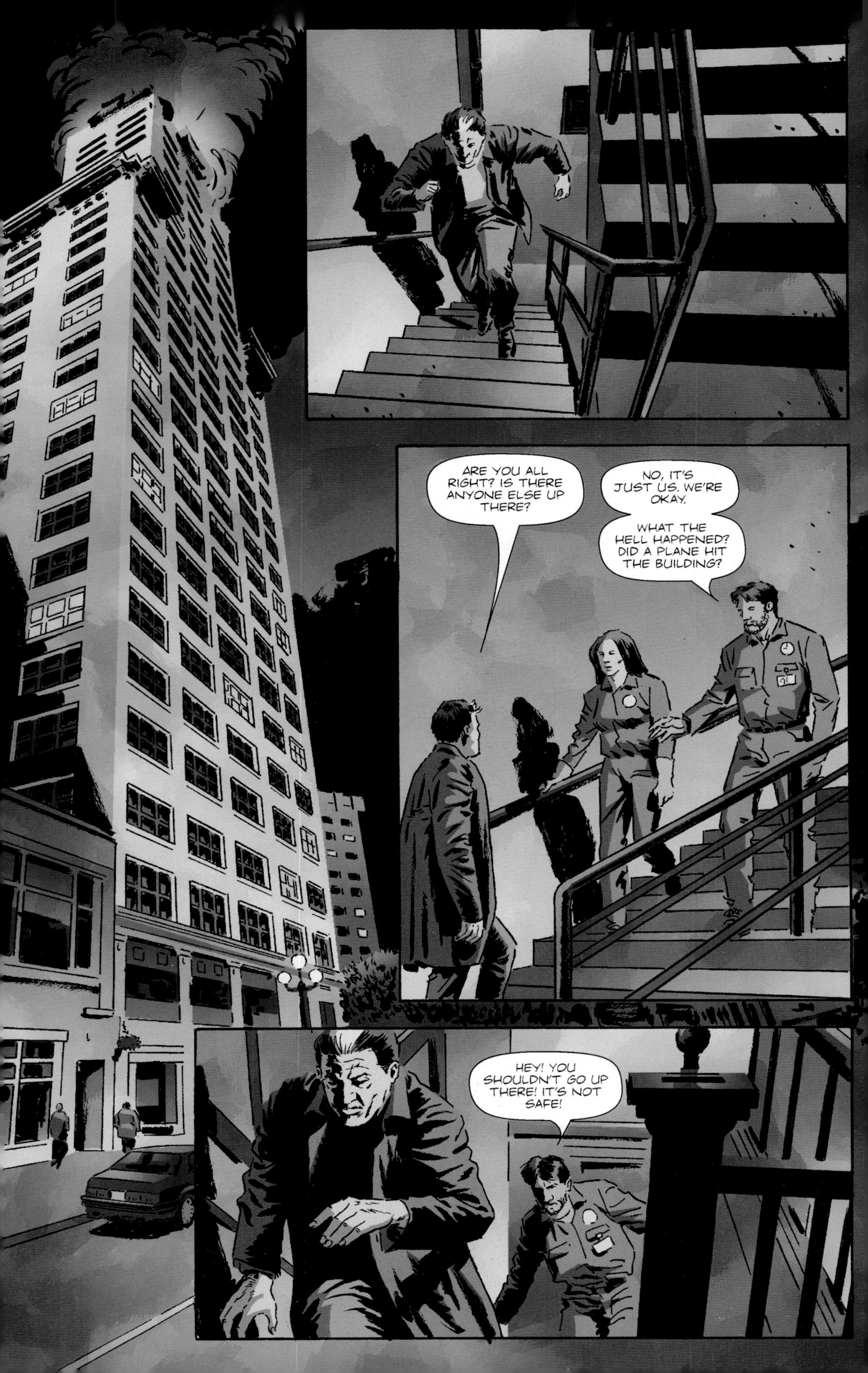
ARE YOU ALL RIGHT? IS THERE ANYONE ELSE UP THERE?
NO, IT'S JUST US. WE'RE OKAY.
WHAT THE HELL HAPPENED? DID A PLANE HIT THE BUILDING?
HEY! YOU SHOULDN'T GO UP THERE! IT'S NOT SAFE!

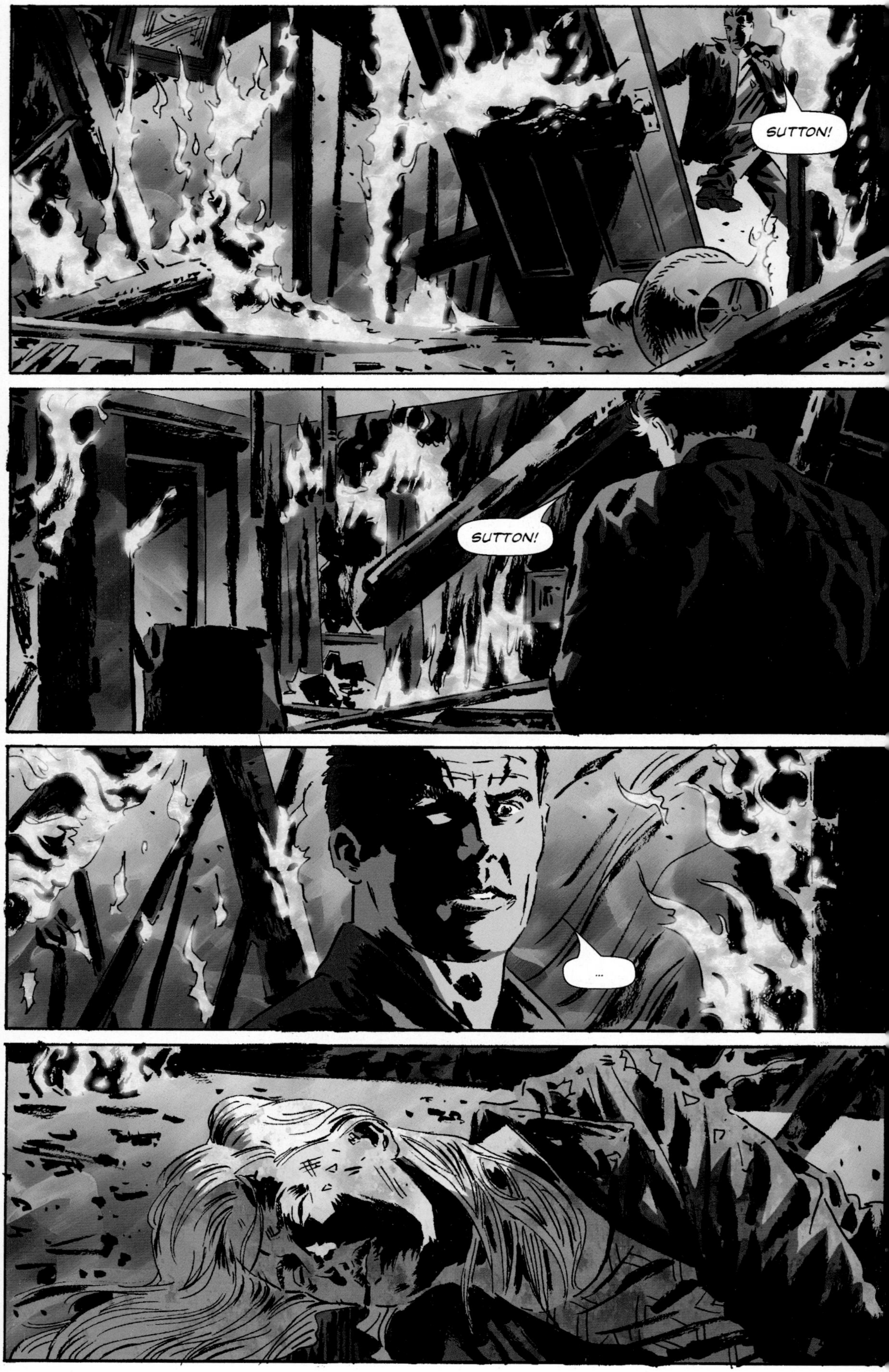
SUTTON!
SUTTON!
...

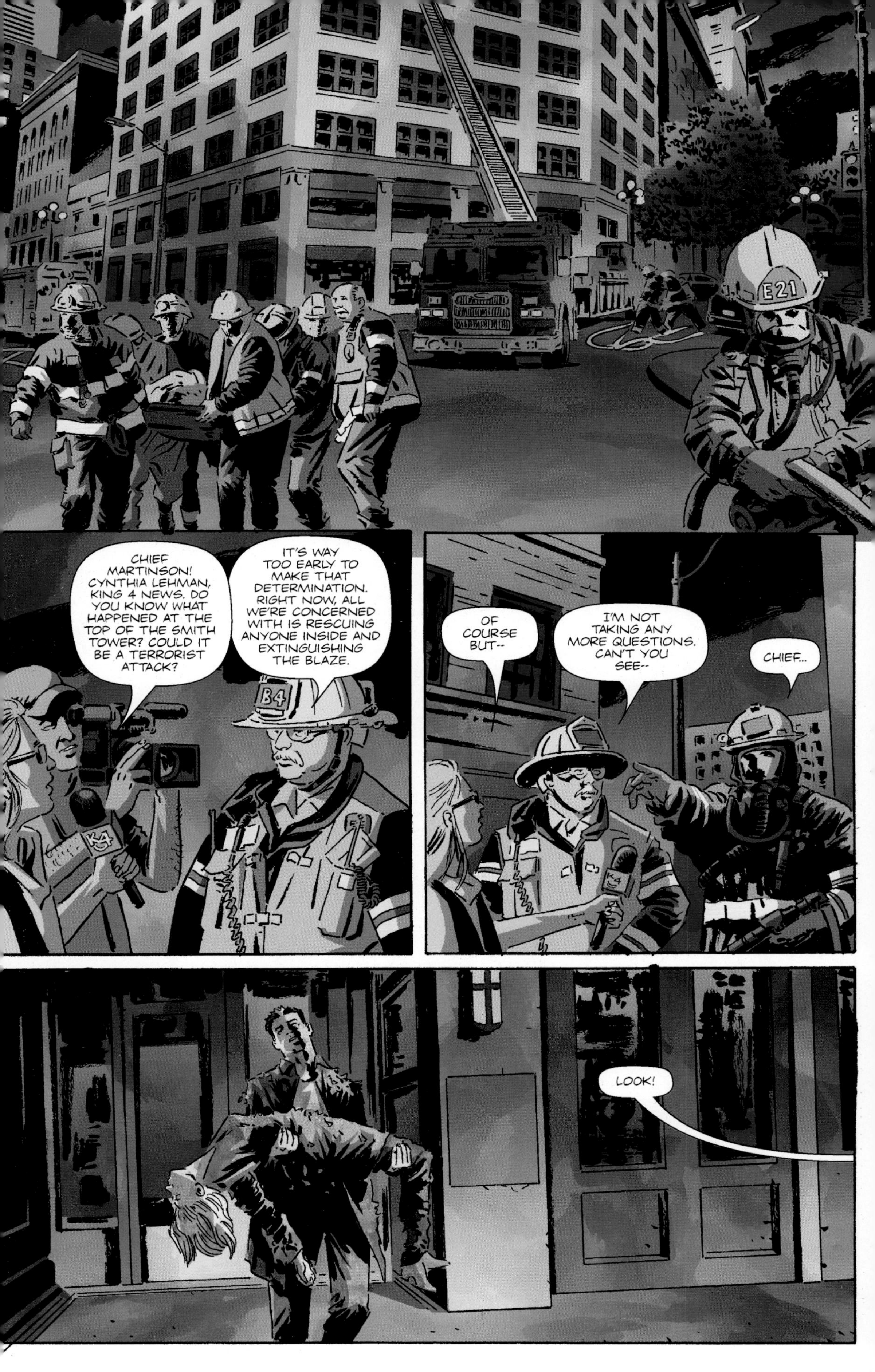
E21
CHIEF MARTINSON! CYNTHIA LEHMAN, KING 4 NEWS. DO YOU KNOW WHAT HAPPENED AT THE TOP OF THE SMITH TOWER? COULD IT BE A TERRORIST ATTACK?
IT'S WAY TOO EARLY TO MAKE THAT DETERMINATION. RIGHT NOW, ALL WE'RE CONCERNED WITH IS RESCUING ANYONE INSIDE AND EXTINGUISHING THE BLAZE.
B4
K4
OF COURSE BUT--
I'M NOT TAKING ANY MORE QUESTIONS. CAN'T YOU SEE--
CHIEF...
LOOK!

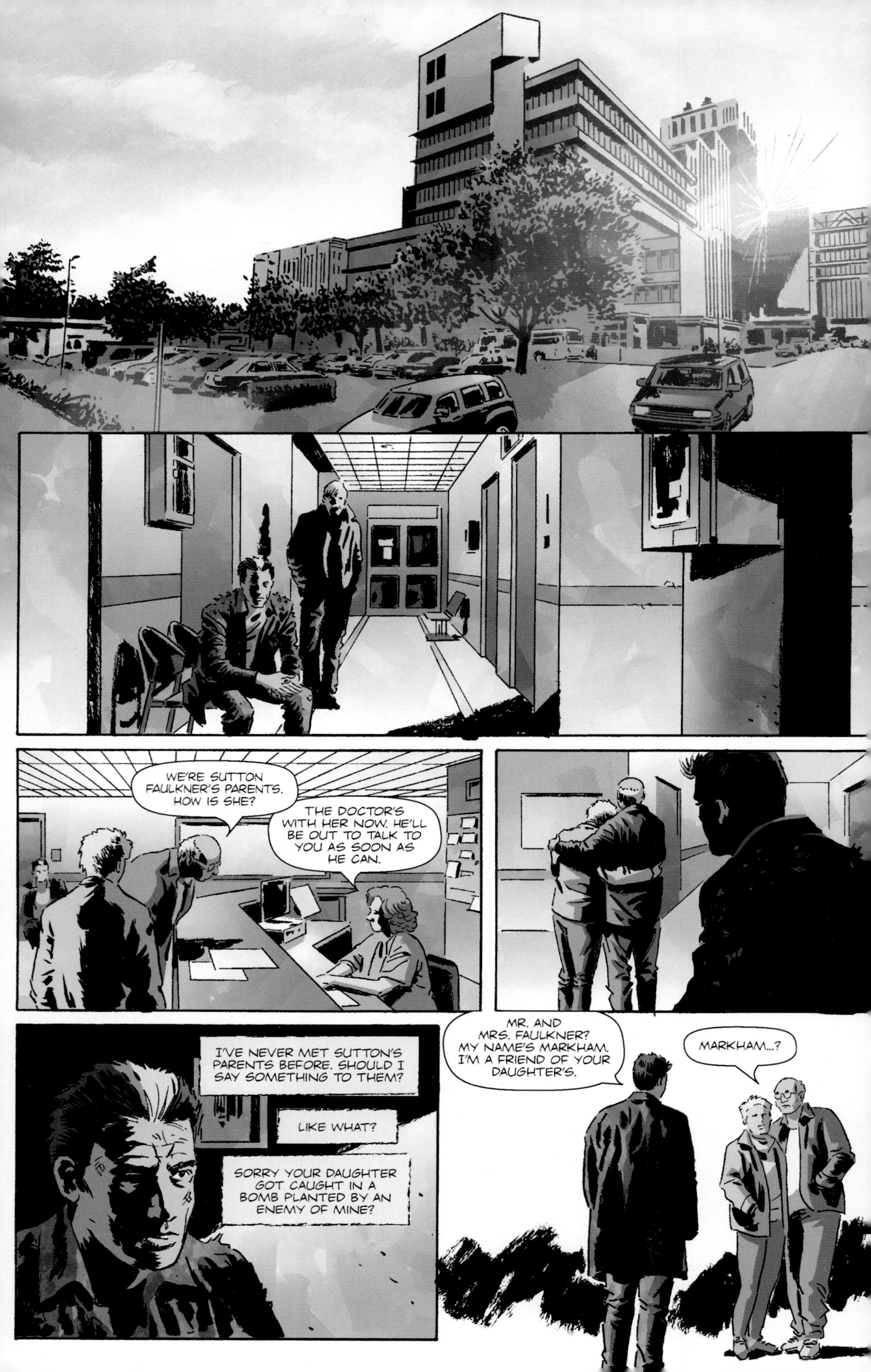
WE'RE SUTTON FAULKNER'S PARENTS. HOW IS SHE?
THE DOCTOR'S WITH HER NOW. HE'LL BE OUT TO TALK TO YOU AS SOON AS HE CAN.
I'VE NEVER MET SUTTON'S PARENTS BEFORE. SHOULD I SAY SOMETHING TO THEM?
LIKE WHAT?
SORRY YOUR DAUGHTER GOT CAUGHT IN A BOMB PLANTED BY AN ENEMY OF MINE?
MR. AND MRS. FAULKNER? MY NAME'S MARKHAM. I'M A FRIEND OF YOUR DAUGHTER'S.
MARKHAM...?

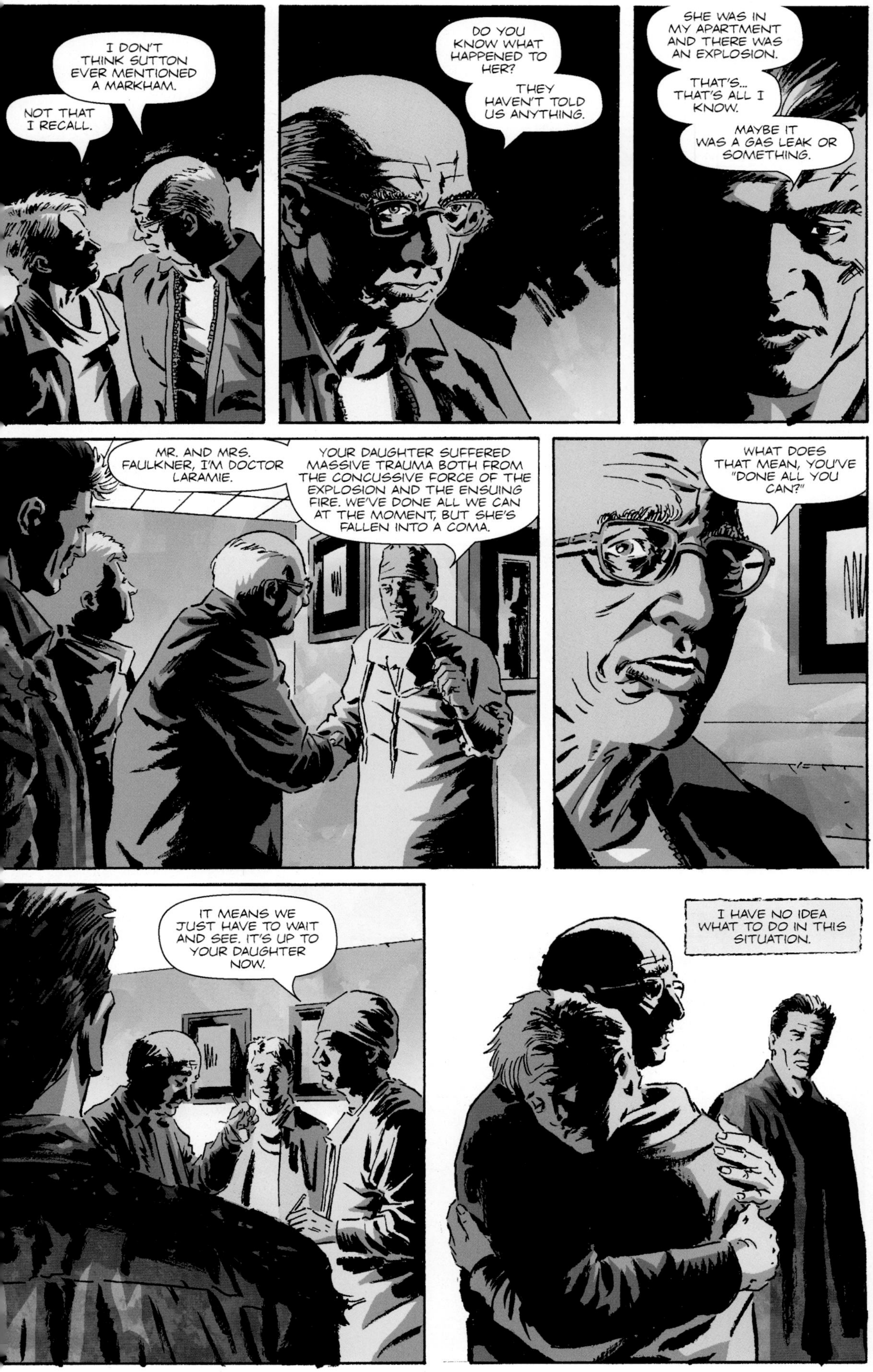
I DON'T THINK SUTTON EVER MENTIONED A MARKHAM.
NOT THAT I RECALL.
DO YOU KNOW WHAT HAPPENED TO HER?
THEY HAVEN'T TOLD US ANYTHING.
SHE WAS IN MY APARTMENT AND THERE WAS AN EXPLOSION.
THAT'S... THAT'S ALL I KNOW.
MAYBE IT WAS A GAS LEAK OR SOMETHING.
MR. AND MRS. FAULKNER, I'M DOCTOR LARAMIE.
YOUR DAUGHTER SUFFERED MASSIVE TRAUMA BOTH FROM THE CONCUSSIVE FORCE OF THE EXPLOSION AND THE ENSUING FIRE. WE'VE DONE ALL WE CAN AT THE MOMENT, BUT SHE'S FALLEN INTO A COMA.
WHAT DOES THAT MEAN, YOU'VE "DONE ALL YOU CAN?"
IT MEANS WE JUST HAVE TO WAIT AND SEE. IT'S UP TO YOUR DAUGHTER NOW.
I HAVE NO IDEA WHAT TO DO IN THIS SITUATION.

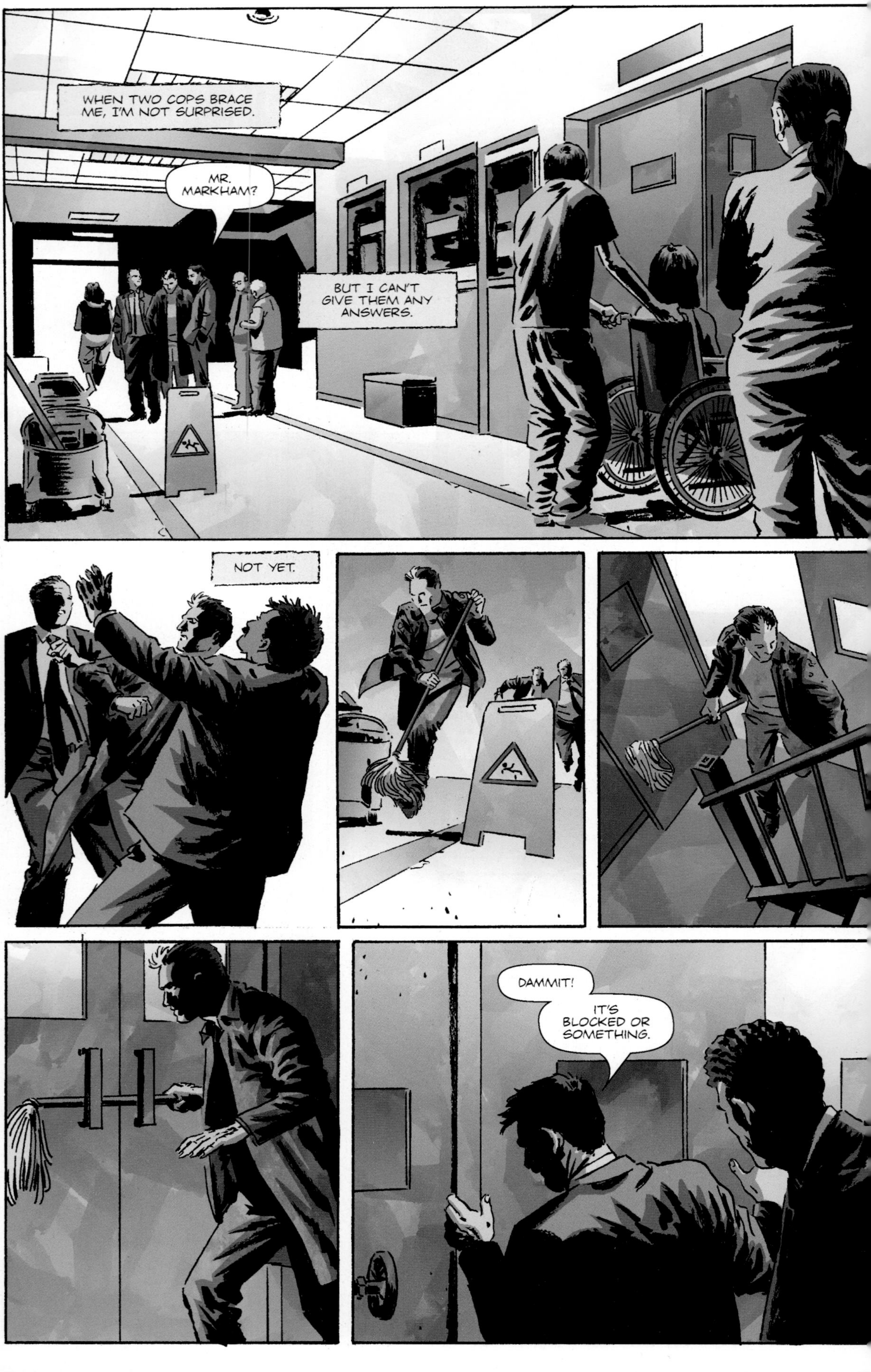
WHEN TWO COPS BRACE ME, I'M NOT SURPRISED.
MR. MARKHAM?
BUT I CAN'T GIVE THEM ANY ANSWERS.
NOT YET.
DAMMIT!
IT'S BLOCKED OR SOMETHING.

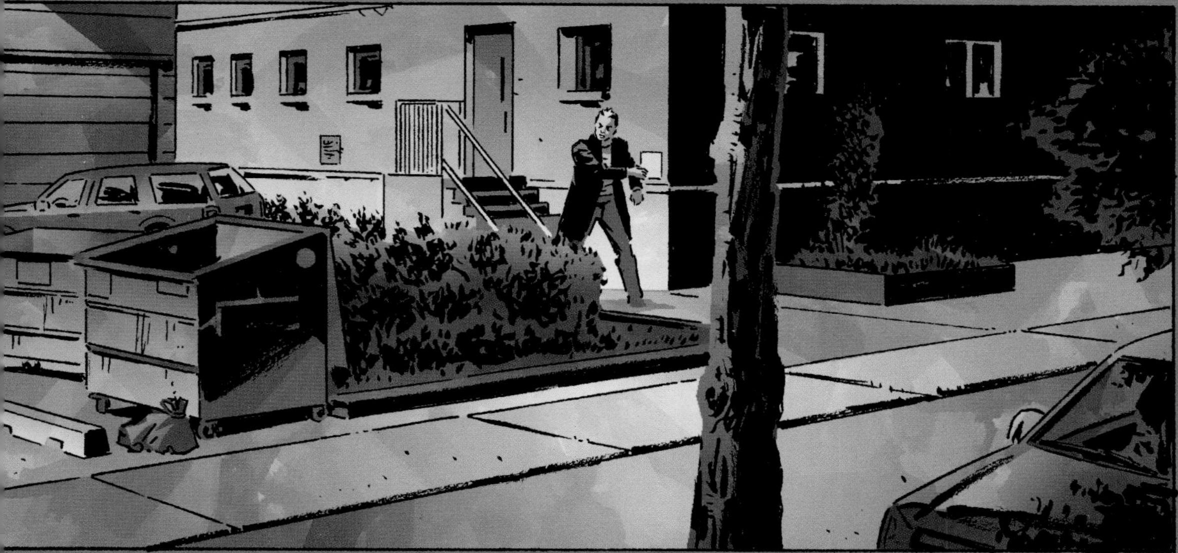

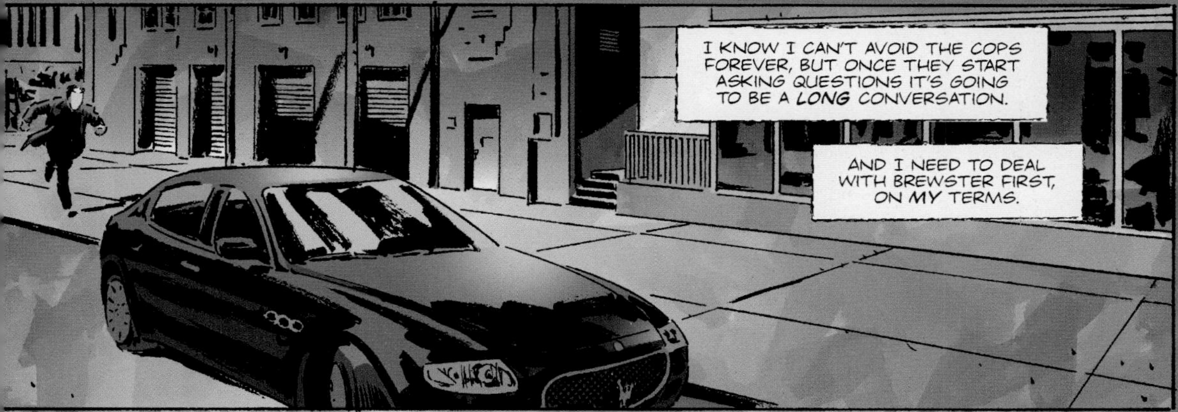
I KNOW I CAN'T AVOID THE COPS FOREVER, BUT ONCE THEY START ASKING QUESTIONS IT'S GOING TO BE A LONG CONVERSATION.
AND I NEED TO DEAL WITH BREWSTER FIRST, ON MY TERMS.

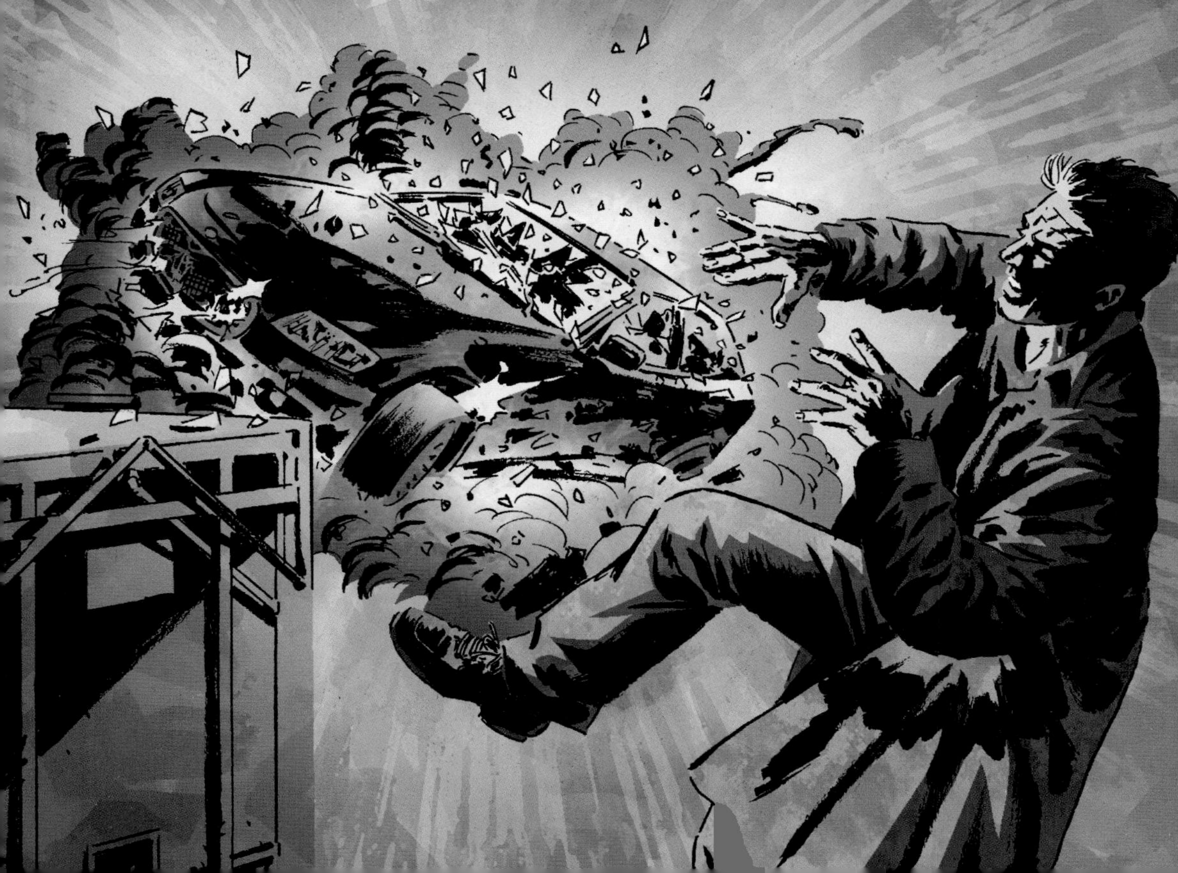

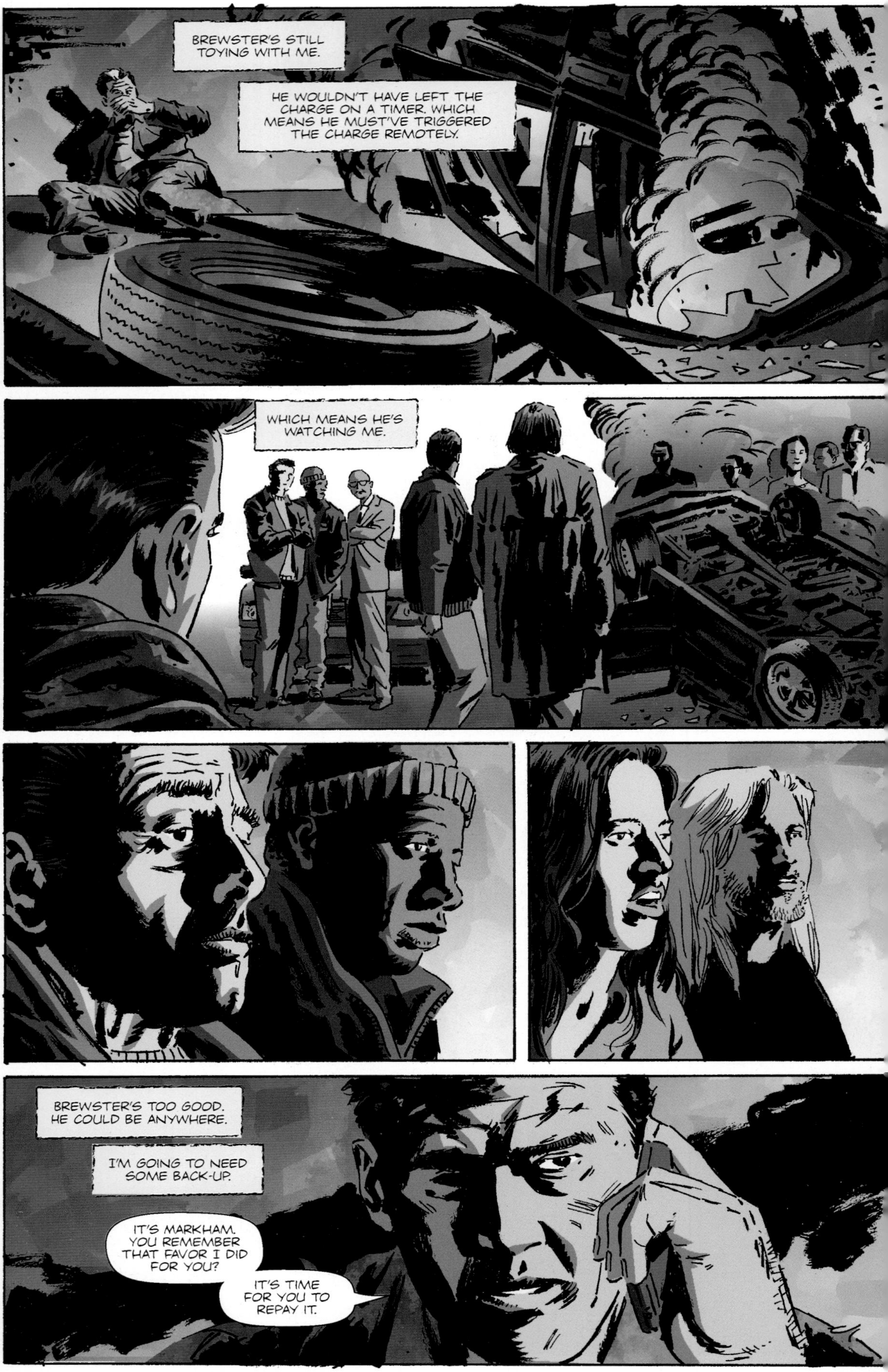
BREWSTER'S STILL TOYING WITH ME.
HE WOULDN'T HAVE LEFT THE CHARGE ON A TIMER. WHICH MEANS HE MUST'VE TRIGGERED THE CHARGE REMOTELY.
WHICH MEANS HE'S WATCHING ME.
BREWSTER'S TOO GOOD. HE COULD BE ANYWHERE.
I'M GOING TO NEED SOME BACK-UP.
IT'S MARKHAM. YOU REMEMBER THAT FAVOR I DID FOR YOU?
IT'S TIME FOR YOU TO REPAY IT.

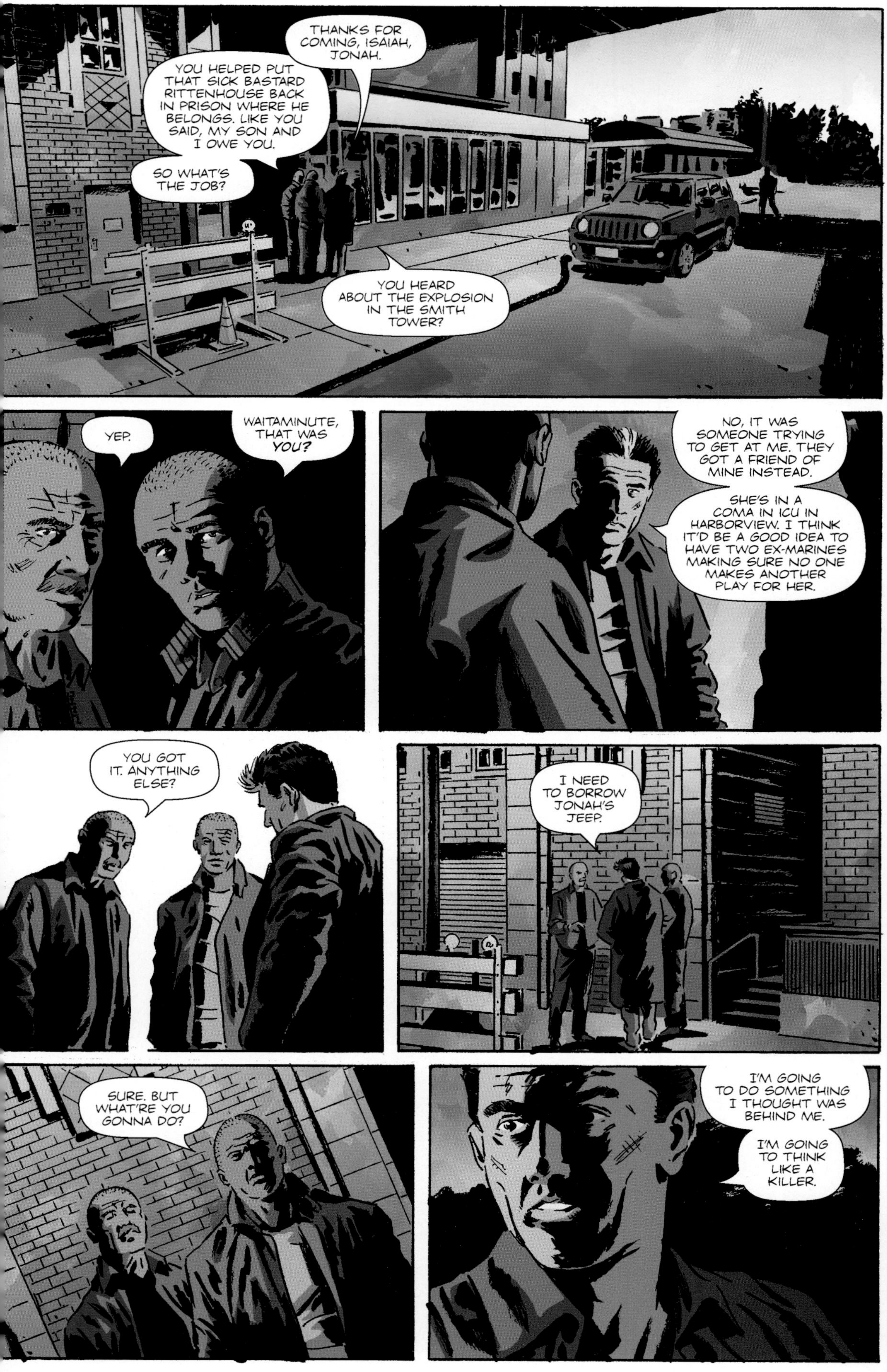
THANKS FOR COMING, ISAIAH, JONAH.
YOU HELPED PUT THAT SICK BASTARD RITTENHOUSE BACK IN PRISON WHERE HE BELONGS. LIKE YOU SAID, MY SON AND I OWE YOU.
SO WHAT'S THE JOB?
YOU HEARD ABOUT THE EXPLOSION IN THE SMITH TOWER?
YEP.
WAITAMINUTE, THAT WAS YOU?
NO, IT WAS SOMEONE TRYING TO GET AT ME. THEY GOT A FRIEND OF MINE INSTEAD.
SHE'S IN A COMA IN ICU IN HARBORVIEW. I THINK IT'D BE A GOOD IDEA TO HAVE TWO EX-MARINES MAKING SURE NO ONE MAKES ANOTHER PLAY FOR HER.
YOU GOT IT. ANYTHING ELSE?
I NEED TO BORROW JONAH'S JEEP.
SURE. BUT WHAT'RE YOU GONNA DO?
I'M GOING TO DO SOMETHING I THOUGHT WAS BEHIND ME.
I'M GOING TO THINK LIKE A KILLER.

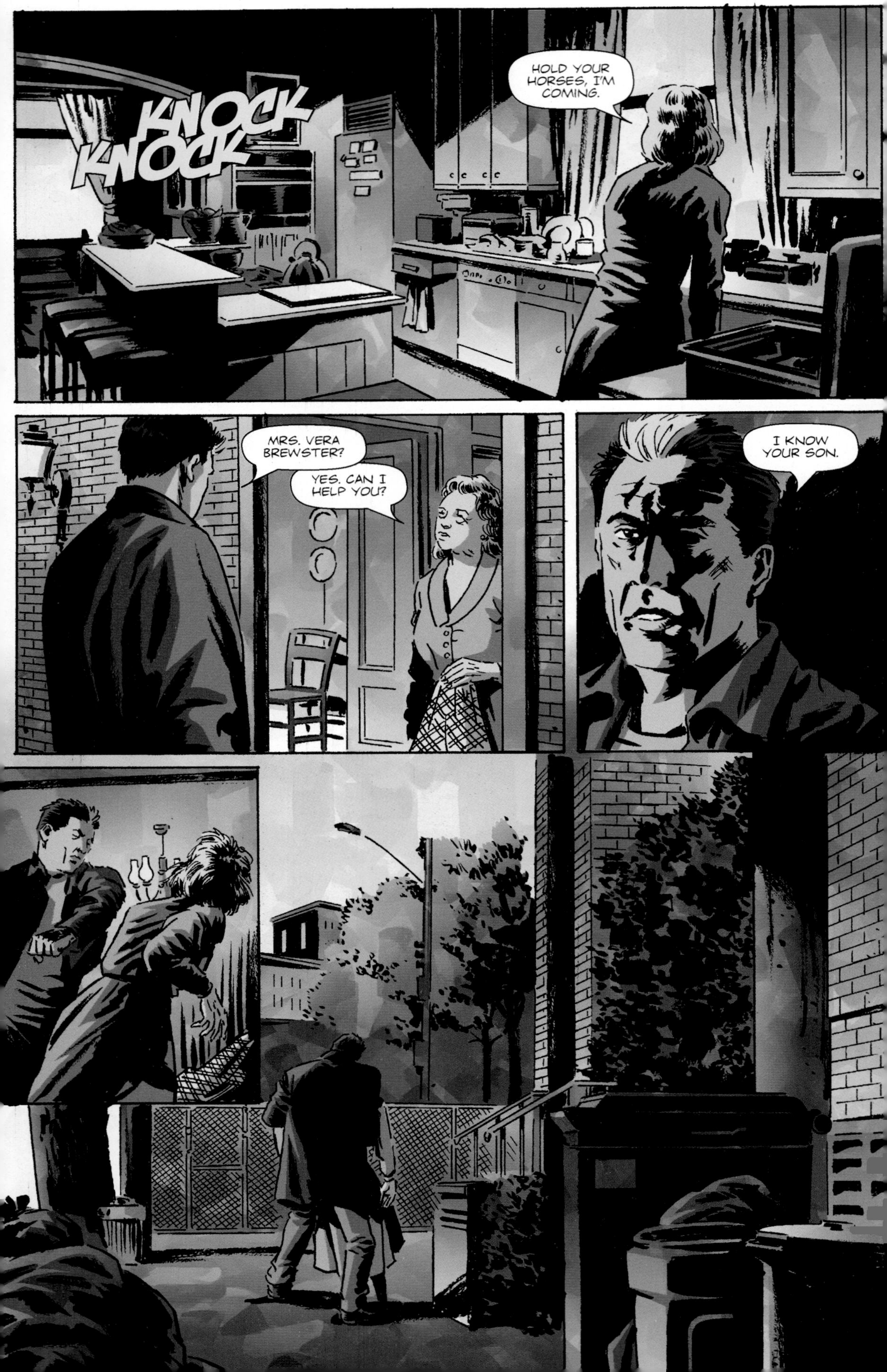
KNOCK KNOCK
HOLD YOUR HORSES, I'M COMING.
MRS. VERA BREWSTER?
YES. CAN I HELP YOU?
I KNOW YOUR SON.

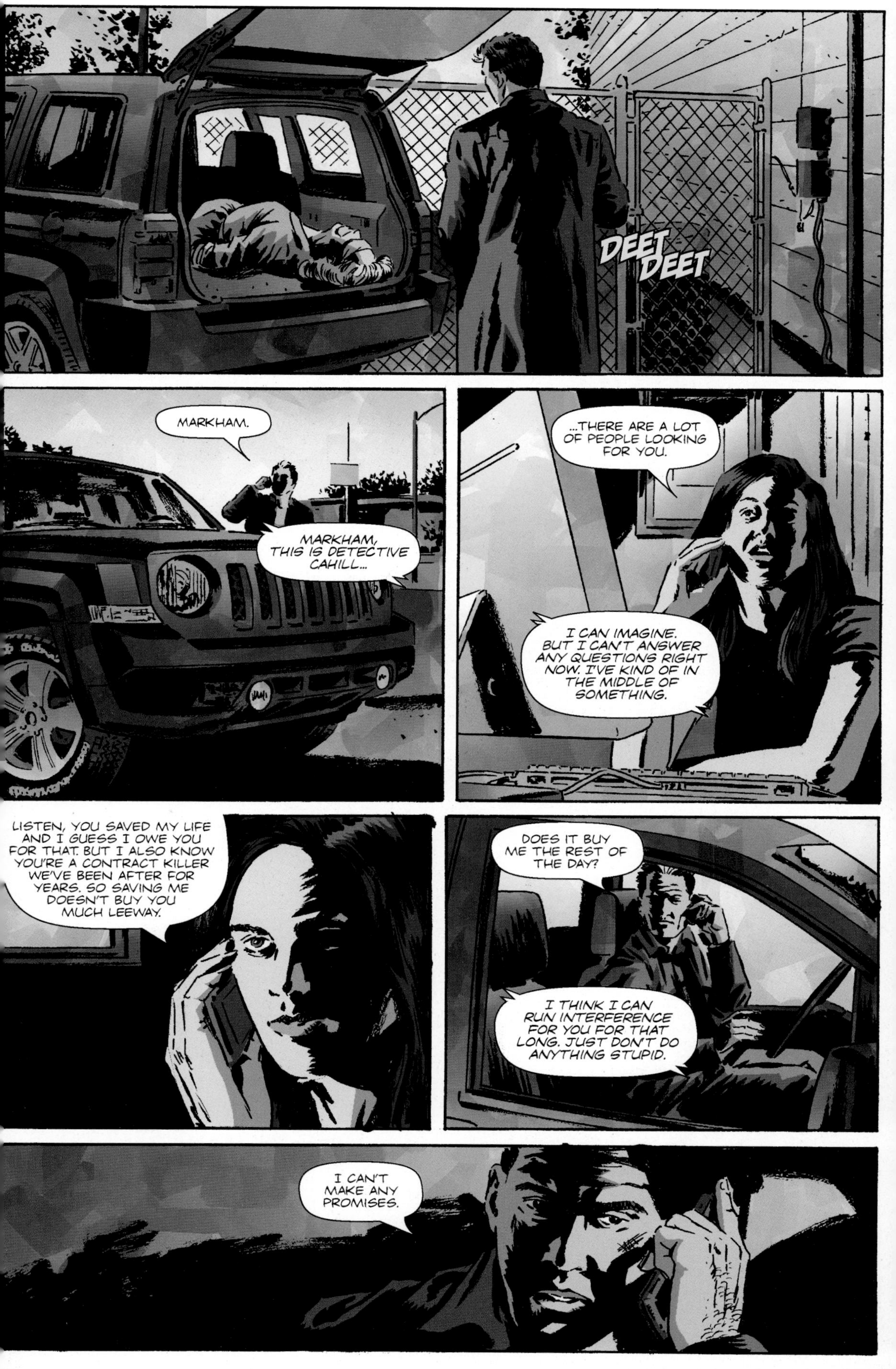

DEET DEET
MARKHAM.
MARKHAM, THIS IS DETECTIVE CAHILL...
...THERE ARE A LOT OF PEOPLE LOOKING FOR YOU.
I CAN IMAGINE. BUT I CAN'T ANSWER ANY QUESTIONS RIGHT NOW. I'VE KIND OF IN THE MIDDLE OF SOMETHING.
LISTEN, YOU SAVED MY LIFE AND I GUESS I OWE YOU FOR THAT. BUT I ALSO KNOW YOU'RE A CONTRACT KILLER WE'VE BEEN AFTER FOR YEARS. SO SAVING ME DOESN'T BUY YOU MUCH LEEWAY.
DOES IT BUY ME THE REST OF THE DAY?
I THINK I CAN RUN INTERFERENCE FOR YOU FOR THAT LONG. JUST DON'T DO ANYTHING STUPID.
I CAN'T MAKE ANY PROMISES.

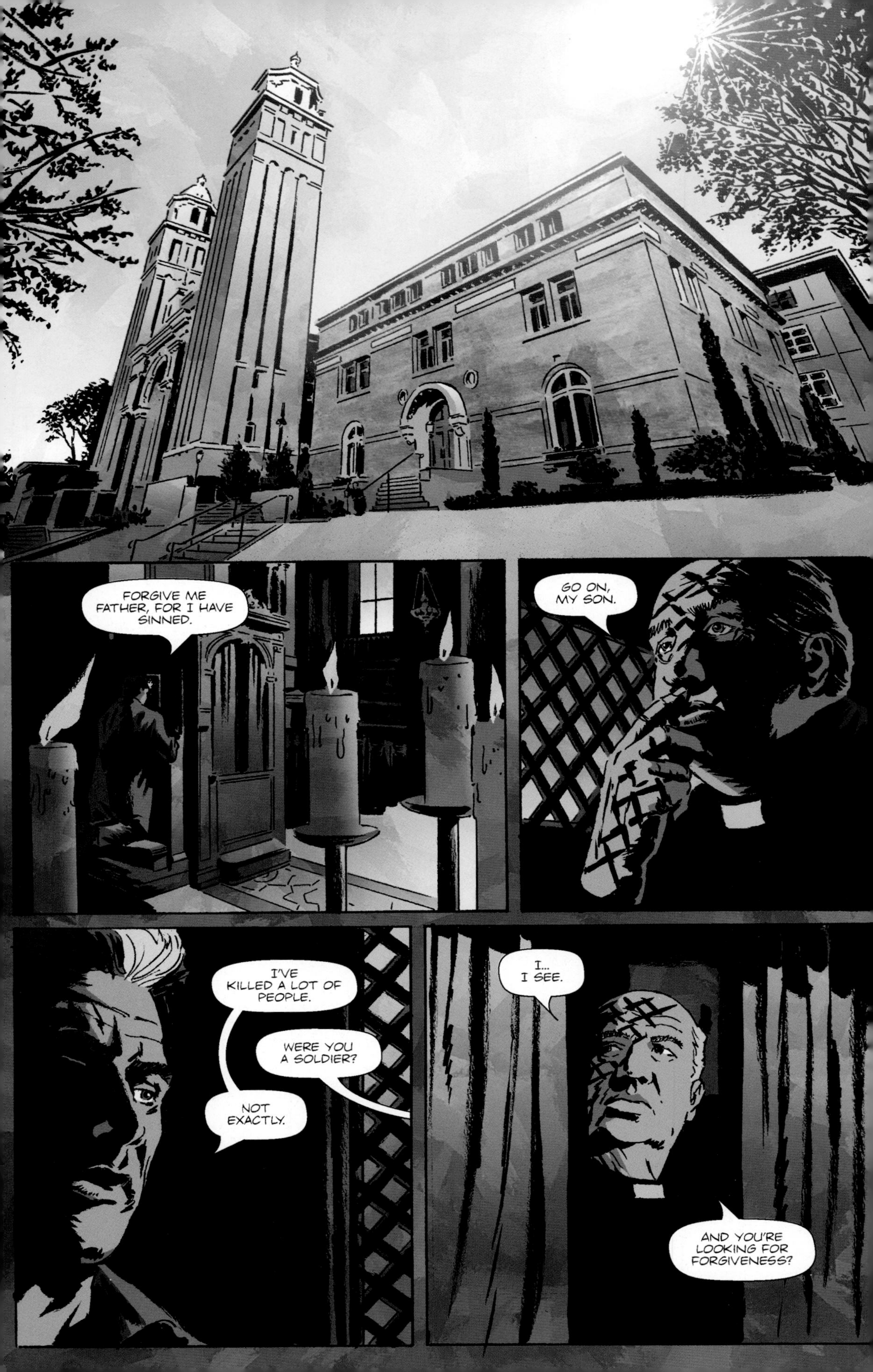
FORGIVE ME FATHER, FOR I HAVE SINNED.
GO ON, MY SON.
I'VE KILLED A LOT OF PEOPLE.
WERE YOU A SOLDIER?
NOT EXACTLY.
I... I SEE.
AND YOU'RE LOOKING FOR FORGIVENESS?

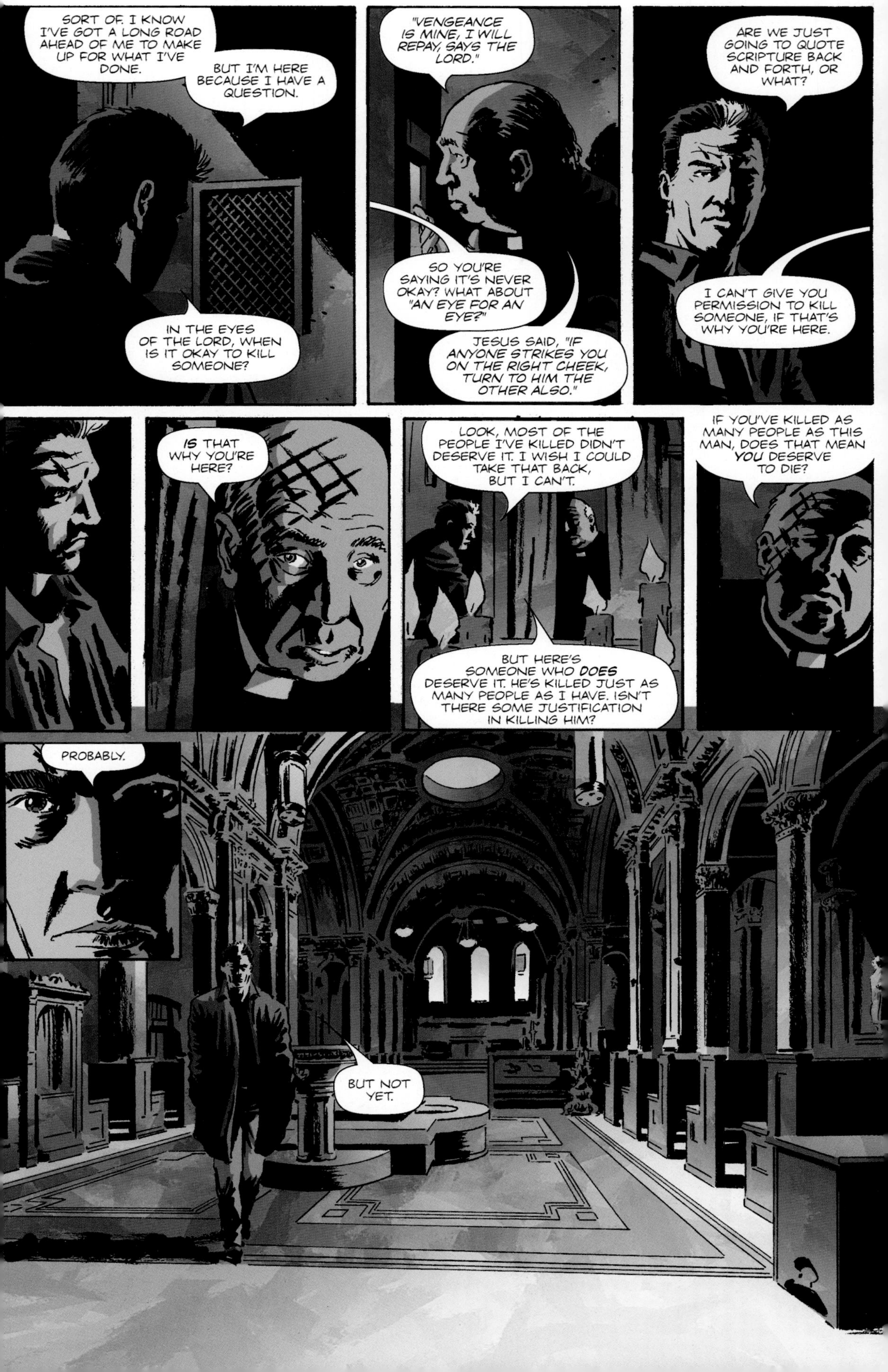
SORT OF. I KNOW I'VE GOT A LONG ROAD AHEAD OF ME TO MAKE UP FOR WHAT I'VE DONE.
BUT I'M HERE BECAUSE I HAVE A QUESTION.
IN THE EYES OF THE LORD, WHEN IS IT OKAY TO KILL SOMEONE?
"VENGEANCE IS MINE, I WILL REPAY, SAYS THE LORD."
SO YOU'RE SAYING IT'S NEVER OKAY? WHAT ABOUT "AN EYE FOR AN EYE?"
JESUS SAID, "IF ANYONE STRIKES YOU ON THE RIGHT CHEEK, TURN TO HIM THE OTHER ALSO."
ARE WE JUST GOING TO QUOTE SCRIPTURE BACK AND FORTH, OR WHAT?
I CAN'T GIVE YOU PERMISSION TO KILL SOMEONE, IF THAT'S WHY YOU'RE HERE.
IS THAT WHY YOU'RE HERE?
LOOK, MOST OF THE PEOPLE I'VE KILLED DIDN'T DESERVE IT. I WISH I COULD TAKE THAT BACK, BUT I CAN'T.
BUT HERE'S SOMEONE WHO DOES DESERVE IT. HE'S KILLED JUST AS MANY PEOPLE AS I HAVE. ISN'T THERE SOME JUSTIFICATION IN KILLING HIM?
IF YOU'VE KILLED AS MANY PEOPLE AS THIS MAN, DOES THAT MEAN YOU DESERVE TO DIE?
PROBABLY.
BUT NOT YET.

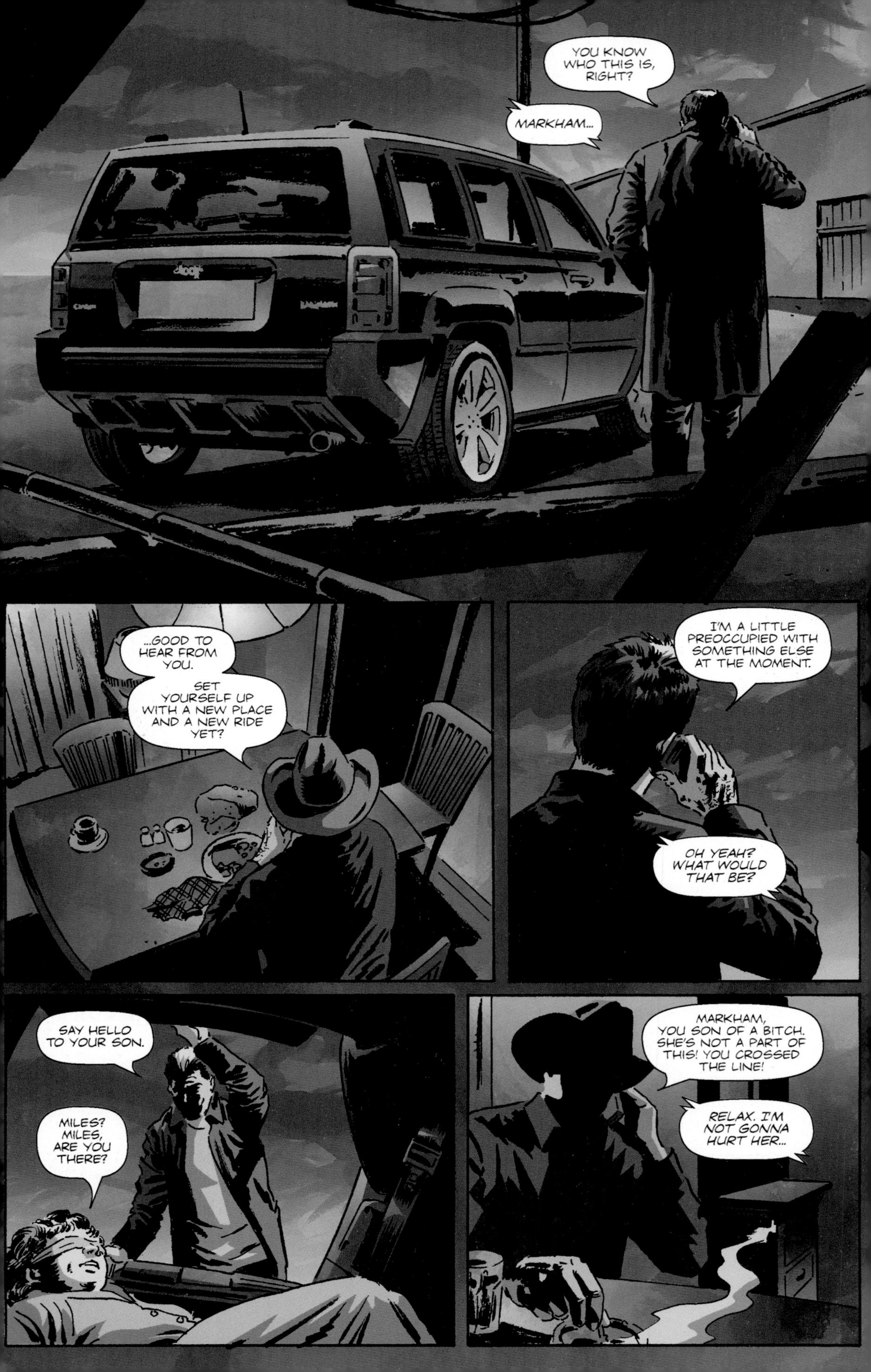
YOU KNOW WHO THIS IS, RIGHT?
MARKHAM...
...GOOD TO HEAR FROM YOU.
SET YOURSELF UP WITH A NEW PLACE AND A NEW RIDE YET?
I'M A LITTLE PREOCCUPIED WITH SOMETHING ELSE AT THE MOMENT.
OH YEAH? WHAT WOULD THAT BE?
SAY HELLO TO YOUR SON.
MILES? MILES, ARE YOU THERE?
MARKHAM, YOU SON OF A BITCH. SHE'S NOT A PART OF THIS! YOU CROSSED THE LINE!
RELAX. I'M NOT GONNA HURT HER...

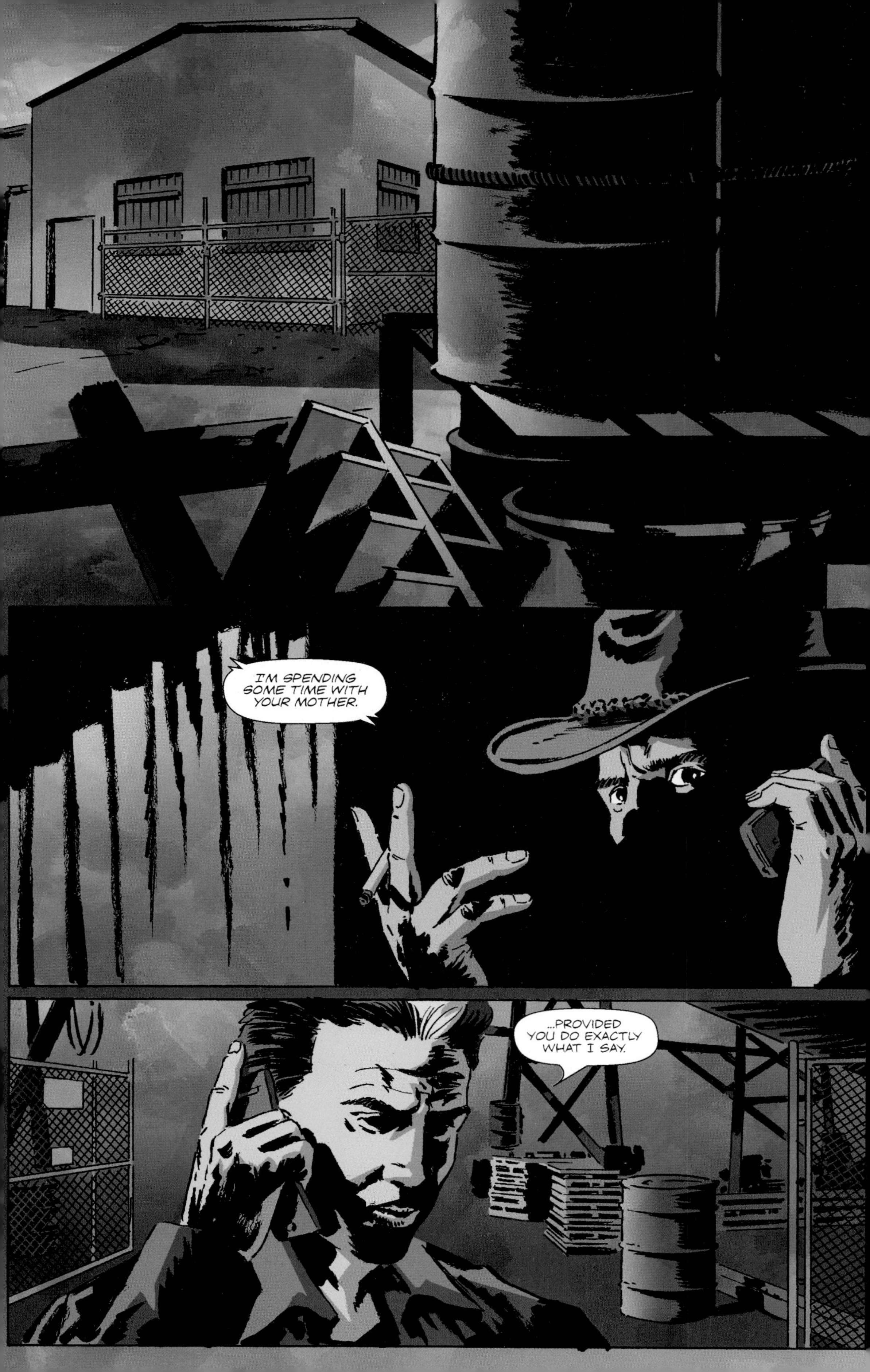
I'M SPENDING SOME TIME WITH YOUR MOTHER.
...PROVIDED YOU DO EXACTLY WHAT I SAY.

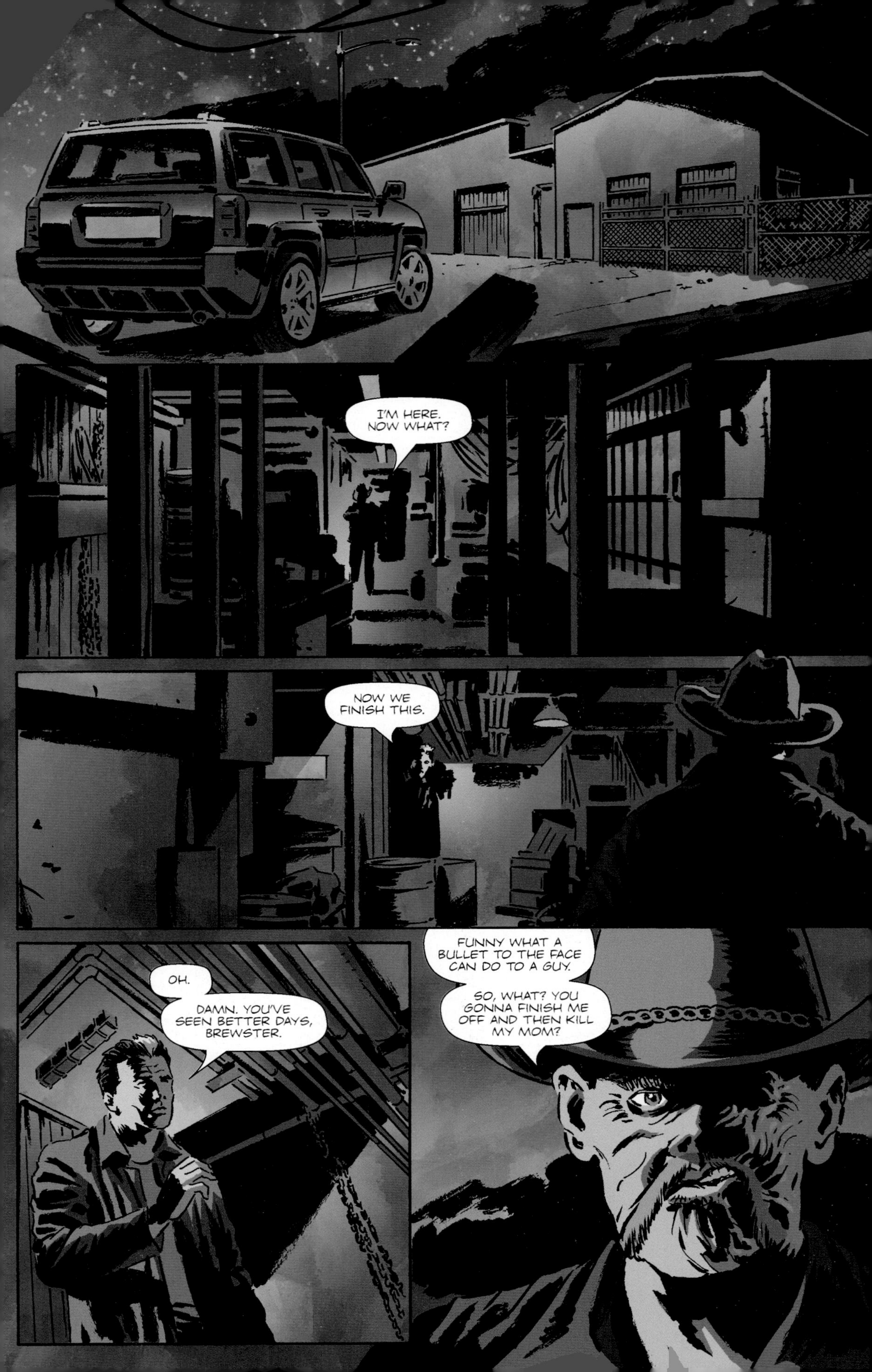
I'M HERE. NOW WHAT?
NOW WE FINISH THIS.
OH.
DAMN. YOU'VE SEEN BETTER DAYS, BREWSTER.
FUNNY WHAT A BULLET TO THE FACE CAN DO TO A GUY.
SO, WHAT? YOU GONNA FINISH ME OFF AND THEN KILL MY MOM?

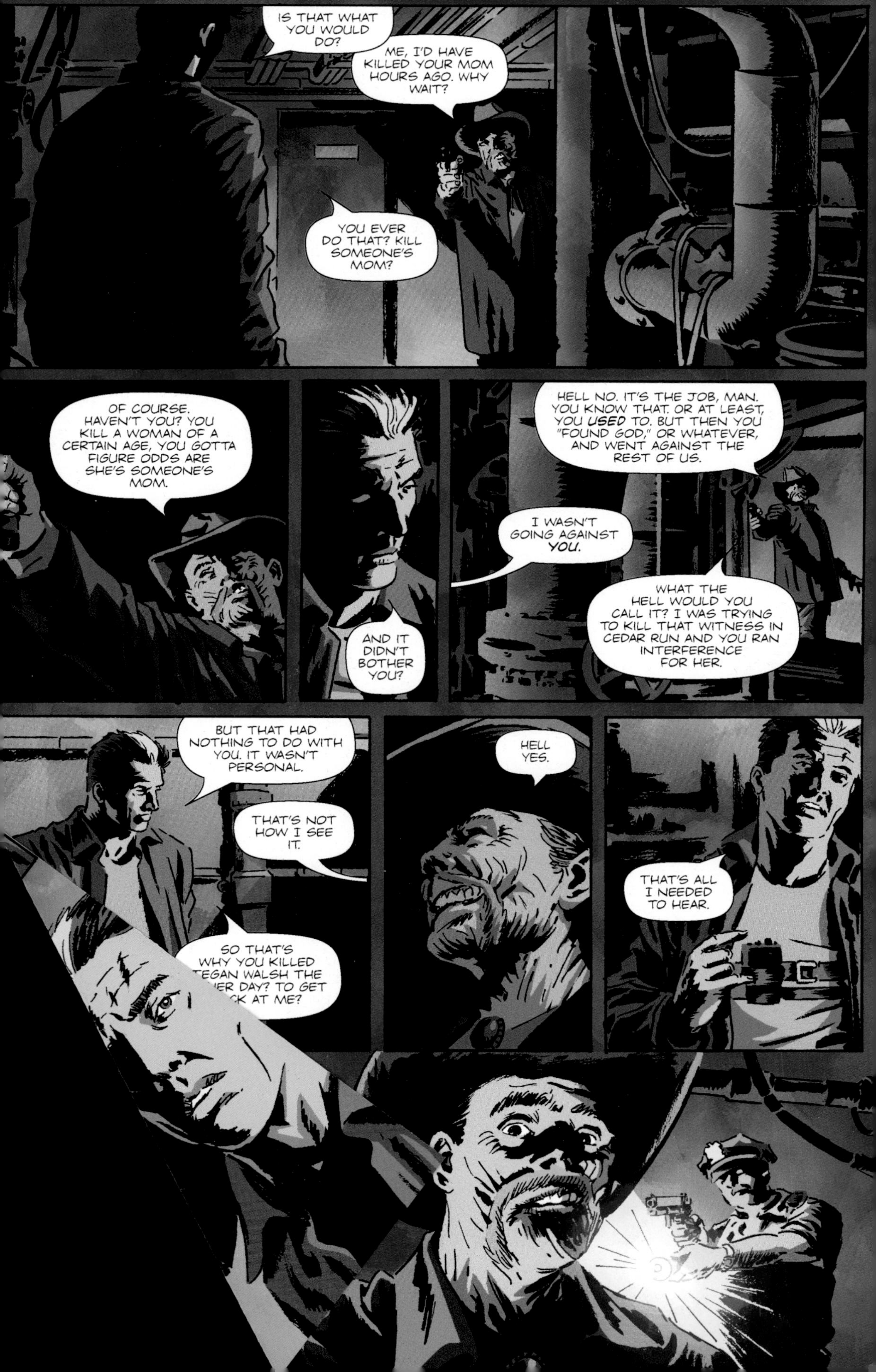

IS THAT WHAT YOU WOULD DO?
ME, I'D HAVE KILLED YOUR MOM HOURS AGO. WHY WAIT?
YOU EVER DO THAT? KILL SOMEONE'S MOM?
OF COURSE. HAVEN'T YOU? YOU KILL A WOMAN OF A CERTAIN AGE, YOU GOTTA FIGURE ODDS ARE SHE'S SOMEONE'S MOM.
AND IT DIDN'T BOTHER YOU?
HELL NO. IT'S THE JOB, MAN. YOU KNOW THAT. OR AT LEAST, YOU USED TO. BUT THEN YOU "FOUND GOD," OR WHATEVER, AND WENT AGAINST THE REST OF US.
I WASN'T GOING AGAINST YOU.
WHAT THE HELL WOULD YOU CALL IT? I WAS TRYING TO KILL THAT WITNESS IN CEDAR RUN AND YOU RAN INTERFERENCE FOR HER.
BUT THAT HAD NOTHING TO DO WITH YOU. IT WASN'T PERSONAL.
THAT'S NOT HOW I SEE IT.
SO THAT'S WHY YOU KILLED TEGAN WALSH THE
HELL YES.
THAT'S ALL I NEEDED TO HEAR.

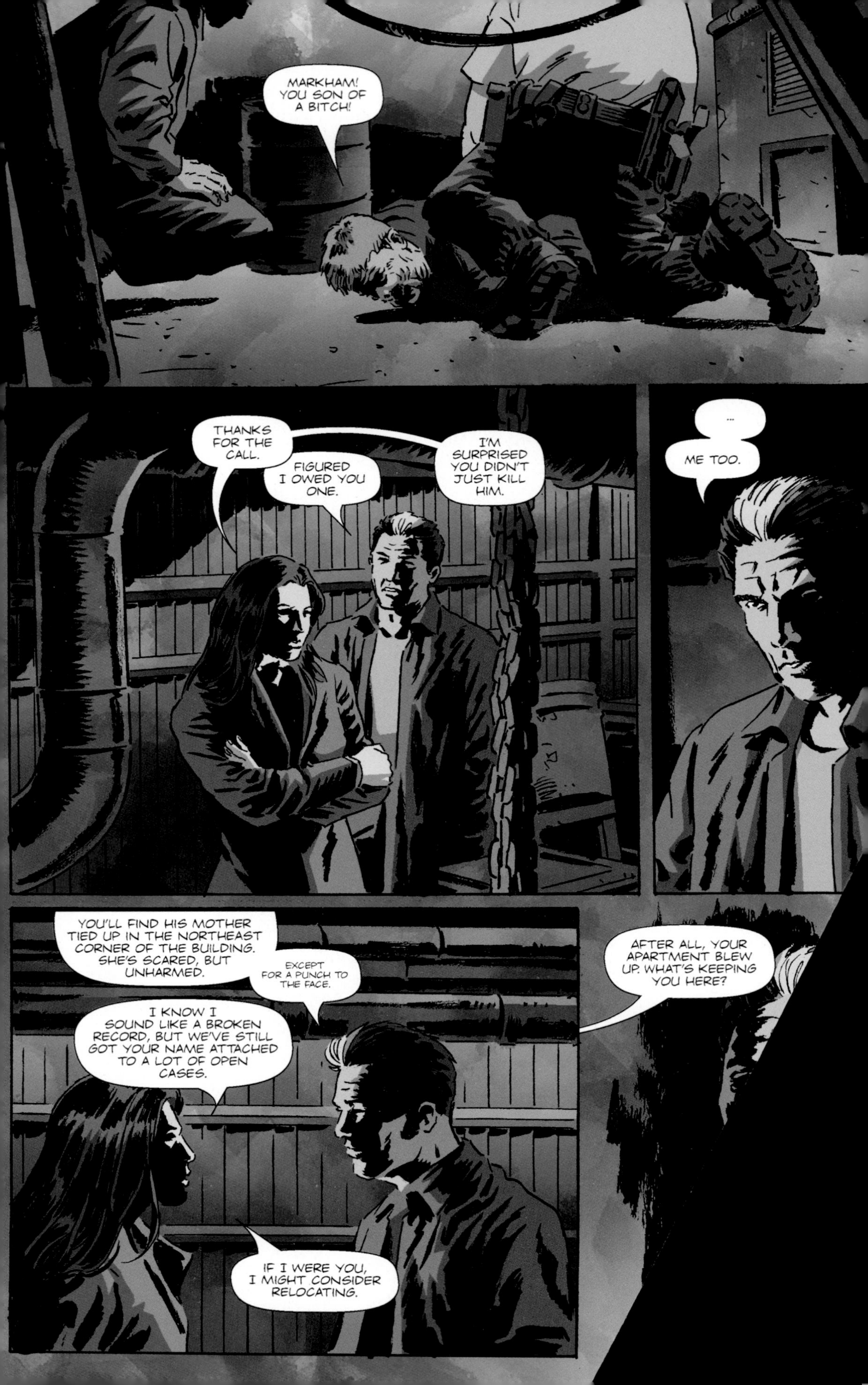
MARKHAM! YOU SON OF A BITCH!
THANKS FOR THE CALL.
FIGURED I OWED YOU ONE.
I'M SURPRISED YOU DIDN'T JUST KILL HIM.
...
ME TOO.
YOU'LL FIND HIS MOTHER TIED UP IN THE NORTHEAST CORNER OF THE BUILDING. SHE'S SCARED, BUT UNHARMED.
EXCEPT FOR A PUNCH TO THE FACE.
I KNOW I SOUND LIKE A BROKEN RECORD, BUT WE'VE STILL GOT YOUR NAME ATTACHED TO A LOT OF OPEN CASES.
AFTER ALL, YOUR APARTMENT BLEW UP. WHAT'S KEEPING YOU HERE?
IF I WERE YOU, I MIGHT CONSIDER RELOCATING.

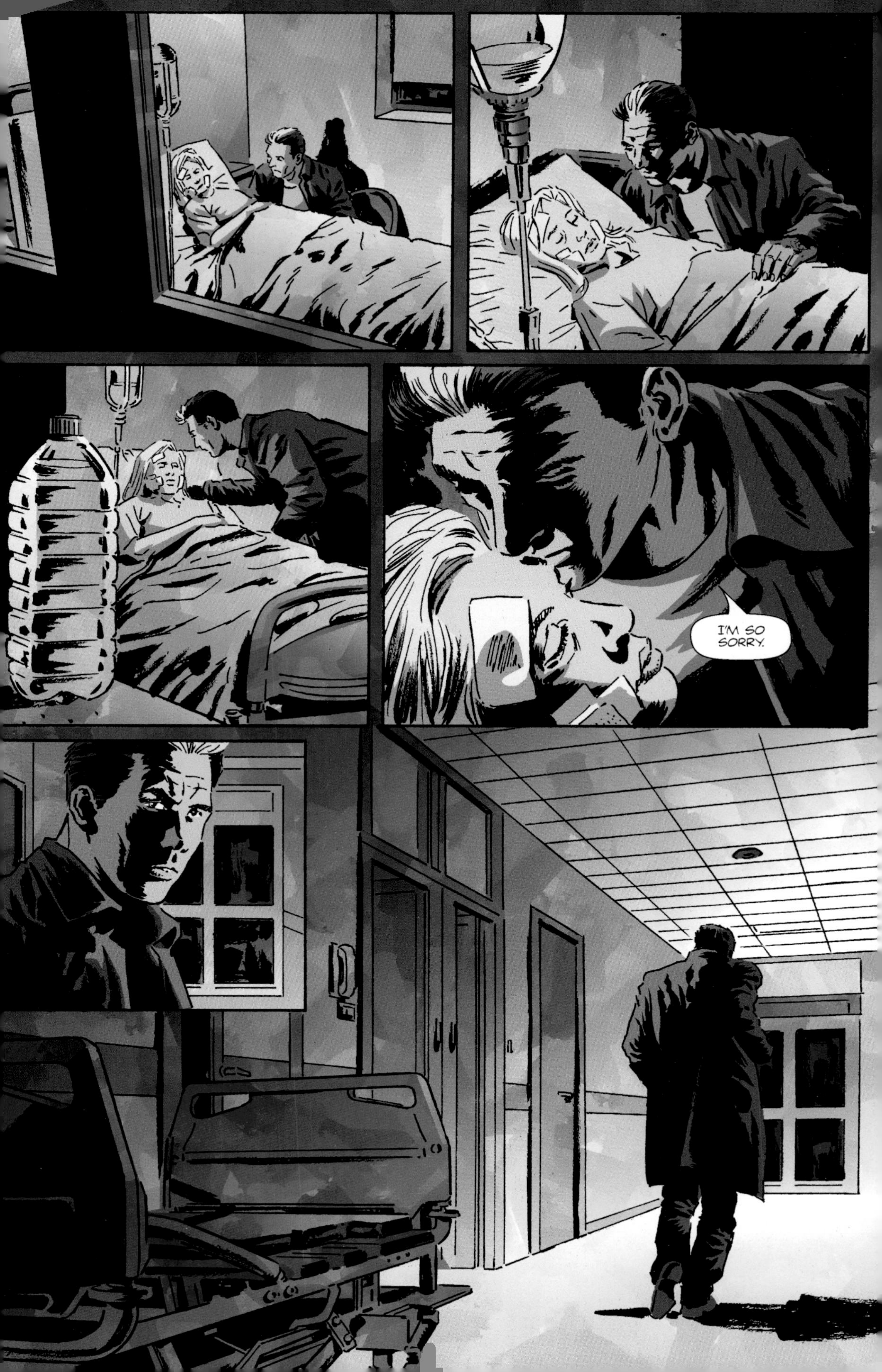
I'M SO SORRY.

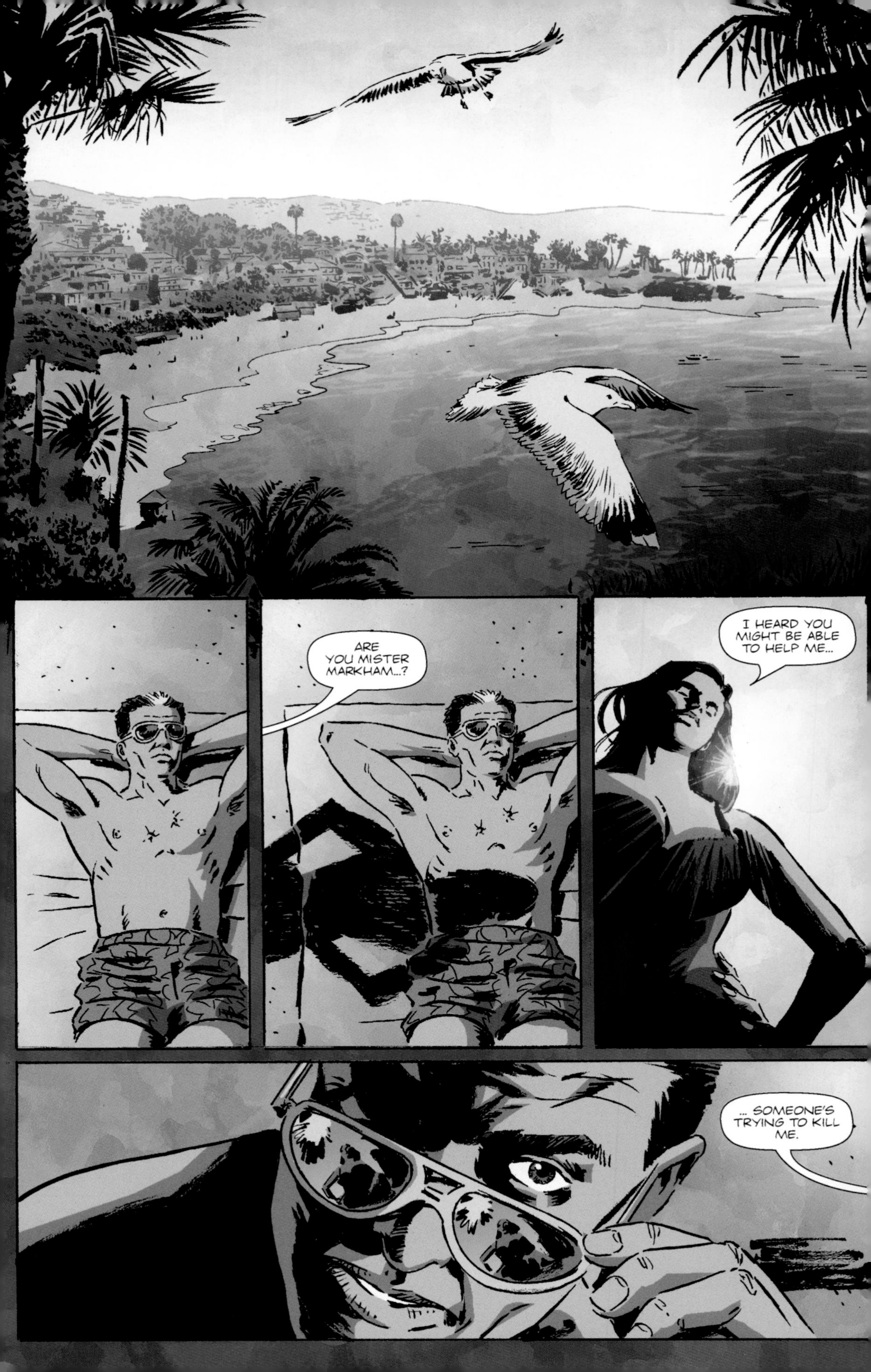
ARE YOU MISTER MARKHAM...?
I HEARD YOU MIGHT BE ABLE TO HELP ME...
... SOMEONE'S TRYING TO KILL ME.

EAR DEATH - ISSUE #1
0-page script
y Jay Faerber
econd Draft 04-29-10

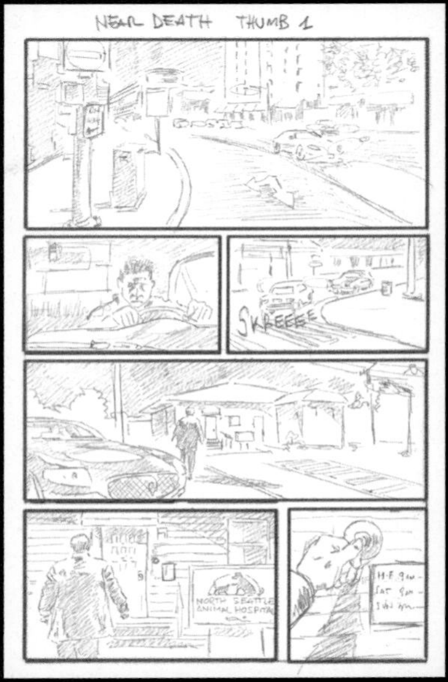
NEAR DEATH THUMB 1
SKREEEE

AGE 1

AGE 1, Panel One
/e open on a shot of Markham's car, driving through the nearly empty Seattle streets in the middle of the ight.

CAPTION: Alec Markham's been in worse situations.

AGE 1, Panel Two
nside the car, Markham is at the wheel. He's leaning forward, gripping the wheel tightly. His eyes are only half-pen. Simone, on these first three pages, Markham's hair is totally black. No white at all.

CAPTION: At least, that's what he keeps telling himself as he tries not to black out.
CAPTION: Luckily for him, the streets are almost deserted this time of night.

AGE 1, Panel Three
ack outside the car again. Markham has drifted into the other lane, and nearly hits an oncoming car. The ther car has to swerve to avoid Markham.

CAPTION: Almost.

AGE 1, Panel Four
larkham's car is parked awkwardly in a small parking lot beside a small, one-story building just outside the ty. Markham is limping away from the car.

CAPTION: As he hobbles towards the front door, he hopes Sutton isn't out on a date or something.
CAPTION: But she's never out on a date. She's never out anywhere.

AGE 1, Panel Five
larkham approaches the front door of the building. We can see a lit sign out front.

CAPTION: It occurs to him that he should take her out more often. Buy her dinner. Take her to a movie. He decides nat if he makes it through this, he will.

TEXT ON SIGN: North Seattle Animal Hospital

AGE 1, Panel Six
lose on Markham's bloody hand as it pushes the doorbell. Next to the bell is a sign.

TEXT ON SIGN: Hours: M-F 9:00am - 7:00pm
Sat 9:00am - 8:00pm
Sun 12:00pm - 5:00pm
After Hours Emergency: Ring Bell

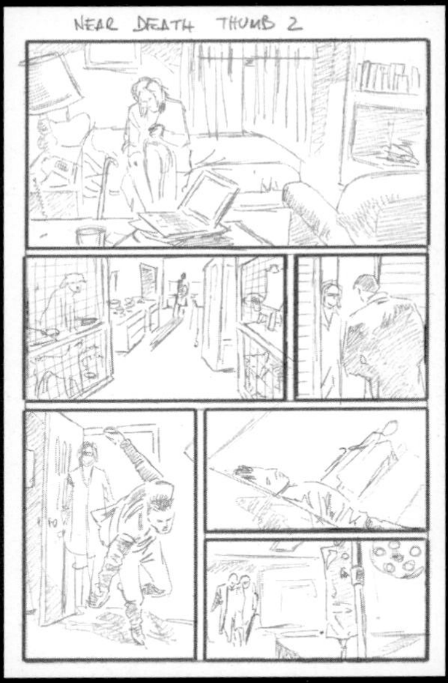
NEAR DEATH THUMB 2

AGE 2

AGE 2, Panel One
ut to the bedroom of Dr. Sutton Faulkner. She's in her 30s, blond, and could be attractive if she put some ffort into it. She's sitting on her bed wearing a long t-shirt, and pulling on a thick robe. Her hair's a mess.

CAPTION: Dr. Sutton Faulkner stopped being a heavy sleeper shortly after she added 24-hour mergency service to her small veterinary hospital.
CAPTION: She lives alone and doesn't have much of a social life, so she figured she may as well enefit from the premium people are willing to pay for late-night visits to the vet.

AGE 2, Panel Two
utton, now clothed in a robe and wearing glasses, moves through the back of her office with the use of a ane. This part of the office is where the injured animals are kept in cages.

CAPTION: But as she makes her way from her apartment to her office, she swears that if the erson ringing the bell turns out to be Mrs. Pretzman complaining that her cat threw up again, Sutton's finally oing to tell the old bitch off.

AGE 2, Panel Three
/e're in the front reception area of Sutton's small animal hospital now. She's opening the front door and sees larkham standing there, shoulders hunched. The door is not all the way open in this shot. She's in the process f opening it.

MARKHAM / weak: Sorry about this, Doc.

SUTTON: Alec, what's --

AGE 2, Panel Four
larkham collapses, falling forward into her office. Sutton is moving quickly out of his way.

SUTTON: Jesus!

AGE 2, Panel Five
larkham lies there on the floor, motionless, as Sutton stands over him, a surprised look on her face.

CAPTION: This isn't the first time Sutton has tended to Alec Markham's wounds, but it *is* the first time he's collapsed before even
reaching her operating room.
CAPTION: She's good in a crisis, and is confident she'll be able to save him once he's on the table.

PAGE 2, Panel Six
Sutton is bent over, her hands under Markham's armpits, as she awkwardly drags him across the floor.

CAPTION: It's *getting* him on the table that's going to be a challenge.

PAGE 3

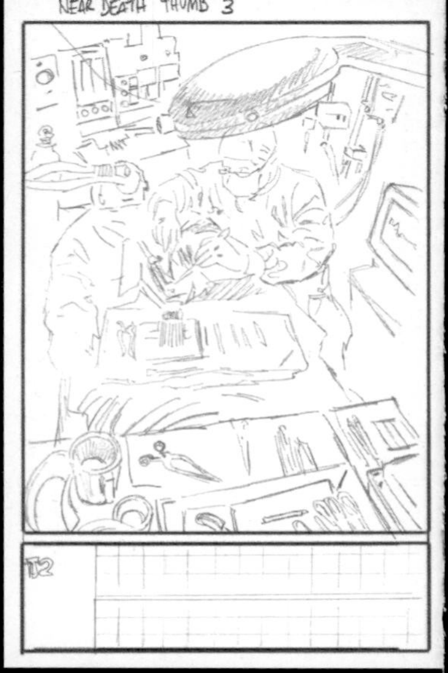
NEAR DEATH THUMB 3

PAGE 3, Panel One
BIG panel, almost a splash -- of Markham lying on Sutton's operating table. He's shirtless, and his chest is all bloody from a bullet wound near his heart. Sutton is standing over him, trying to dig the bullet out. I think this would look cool as a downshot, but it's up to you.

CAPTION: It's three hours before Sutton has the bullet removed from Markham's chest. She thinks the worst is over.
CAPTION: She's wrong.

PAGE 3, Panel Two
This is a long, thin panel across the bottom of the page. It's black, save for a EKG rhythm readout. Only Markham has "flatlined," so the line is straight, with no peaks or valleys.

NO COPY

PAGE 4

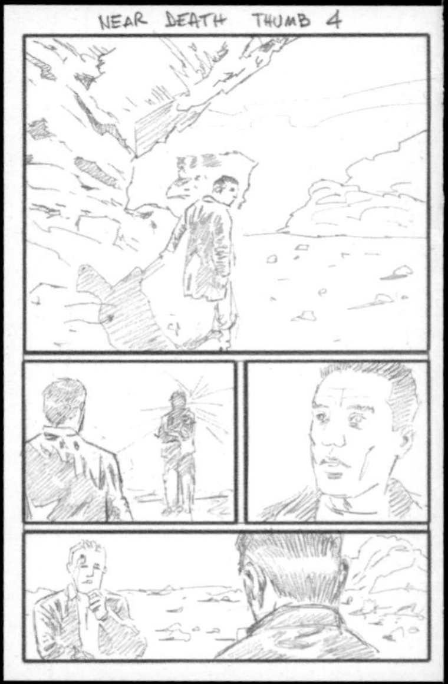
NEAR DEATH THUMB 4

PAGE 4, Panel One
Cut to Markham, with his hair still black (no white at all), dressed in the same clothes he was in in the last scene, wandering through a bleak, barren landscape. His clothes are fine -- no blood on them or anything, and he's not injured. I'm picturing the landscape being all rocky and hard and empty. This should be the biggest panel of the page.

Color note: This scene (pages 4-7) should be colored in stark contrast to the rest of the book. Not b&w, but muted or different in some other way.

NO COPY

PAGE 4, Panel Two
Markham sees a man in the distance. This can be an over-the-shoulder shot.

MARKHAM: Hey!

PAGE 4, Panel Three
Markham approaches the man, and is shocked by what he sees. Frame this shot so we can't see the man's face. It's off-panel. Maybe all we can see is his shoulder or something.

MARKHAM: Do you know --
MAKRHAM: Oh.

PAGE 4, Panel Four
Reveal the man, as we get our first good look at him. He's a normal-looking man, except for the huge bullet hole in his head. The bullet hole on his forehead is small (an entry wound) but the back of his head is blown out (the exit wound).

DEAD MAN: Hi, Markham.
DEAD MAN: Long time.

PAGE 5

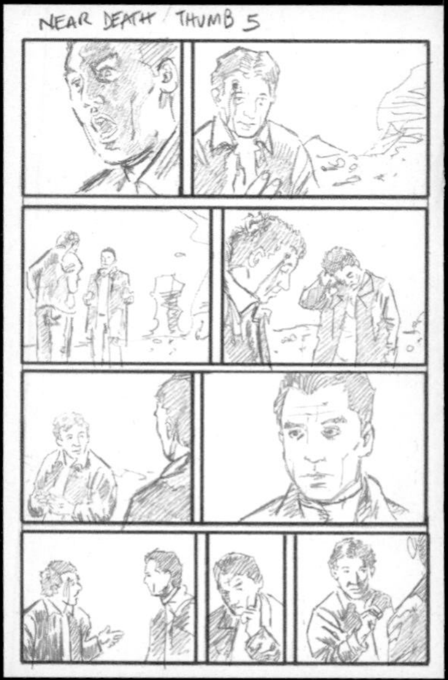
NEAR DEATH THUMB 5

There's a lot of panels on this page, and it might work best as a nine-panel grid, but I'll leave it up to you to decide the best layout.

PAGE 5, Panel One
Markham is shocked.

MARKHAM: You ... how ...

PAGE 5, Panel Two
Back on the dead man.

DEAD MAN: How? You killed me, that's how.
DEAD MAN: I was your first, right? Guess that makes me special.

PAGE 5, Panel Three
On both of them.

MARKHAM: Where am I? I don't understand.

DEAD MAN: What did you think was gonna happen after you died? Heaven?

MARKHAM: I ... I never believed in that stuff.

DEAD MAN: That doesn't appear to be relevant, now does it?

DEAD MAN: Yeah? If you had known...?

MARKHAM / from off: Well I ... I'd have behaved
[dif]ferently.

DEAD MAN: You mean that?

[P]AGE 5, Panel Six
[Ba]ck on Markham.

MARKHAM: Sure. Yes.
MARKHAM: Why?

[P]AGE 5, Panel Seven
[Ba]ck on the dead man.

DEAD MAN: Because maybe there's still time.
DEAD MAN: Maybe you can undo what you did.

[P]AGE 5, Panel Eight
[O]n Markham.

MARKHAM: Like, balance the scales?

[P]AGE 5, Panel Nine
[O]n the dead man.

DEAD MAN: If that's now you want to think of it, yeah.
DEAD MAN: But just remember ...

HEAR DEATH THUMBS 6-7

[P]AGES 6-7

[P]AGES 6-7, Spread
[Th]is is a spread of ALL the people Markham's killed, suddenly standing behind the first dead man. This is asking a lot, but draw as many people as you can -- close
[to] a hundred, if not more. They've all got various wounds: mostly gunshot wounds, but some have been burned, some have broken necks, slit throats, etc. We don't
[ne]ed to see them all very clearly -- you can use cheats and shortcuts to put a lot of them in the background. But the important thing is that we hit the reader with just
[ho]w many people Markham's killed.

DEAD MAN: ... you've got a LOT to make up for.

[P]AGE 8

[P]AGE 8, Panel One
[C]ut back to Sutton's operating table, moments after we left. She's just used the defibrillator paddles to re-start
[M]arkham's heart. So the paddles are no longer touching his chest, but she's standing next to his bed, the
[pa]ddles in her hands, having just used them. Markham's sitting bolt upright, eyes open, surprising Sutton. His
[h]air has the white patch in it now.

MARKHAM: Aah!

SUTTON: Oh!

[P]AGE 8, Panel Two
[M]arkham tries to get off the table, but Sutton stops him.

MARKHAM: I need to --

SUTTON: Wait, you can't --

MARKHAM: But I --

[P]AGE 8, Panel Three
[M]arkham slumps back down on the operating table.

MARKHAM: Ow ...

[P]AGE 8, Panel Four
[S]utton stands next to the table.

NEAR DEATH THUMB 8

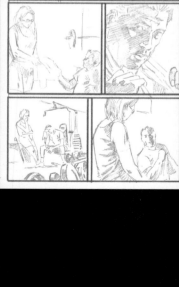

AGE 9

AGE 9, Panel One
ut to a shot of the sun rising over the Seattle skyline.

NO COPY

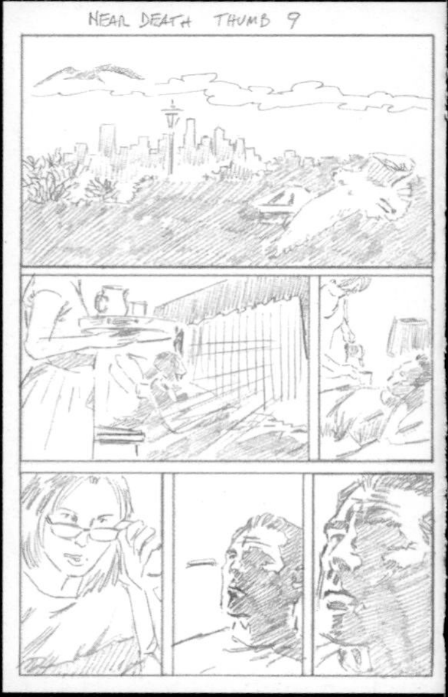
NEAR DEATH THUMB 9

AGE 9, Panel Two
ut Markham lying in the bed in Sutton's extra bedroom. This isn't a hospital room -- just a normal bedroom. e's shirtless, and his chest is bandaged. Sun is streaming into the room through the window. Sutton is tering the room carrying a glass of juice.

SUTTON: You're awake.

AGE 9, Panel Three
tton sets the juice on a small bedside table. Markham's looking up at her.

SUTTON: You've been out for a day and a half. I already know what you're going to say, but I ve to say this anyway. You should go see a real doctor.

MARKHAM: Do you believe in God?

AGE 9, Panel Four
tton looks surprised. She wasn't expecting that question.

SUTTON: Um...
SUTTON: Well, no. I don't think I do.

AGE 9, Panel Five
n just Markham.

MARKHAM: I never did either. But when my heart stopped, I ... I think I died. That's how it works, right?

SUTTON / from off: Yes, but your heart was stopped for less than a minute.

MARKHAM: Well, it was long enough. I saw something, Sutton.

AGE 9, Panel Six
oser in on Markham. Maybe just his eyes, for dramatic effect.

MARKHAM: Something I don't ever want to see again.

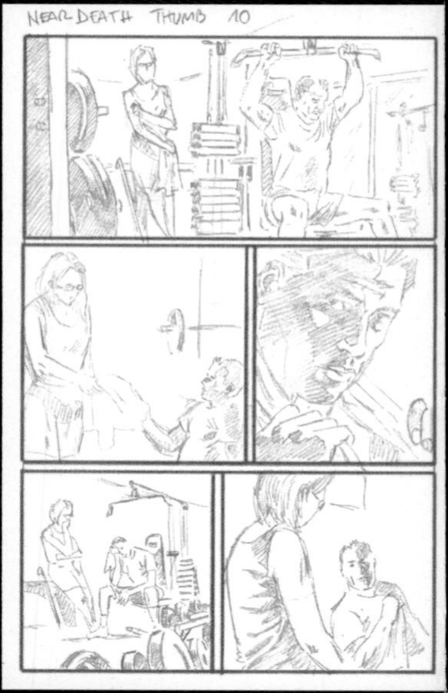
NEAR DEATH THUMB 10

AGE 10

AGE 10, Panel One
ut to a shot of Markham working out on universal gym-style equipment in Sutton's apartment. Sutton is anding by, watching him. He's really pushing himself and is soaked in sweat.

CAPTION: They didn't talk any more about what Markham saw when his heart stopped. But hatever Markham saw changed him. He'd been a driven man for as long as Sutton had known him, but this as something else.
CAPTION: For the next week and a half, Markham pushed himself every day. He exercised rder. Longer. Almost like he was in training for something.

AGE 10, Panel Two
tton hands Markham a towel as he sits up, finished with his workout.

MARKHAM: Thanks.

SUTTON: Sure.

MARKHAM: No, I mean ...

AGE 10, Panel Three
very close on just Markham, a serious, earnest expression on his face.

MARKHAM: THANKS.

AGE 10, Panel Four
tton stands there, and Markham sits there, an awkward silence between them.

NO COPY

AGE 10, Panel Five
new angle on the two of them.

SUTTON: So ... are you getting ready to go back to work?

MARKHAM: Sort of.

AGE 11

AGE 11, Panel One
ut to a daytime shot of Pioneer Square, where Max and Markham stand under the pergola, an old, covered walkway. The crowd is a mix of homeless people and urists. Max can look however you want him to look, but he should have some sort of defining characteristic. He's a quirky sidekick, not a big hero or big villain. So

MAX: You're looking good for a guy who almost died.

MARKHAM: Thanks, Max.
MARKHAM: I need to know about the contract I was on when I got shot.

PAGE 11, Panel Two
Another shot, closer in, of the two of them talking.

MAX: Mr. Novak already got someone else. You don't need to worry about it. As soon as you're feeling up to it, there'll be plenty of work for you.

MARKHAM: This "someone else." He done the job yet?

MAX: As a matter of fact, he hasn't. The mark went off the grid, and it's taken some time to find her.

MARKHAM: But he HAS found her?

PAGE 11, Panel Three
Max looks suspicious.

MAX: Got a lead on her yesterday, yeah. Why do you care? It's not your concern.

PAGE 11, Panel Four
On just Markham.

MARKHAM: It's the first job I didn't finish myself. I'm having a hard time letting it go.
MARKHAM: Who's my replacement?

PAGE 11, Panel Five
Back on just Max.

MAX: You know Brewster, right? Of course you do. Everyone knows Brewster. Well, he took the gig.

PAGE 11, Panel Six
Back on Markham.

MARKHAM: And he's moving now, I bet.

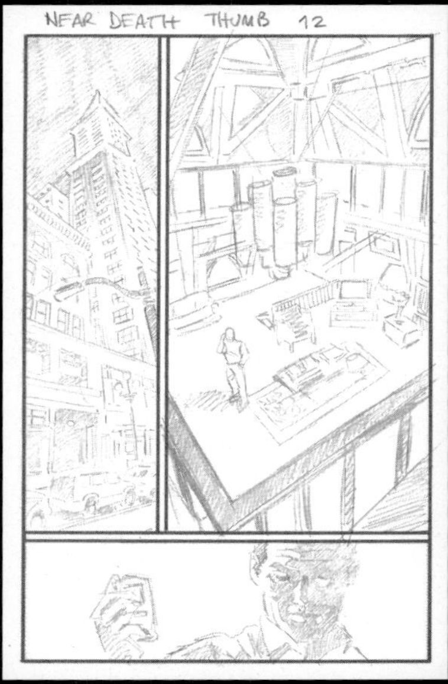

PAGE 11, Panel Seven
On both of them again.

MAX: Like I said, he got a lead on her yesterday.

MARKHAM: Good. I'm glad the job's in good hands. Brewster will come through, no doubt about it.

MAX: So what about you? You ready to take some new jobs?

PAGE 11, Panel Eight
On Markham.

MARKHAM: Not just yet. I'm still recuperating, you know? Doc says I shouldn't exert myself. But thanks for telling me about Brewster. I'll sleep easier knowing he's on the job.

PAGE 11, Panel Nine
End on Max, again looking very suspicious.

MAX: If you say so...

PAGE 12

PAGE 12, Panel One
Cut to a nighttime establishing shot of the Smith Tower, where Markham lives. I've already sent you reference for this Seattle landmark.

FROM INSIDE TOP OF SMITH TOWER: Hey, Brewster, it's Markham.

PAGE 12, Panel Two
Cut inside, where we get our first look of Markham's amazing penthouse, a 3-story loft inside the top pyramid of the tower. I sent you some reference for this as well, but very few interior photos exist, so I'm fine if you want to just make it up. Markham is in the loft, talking on his cellphone. He can be very small in this shot, as the focus is on the architecture of his penthouse. This is the biggest shot of the page.

MARKHAM: Yeah, you heard about that, eh?
MARKHAM: Well, thanks. I'm doing much better. So listen, I heard you took over the contract and that you're in town.
MARKHAM: Oh, really? Guess I heard wrong. Cedar Run, huh? Not much of a nightlife there.
MARKHAM: You can say that again. I had a hell of a time tracking her. The Marshals service is pretty damned good at hiding these witnesses. How'd you manage to find her?
MARKHAM: Nice. Very smart. Well, listen, I won't keep you. I was just going to offer to buy you a drink if you were in town.
MARKHAM: Yeah, that's cool. Happy hunting.

PAGE 12, Panel Three
Markham switches off his phone, and we can see he's seriously considering something. Maybe scratching his chin while he thinks?

NO COPY

PAGE 13

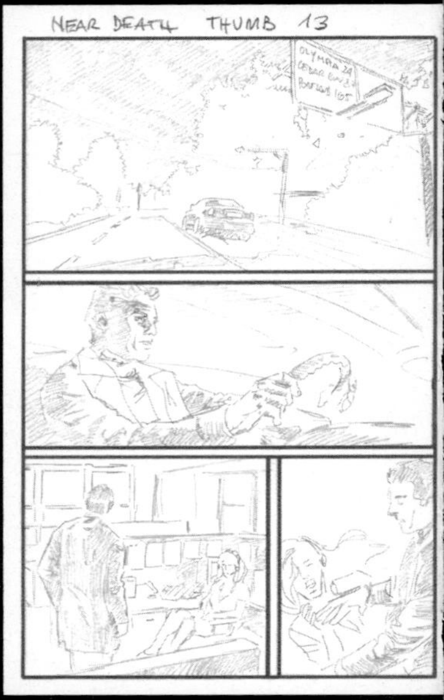
NEAR DEATH THUMB 13

PAGE 13, Panel One
Cut to a nighttime shot of Markham's car -- something expensive, a Lexus or something -- driving away from us, down the freeway past a freeway sign.

FREEWAY SIGN: Olympia 24
Cedar Run 87
Portland 165

PAGE 13, Panel Two
Cut to inside Markham's car, as he drives.

CAPTION: People in Markham's profession have habits and routines and methods just like any other professionals. Different people have different ways of approaching their jobs, and they also have different quirks.

CAPTION: Everyone who knows Brewster knows about his particular quirk. Whenever he's in town for a job, he calls the local escort service with very specific request: he wants one white woman, and one black.

PAGE 13, Panel Three
Cut to Markham inside the office of an escort service. He's talking to a woman sitting in a small cubicle wearing a headset.

CAPTION: Cedar Run is too small of a town to have its own escort service, so Markham visited three escort services in the closest city until he found one that admitted to fulfilling Brewster's request.

PAGE 13, Panel Four
Markham backhands the woman across the face.

CAPTION: These places depend on discretion and don't give out client information.

CAPTION: Unless you know how to ask.

PAGE 14

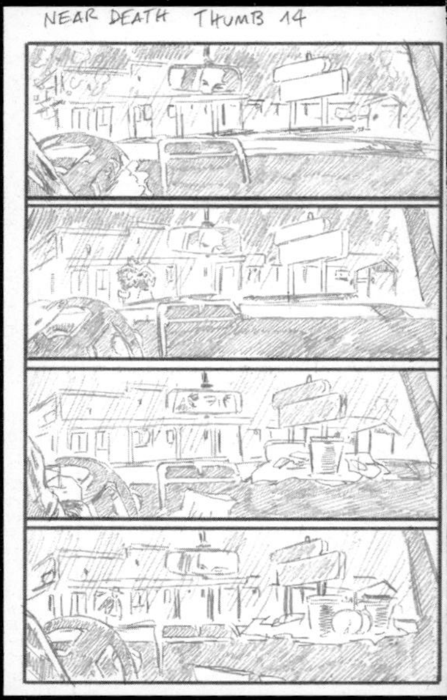
NEAR DEATH THUMB 14

Simone, I picture this page as being four "letterbox" panels of equal size, stacked one on top of the other. You can even use the same image of the motel if you want, and just change the elements that need to be changed in each panel. Whatever's easiest for you.

PAGE 14, Panel One
Cut to Markham sitting in his car, across the street from a small motel. It's nighttime and raining hard. He's slouched in his seat, barely awake.

NO COPY

PAGE 14, Panel Two
The two prostitutes -- one white, one black -- emerge from Brewster's room, their jackets pulled up over their heads to protect them from the rain.

NO COPY

PAGE 14, Panel Three
It's daytime now, and the rain is still coming down hard as Markham remains in his car, waiting and watching.

NO COPY

PAGE 14, Panel Four
Brewster emerges from his motel room, and we see him for the first time. He's a white man in his 30s. He's got a big, thick mustache and is wearing a cowboy hat. It's still raining.

NO COPY

PAGE 15

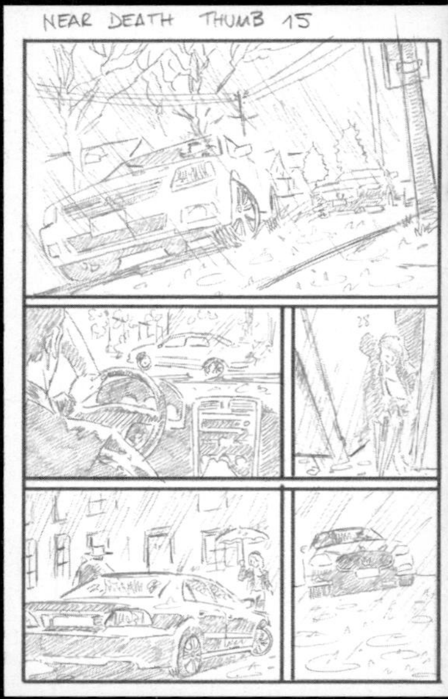
NEAR DEATH THUMB 15

PAGE 15, Panel One
Cut to Markham's car following Brewster's rental car (a simple sedan) through the small town. It's still raining.

CAPTION: For a job like this, where there's a single target, the preferred method of most professionals would be to sit a safe distance away and use a high-powered rifle with a scope.

CAPTION: But the rain makes visibility terrible, and the weather forecast says it's supposed to keep up all week.

CAPTION: Markham knows Brewster will need to get in close, which means he'll lead Markham right to the target. Markham just needs to make sure he gets to her first.

PAGE 15, Panel Two
We're in Markham's car, and through his windshield we can see Brewster's car parked up ahead on the side of the road.

CAPTION: Brewster leads him to a quiet neighborhood a few miles outside town.

CAPTION: Markham parks half a block behind Brewster.

PAGE 15, Panel Three
A woman in her late 20s comes out the front door of one of the houses. She's holding an umbrella.

NO COPY

PAGE 15, Panel Four
Brewster gets out of his car, and from this angle we can see that he's parked right in front of the woman's house. She's walking from her front door towards him.

NO COPY

PAGE 15, Panel Five
Markham's car comes hurtling down the street, at great speed.

NO COPY

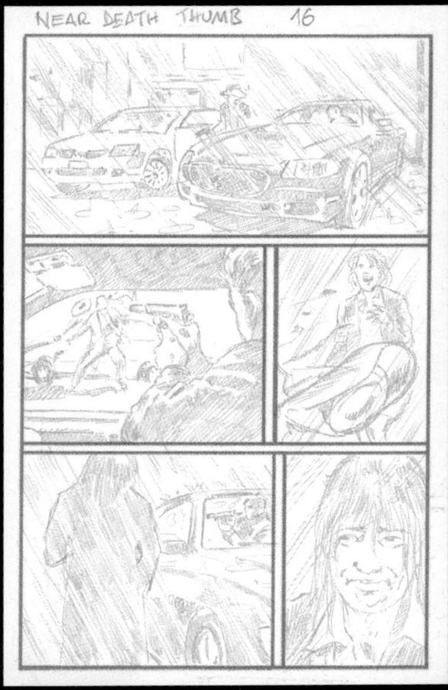
NEAR DEATH THUMB 16

PAGE 16

PAGE 16, Panel One
Markham stops the car in the street right next to Brewster, who's on the passenger side of Markham's car. The passenger-side window of Markham's car is down, and Markham is yelling out of it. We can see that Brewster clearly has a gun in his hand.

MARKHAM: Brewster!

PAGE 16, Panel Two
Markham fires his pistol -- equipped with a silencer -- through the passenger-side window, hitting Brewster in the face.

SFX: =FFT=

PAGE 16, Panel Three
The woman screams.

WOMAN: OH MY GOD!!

PAGE 16, Panel Four
Markham aims his gun at her.

MARKHAM: Get in.
MARKHAM: Now.

PAGE 16, Panel Five
Close on the woman's face, terrified.

NO COPY

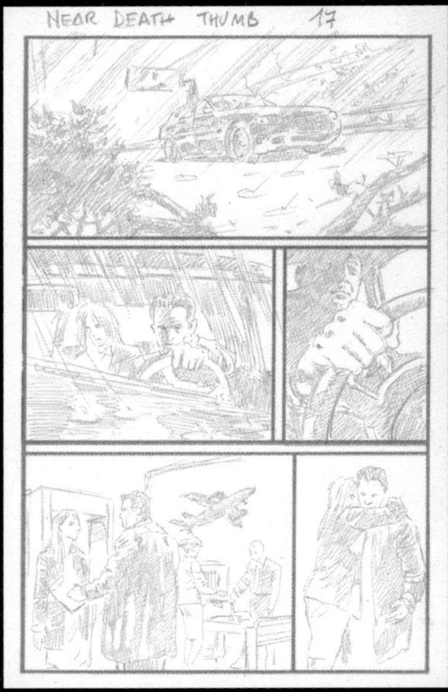
NEAR DEATH THUMB 17

PAGE 17

PAGE 17, Panel One
Cut to Markham's car, racing down the highway in the rain.

FROM CAR: The Marshals. You need to take me to the Marshals. I'm a protected witness. They have --

PAGE 17, Panel Two
Cut inside the car, with Markham at the wheel and the woman in the passenger seat. She's still very scared. Markham is calm and cool.

MARKHAM: You can't go to the Marshals. There's a leak in their department. That's how Brewster found you. The man who hired Brewster will keep sending people until they get you.
MARKHAM: You put a very important person in jail with your testimony, and he's got a lot of friends. So I need to make you disappear.

WOMAN: Who ARE you? Why are you doing this?

PAGE 17, Panel Three
Close on Brewster, behind the wheel.

MARKHAM: ...
MARKHAM: It's complicated.

PAGE 17, Panel Four
Cut to Markham and the woman in a small airport terminal. He's handing her an envelope.

CAPTION: Markham buys the woman three plane tickets, to three different destinations. He tells her to pick a place, and go. He doesn't want to know where.
CAPTION: He also gives her $10,000, a good start on a new life.
CAPTION: From here on out, she's on her own. There will be no Marshals to check in on her, no US Attorneys needing her testimony.
CAPTION: She'll be a blank slate, and he tells her to make the most of it.

PAGE 17, Panel Five
The woman hugs Markham with great emotion and he just stands there, arms at his side, totally not used to this type of interaction.

CAPTION: As he turns to leave she touches his arm and then does something no one has done to Markham in a long, long time.

PAGE 18

PAGE 18, Panel One
Cut to Markham and Max, sitting on a bench at Kerry Park in Seattle, in the daytime.

MAX: You hear about Brewster?
MARKHAM: Yeah. Shame.
MARKHAM: What about the girl?

MAX: In the wind.

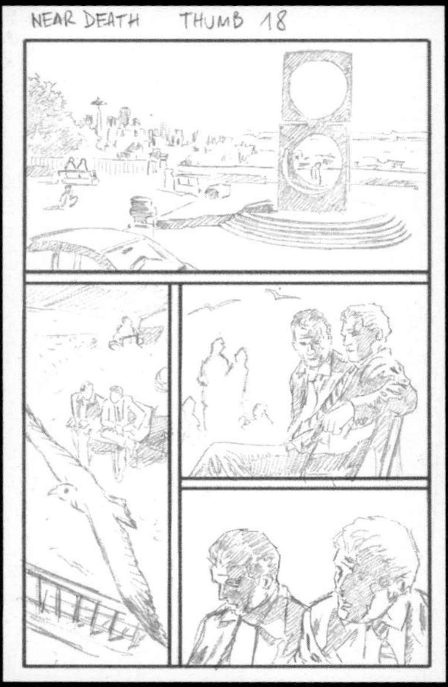
NEAR DEATH THUMB 18

PAGE 18, Panel Two
Markham looks at Max with a sideways glance, trying not to give away how interested he is in the answer to his question.

MARKHAM: Any idea what happened?

PAGE 18, Panel Three
On Max, looking out at the city, not making eye contact with Markham.

MAX: Nope. But Mr. Novak is PISSED.
MAX: If he finds out who interfered there's gonna be HELL to pay.

PAGE 18, Panel Four
Now we're on Markham, his expression not betraying what he really knows.

MARKHAM: Well if I hear anything, I'll be sure to let you know.

PAGE 19

PAGE 19, Panel One
Cut to a nighttime establishing shot of the Smith Tower, Markham's residence.

NO COPY

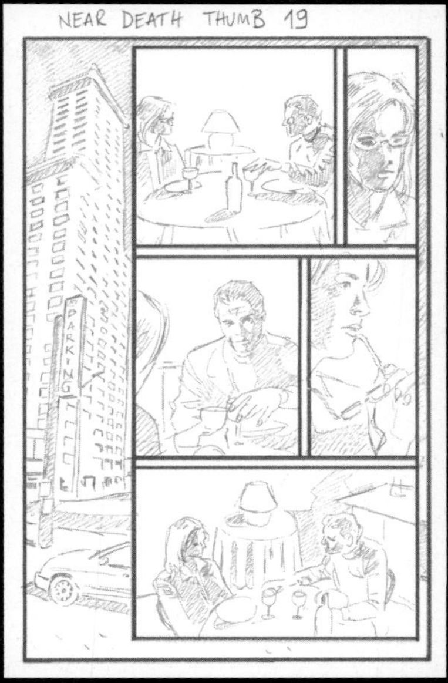
NEAR DEATH THUMB 19
PARKING

PAGE 19, Panel Two
Inside, Markham and Sutton are each enjoying a glass of wine.

SUTTON: So you're not going to kill people anymore.

MARKHAM: Not for money. And not if I can help it. But I guess I've got no problem with killing to save a life.
MARKHAM: Although honestly, I've got no problem with killing, period.
MARKHAM / small: I just don't like where it leads.

PAGE 19, Panel Three
On just Sutton.

SUTTON: So ... how did it feel? To save someone?

PAGE 19, Panel Four
On just Markham, looking at Sutton.

MARKHAM: You're a doctor. You've saved me more than once.

PAGE 19, Panel Five
Back on Sutton.

SUTTON: Yeah, but I'm asking you how it felt FOR YOU.

PAGE 19, Panel Six
A long shot on both of them, maybe in silhouette?

MARKHAM: Honestly?
MARKHAM: I didn't feel anything.

PAGE 20

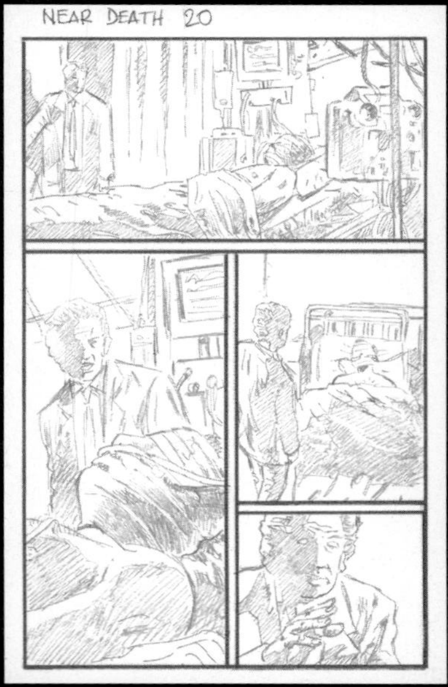
NEAR DEATH 20

PAGE 20, Panel One
Cut to a shot of Brewster, lying in a hospital bed, hooked up to all kinds of machines. His face is completely bandaged so we can't recognize him in this panel.

NO COPY

PAGE 20, Panel Two
Max enters the room.

MAX: Hey, Brewster?
MAX: It's me, Max.

PAGE 20, Panel Three
Max stands next to Brewster's bed.

MAX: Listen, Mr. Novak is real sorry about how this all went down. And he's gonna do whatever he can to make things right with you.

PAGE 20, Panel Four
Closer in on Max, looking sinister.

MAX: Starting with the name of the guy who shot you.

CAPTION: To Be Continued...